Cohesive Story Building

3D Fiction Fundamentals Collection, Volume 2

Karen S. Wiesner

Writers Exchange E-Publishing
http://www.writers-exchange.com

3D Fiction Fundamentals Collection, Volume 2: *Cohesive Story Building*

Writers Exchange E-Publishing
PO Box 372
ATHERTON QLD 4883

Third Edition

Originally published September 2008 as *From First Draft to Finished Novel* {A Writer's Guide to Cohesive Story Building}

Cover Art by: German Creative

Published by Writers Exchange E-Publishing
http://www.writers-exchange.com

TABLE OF CONTENTS

Author's Note

When I first sold this book to Writer's Digest Books, the title was *Cohesive Story Building*, which seemed like the perfect title given the subject matter inside. Alas, it was changed to *From First Draft to Finished Novel* {A Writer's Guide to Cohesive Story Building} during production, something that never seemed right to me since all my writing reference manuals can work equally well for any other size of fiction. I'm excited to offer the revised reissue with the most fitting title in this collection. The one thing all seven volumes have in common is that they're about teaching cohesive three-dimensional writing, whether it's in the pages of a single story, all the series installments, or even just in a book blurb. Here, each one of my writing reference manuals builds on the one that came before, overlapping sometimes because solid three-dimensional writing needs a strong foundation every single time, always offering a new focus of development.

Believe me, writing craft manuals isn't something anyone does for money (though that's nice). It's all about paying it forward, wanting to help other writers navigate their way forward on what can sometimes be a dark and murky path. One reviewer described my craft titles like this: "Karen speaks to you directly, frankly, cheerfully, and writes in a wonderfully entertaining style. She shares all her secrets and lets you look over her shoulder as she does. She never sounds patronizing. Instead, she points out that there is no wrong way to write a book, but that some ways are too ineffective for a writer who wants to write salable books on a regular basis. She doesn't bore you with theories. Karen is like a dance instructor who knows how to make people tango with grace even when they have two left feet." Encouraging you as a writer is what I hope you gain from using my methods.

Happy and productive writing!

Karen S. Wiesner

Collection

by award-winning author Karen S. Wiesner
covers the A to Z's of crafting the highest quality fiction including how to:

- Brainstorm and work productively to ensure that each stage in the writing process from prewriting to polishing produces masterful results the first time around.
- Create an outline so complete it actually qualifies as the first draft of your book, allowing your first written draft to be final-draft quality.
- Develop realistically three-dimensional and cohesive characters, plots, settings, relationships, and scenes so life-like and memorable your readers will be diehard fans.
- Effectively prepare for a series in advance to prevent painted-in-a-corner scenarios in order to keep fans coming back eagerly for each and every installment.
- Learn innovative techniques to write a complex sequence of stories that require overarching series arcs and immense world- and character-building.
- Craft sizzling back cover, series, and high-concept blurbs for describing, promoting, and selling your books.
- Maximize your potential and momentum for becoming a career author indefinitely.

With step-by-step guidelines, instructions, and tips throughout that are flexible and clearly written, imparting a layman's ease of understanding and can-do motivation, this collection may be the only writing craft books you'll ever need. Each volume has a free bonus companion ebooklet, presented in editable digital format that includes all the aids from the main book you can use in your own writing--and extras! A print edition is also available.

The seven volumes and bonus companion booklets in this collection are:

1. ***First Draft Outline*** formerly published by Writer's Digest Books as *First Draft in 30 Days* {A Novel Writer's System for Building a Complete and Cohesive Manuscript}

2. ***Cohesive Story Building*** formerly published by Writer's Digest Books as *From First Draft to Finished Novel* {A Writer's Guide to Cohesive Story Building}

3. ***Writing the Standalone Series*** formerly published by Writer's Digest Books as *Writing the Fiction Series* {The Complete Guide for Novels and Novellas}

4. ***Writing the Overarching Series*** {or How I Sent a Clumsy Girl into Outer Space}

5. ***Three-Dimensional Fiction Writing*** formerly published by Writer's Digest Books as *Bring Your Fiction to*

Life {Crafting Three-Dimensional Stories with Depth and Complexity}

6. ***CPR for Dead or Lifeless Fiction*** {A Writer's Guide to Deep and Multifaceted Development and Progression of **C**haracters, **P**lots, and **R**elationships}

7. ***Writing Blurbs That Sizzle--And Sell!***

3D Fiction Fundamentals Complete Series Collection (7 books in 1 volume)

Find out more here: http://www.writers-exchange.com/3d-fiction-fundamentals-series/

About the Author

In addition to having been a popular writing reference instructor and writer, professional blurbologist and freelance editor, Karen s. Wiesner is the accomplished author of 156 titles published, which have been nominated/won for over a hundred and thirty awards. The books Karen has edited have won multiple awards, and she's judged numerous writing contests.

Her nonfiction has included more than a half-dozen writing reference manuals that teach writers story crafting techniques as well specific facets of the book industry, such as author promotional techniques and the ins-and-outs of electronic publishing.

Karen is the author of sixteen fiction series which cover such genres as women's fiction, romance, mystery/police procedural/cozy, suspense/thriller, paranormal/supernatural, futuristic, fantasy, science fiction, gothic, inspirational/Christian, thriller, horror, chick-lit, and action/adventure. She also writes children's books and poetry. Karen will begin illustrating children's books starting in 2025.

Visit Karen's website and blog at https://karenwiesner.weebly.com/. Check out her Facebook author page here: http://www.facebook.com/KarenWiesnerAuthor. Visit her Writers Exchange E-Publishing author page at http://www.writers-exchange.com/karen-wiesner/.

INTRODUCTION
Principles of Building a Story

THE ESSENTIAL PROCESS OF LAYERING

In his book *The House You Build: Making Real-World Choices to Get the Home You Want,* architect Duo Dickinson suggests several crucial principles in successful planning and building, such as using standard materials creatively, not hurrying, preparing an on-spec budget, building in phases, and designing something you would want to own for a long period of time.

The process of planning and writing a book shares many of the same principles. When an author builds a story, he doesn't need fancy tools. He just needs to creatively use the tools he has to come up with his own unique design. He writes what he knows and feels. While a story will be written on its own timetable, this doesn't mean the author shouldn't be goal-oriented and disciplined. After all, just as a house that doesn't get built is never lived in, a book that doesn't get written will never be read. Additionally, building a story in phases, adding layer upon layer and making sure that the layers cohere, is the most productive, efficient way to complete a story. Certainly all writers want to offer a book that they're proud to call their own indefinitely.

When Building a House

Even the steps in building a house are similar to those in writing a story. When building a house, the designer (or the one who will be living in the house) comes up with ideas for his dream house, he makes very specific plans to lay the groundwork for the project, and only then will he break ground in order to lay the foundation. Framework is done inside and out, then electrical, plumbing, and ventilation systems can be installed.

The making (and breaking) of a house is based on the solidity of the foundation and framework. I remember when my husband and I were looking at houses in hope of purchasing our dream home. Our realtor showed us a house that had been decorated beautifully--the very best appliances, cabinets, carpeting, even a hot tub. But there was quite obviously something not right about the whole package. There were deep cracks running throughout the walls and ceiling, and the structure seemed to be slanting--not simply because it'd been built on a hill.

The realtor told us that the builder had been inexperienced, and, initially, cheap. When making the foundation, he poured a thin layer of concrete in a slab, the way it would be done for a sidewalk. What he should have done was dig footings below the frost line and then build the house on the solid foundation of those footings. Because he didn't, when the ground under the foundation froze in the winter, the water in the ground naturally froze, as well, and expanded, lifting the house in the places it froze. The frost heave caused violent cracks to form in the walls and ceiling. Other problems occurred, as direct or indirect results of the shoddy foundation, including pipes bursting (because the house lacked a properly heated basement in a climate where winter normally fell to frigid temperatures) and water damage. Additionally, there were major problems with the substandard-quality heating system installed on the main floor.

In order to sell the house, this builder attempted to go back and cover up the problems by filling the house with an irresistible selection of decorations, like expensive furnishings and appliances (that whirlpool bathtub turned my head more than once in the walk-through). Ultimately, for my husband and I, nothing could change the fact that this house wasn't solid enough to live in.

The builder had three options to fix what he'd done. The first wasn't truly a fix since it essentially meant tearing the house down and starting from scratch--this time with a solid plan, quality materials, and a strong foundation.

The builder could have opted to jack up the main house and go back under to build a solid foundation. This option would have eliminated future problems but nevertheless brought a lot of unpredictability. He must have surely realized that the lack of a good foundation was the crux of the house's problems--one that could never be fully corrected unless he went with the first and best option of starting from scratch and doing it right this time. But jacking up the house and making himself a good foundation wouldn't fix the issues the bad foundation had already caused. At this point, the house had become a money and time dump, considering how few people would want to live in something so flawed. I honestly don't know how the house passed inspection.

This builder didn't choose either of the first two options. Instead, he chose an option that shouldn't have even been an option. Out of cheapness (because he'd already poured so much cash into the house, trying to fix and cover up underlying problems), or maybe even sentimental reasons, he felt that the main level of the house was salvageable and he could sell it cheap as is. *Hey, let someone else deal with the problems that'll plague this house for years*, he may have thought. And then, of course, the guy got lucky and someone bought the sinkhole, which meant this builder probably thought he got away with not doing it right the first time, and he might not have learned his lesson for the next time he put a house up.

A quality builder stresses the importance of laying the groundwork right the first time. Only then can building begin with framework, the installation of drywall, cabinets, and interior trim. Decorating the house is the final step in the process. The layering steps must be done in the right order--and are ideally not done simultaneously--to complete a solid, pleasing home someone would want to live in for the rest of his life.

When Building a Story

When building a story, an author dreams up ideas through a process called brainstorming. When he has sufficient ideas to warrant actual physical work being done, he makes very specific plans to lay the groundwork for the project, and only then will he break ground in order to lay the foundation. Essentially, he creates a blueprint in some form--pre-writing or an outline--and this is the true solid foundation for any story. Only rarely will a job done right turn out wrong.

If a writer opts to skip the solid foundation of pre-writing, he'll probably have trouble all through the project, especially at the end, when he has a massive stack of pages that somehow have to be fixed. An experienced writer may well be able to correct the crux of a story's problems without starting from scratch, but this won't necessarily make the problems caused by the initial, bad foundation go away. Without a doubt, the writer will dump a lot of blood, sweat, and tears into re-working and revising the manuscript, possibly many times.

No amount of decoration will fix a story that's seriously flawed. In *Novelist's Essential Guide to Creating Plot,* J. Madison Davis calls this kind of fixing "patching" the story. The writer relies on patching rather than a good design. The patch drops out of nowhere into a story and forces things to go where the author wants them to. The outcome is never convincing.

Rejection from agents and editors is inevitable when a story is fundamentally flawed. Luck-makes-a-bad-choice-worth-it scenario: The author sells the work to a publisher. Reviewers will then probably do what they always do--without mercy--and perhaps the author will see the wisdom of starting each future project with a solid foundation. For a published author with a supportive publisher, we can only hope that, if readers don't come back for more, the author doesn't give up, but instead endeavors from that point on to build soundly from the get-go.

It's never productive to plunge into a story and write endless pages that either get discarded or have to be laboriously reshaped. If you know your story and conflicts before you start writing, you can focus on scenes that work and advance the plot. Knowing your story from start to finish before writing the first draft will allow you to convey the character's emotions more clearly through whatever he faces. Knowing your story gives you the edge to create tense scenes because you'll be aware of what's at stake in the end. Additionally, effective foreshadowing is done best when you know where the story is going from the first word written. You'll know your character so intimately, you'll have no doubt how he'll react to each obstacle you put in his path.

First, make certain you have a story foundation that can support the framework you build onto it afterwards. Don't move forward into writing the first draft until you have that.

Revising a story, like decorating a house, should be the final step in the process. These layering steps should done in the right order--never simultaneously--to complete a solid, pleasing story that is fully realized and irresistible.

LAYERING TO GAIN COHESION

We've established, from comparing the process of building a house to the process of building a story, that there are three distinct layering steps. In building a house, these are:

Stage 1: Planning for and laying a foundation
Stage 2: Building
Stage 3: Decorating

In building a story, there are three distinct layering steps:

Stage 1: Planning for and laying a foundation
Stage 2: Writing
Stage 3: Revising

Each stage in building a house involves a variety of steps, such as picking out a plot to build on, working plans around the unique aspects of that plot, excavation, and a variety of installations. In writing, each of the three layering stages is distinct, and also consists of several steps. The first layer, planning and blueprinting, has four steps:

1. Brainstorming
2. Researching
3. Story blueprinting
4. Setting the story blueprint aside

Writing, like framework in building a house, is the second layer, and also involves four steps:

1. Building a cohesive story with a Story Plan Checklist
2. Evaluating the blueprint
3. Writing the first draft
4. Creating a punch list

Finally, the third layer, revising, requires four distinct steps:

1. Revising
2. Involving critique partners
3. Setting the final draft aside
4. Final editing and polishing

Then we get to Layer IV--which involves preparing your work for submission. This layer isn't about crafting your story, per se, but it's too important to ignore. Think of it as preparing to sell the house you worked so hard to build.

The Merits of Layering

Without layering, a story is one-dimensional, unbelievable, boring. But with proper layering, the characters will become so lifelike, readers may believe they're fully capable of stepping right off the pages into the room. Layering means strength in story-building just as it does in house-building: stronger plots, suspense, intrigue, emotions, motivations, stronger *everything*. More reason for editors to love you and for readers to come back again and again.

Layering has another component that writers should take into account. Layering a story produces cohesion between all of the story elements.

The word *cohesive* brings to mind many concepts. You might think of the cohesion of a symbiotic relationship. The symbiont becomes one with its host. Separating the two is difficult (if not impossible) and, in some instances, unwise, as both may lose something vital they can no longer live without. The elements of a story work together in symbiotic cohesion.

Some dictionary definitions that really show the perimeters of the wonderful word *cohesive* are: "logically connected, consistent;

having a natural agreement of part, harmonious; the act or state of uniting and sticking together; the molecular force between particles within a body or substance that acts to unite them; of or pertaining to the molecular force within a body or substance acting to unite its parts."

I particularly like that last part because it so perfectly describes what happens when all the elements of your story fit together. It's as if some elemental force draws each part of a story together and then fuses them until they become one and are unable to be separated.

The amazing part of this process is that it works *uniquely* for every single writer. In other words, if you gave the same basic idea to writers in every genre, each would come up with something different. In *Breathing Life Into Your Characters*, Rachel Ballon says, "There is nobody else in the world exactly like you, and nobody but you can write the story you want to tell." We'll test that in the exercises included in Appendix E.

A builder knows the best supplies to use to produce a sound house, just as plumbers and electricians follow the guidelines and regulations of their professions. And a home decorator would never put together elements that are grossly at odds. His job is to create something that's both pleasing to the eye and perfectly suited to the individuals in the home.

In the same way, the three main story elements of character, plot, and setting *must* be cohesive and work together in such a way that taking away a single element would be impossible because all of the elements have seamlessly become a part of each other. They complement each other and work together to make the plot impenetrable and airtight.

The best reason I've heard for building cohesion into your story is from Debra Dixon in *Goal, Motivation & Conflict* (*GMC*): If characters, conflicts, goals and motivations don't intersect and collide, you're writing separate books *in the same manuscript*. The process by which a writer builds cohesion is one of layering and building up and bringing *together* the strengths of all aspects within his story.

HOW TO USE THIS BOOK

The purpose of *Cohesive Story Building* is to show you the three distinctive layers of a story and how to build utterly solid, cohesive story elements. Cohesion needs to start immediately, even during the brainstorming phase, and it's crucial that it be maintained throughout the preliminary sketching and outlining of your story. Characters must blend in naturally with your setting, just as your plot must be an organic part of your character and setting. If a story doesn't work, it very likely because your story elements aren't cohesive. In this book, I'll show you how each element depends on the other two, and how to mix them until they fuse irrevocably.

This book is broken down into four main chapters, or layers, followed by six appendices.

Layer I focuses on planning for and laying the foundation of a book, and will give you a concise guideline to creating an outline that includes each scene of your book.

Layer II is actually divided into two separate parts: A and B. Part A explores the steps involved in building on the foundation with the development of a Story Plan Checklist, which essentially functions as the cohesive framework of your story. Then you'll evaluate this blueprint you've created to guide the writing of your book. In Part B, we'll discuss writing the first draft using the outline and Story Building Checklist, and, finally, creating a final list of work to be done with the revision.

Layer III covers the final layer of a story--specifically, revising, editing, and polishing.

Layer IV acts as a thorough walk-through of the three steps involved with preparing a proposal (and creating a synopsis based on your Story Plan Checklist).

The seven appendices contain all the supplemental materials you'll need to work your way through the story-building process:

- *Appendix A* contains a glossary that includes key terms discussed within this book. If you ever get confused about what a term means, just consult the glossary.
- *Appendix B* provides blank worksheets and sketch

forms from my book *First Draft Outline* that you'll find helpful in the process of building your story.

- *Appendix C* contains crucial checklists to see you through the building phase (such as a Story Plan Checklist template).
- *Appendix D* contains Story Plan Checklist examples of several popular novels.
- *Appendix E* gives a Story Plan Checklist exercise to help build your cohesion skills.
- *Appendix F* gives a number of passages to help you to refine your editing and polishing skills.
- *Appendix G* contains submission package examples.

Using *First Draft Outline* and *Cohesive Story Building* Together

Many who have read my writing reference on outlining, *First Draft Outline* will find *Cohesive Story Building* a perfect companion to that book. By default, an in-depth system for story writing like the one in *First Draft Outline* encourages and supports story consistency and cohesion.

In an ideal situation, a writer goes through the following twelve steps to get a finished book:

1) Brainstorming
2) Researching
3) Outlining
4) Completing a Story Plan Checklist
5) Setting aside the project
6) Evaluating the outline
7) Writing the first draft
8) Setting aside the project
9) Revising the first draft
10) Setting aside the project
11) Editing and polishing
12) Creating a proposal

Cohesive Story Building will take you through every single one of these steps--without duplication what's already been covered in *First Draft Outline.*

Layer I of *Cohesive Story Building* touches on some of the same processes examined in-depth in *First Draft Outline*. In that book, I talked widely about the essential requirements of brainstorming, pre-writing and, yes, outlining to write a solid story. Why revisit that topic here? Because it's that important and it's an essential part of completing a first draft and a finished book! An outline has the dual purpose of creating a firm foundation for a story as well as putting the hard work of writing where it belongs--at the beginning a project. If you work out the kinks in the story at the get-go (using whatever form of a guide you prefer to work with), you ensure that the writing and revising are the easy parts. Best of all, what you end up with is utterly solid, requiring only minor editing and polishing to make it publishable.

However, I do want to stress that *Cohesive Story Building* is not another outline book, like *First Draft Outline*. This new book focuses on ensuring cohesion between character, setting and plot. The Story Plan Checklist, covered in Layer II, is the means in which you'll do that. Why is this checklist so essential? Because it's vitally important that you see the major points of your story in condensed form in order to gain cohesion of characters, settings and plot in your own work. This checklist connects all the dots and thereby guarantees cohesion. Used together, your outline and Story Plan Checklist will help you write a "final draft quality" first draft that really will be something amazing.

Following the Layer I preliminary sketching and outlining discussion, we'll move on to Layer II and start the story-building process with the Story Plan Checklist, which leads us to where, in many ways, *First Draft Outline* left off--the writing of the book. *Cohesive Story Building* goes deeper than the natural cohesion that weaves together a story during outlining, completing the Story Plan Checklist, and writing.

The reason I've placed the elements of cohesion in Layer II of this book, instead of in the planning stage (Layer I), is because in completing a Story Plan Checklist you're really going to see the miracle of wonderfully intersecting character, setting, and plot.

The checklist will complete both your outline and your first draft by confirming that you've connected every cohesive dot from start to finish.

If the *First Draft Outline* method worked for you and you want to enhance your story-building, use both books together. While it's not necessary to actually merge your outline and Story Plan Checklist into the same document, I will give you an example later in this book of how to use the two together to write your first draft.

See the Story Plan Checklist Method in Action

Speaking of the Story Plan Checklist in Layer II, you'll get the chance to see it in action when I use a best-selling mystery novel to demonstrate each step in creating a checklist of your very own.

I do want to assure you that the Story Plan Checklist is versatile. I use a mystery novel as the main example in Layer II, but you can use the Story Plan Checklist for every single genre of fiction, no matter how short or long your work is. I've included example checklists in Appendix D for an action/adventure romantic suspense novel, a horror novel, a young adult fantasy novel, and a mainstream literary fiction novel.

Please note that all of the examples in this book contain major spoilers. If you haven't already read the books used and want to, do so before you go over the examples, as the checklist contains the entire plot of each book in consolidated form.

Whether You're Starting a New Project or Working on an Old One...

Though this book assumes you'll be using this method for a brand new project, you might be wondering if you can use the Story Plan Checklist with a book you've written one or more drafts of that needs more work. Yes! Those previous drafts are the basic "outline" you need. The checklist will then help you pinpoint the problem areas and/or a lack of cohesion that plagued previous drafts of your story.

Also, in an attempt to clear up any confusion that may be caused later, I want to point out that the Story Plan Checklists created in this book from bestselling novels are very detailed and long. The reason that is because these examples have to make sense of the stories presented and something much shorter might have confused readers. (Remember: Your Story Plan Checklist probably *won't* make much sense to anyone but you, at least not until you turn it into a synopsis, and we'll talk about that in Layer IV.) While you might get the impression from these that most checklists of this kind are detailed or long, the fact is that your own (if written in conjunction with your outline) will probably be very short, at maybe five page--ten at the absolute most. Compare that to a 35-50-page outline of a 75,000- to 100,000-word novel. The checklist hits the major points while the outline covers the book scene by scene. Used together, you'll absolutely eliminate the guesswork involved in writing your book.

GETTING STARTED

If your character, setting, and plot are truly cohesive, writing your story will take your breath away. It'll fill your every waking thought, infuse you with constant inspiration and the desperate need to enter the irresistible world you've created to see what happens next. You won't want to leave it--who needs to sleep and eat? It will no doubt even affect your moods as you feel everything your characters do. You may find yourself muttering odd things that make sense only to you. Friends will comment on the faraway look in your eyes. Those who know you well will surely understand that you're off in writers' la-la land again--best not to disturb you until you're bursting to tell them what you've discovered. These things are what make writing both crazy and wonderful.

My hope is that *Cohesive Story Building* will give you a solid plan of action from start to finish through in-depth examples and exercises, and that the leave-no-stone-unturned checklists will help you take the plan into your own writing. This layering process sets up the stages necessary to complete a cohesive, irresistible dream-book that is hauntingly unforgettable to everyone who reads it.

One final note: The worksheets, checklists, and other aids used in this book are available separately in an editable file you can use for your own writing. It's called "*Cohesive Story Building Bonus Companion Booklet*", available free from the publisher of this book. A print edition can be purchased as well.

LAYER I
Planning for and Laying a Foundation

A builder always starts with ideas that eventually get moved to paper in the form of a blueprint. At that point, he can begin excavating and grading the chosen lot and putting in a basement. He'll put the footings, foundation, or supports in place, and then install drainage tiles around the foundation.

In writing, we have similar layering steps involved in the planning and foundation-laying of a story. In the introduction, we talked about the stages involved, including:

1. Brainstorming
2. Researching
3. Story blueprinting
4. Setting the story blueprint aside

Let's look at each one in-depth.

STAGE 1: BRAINSTORMING

Who could ever describe the process of brainstorming as poetically and aptly as Terry Brooks does in *Sometimes the Magic Works*? He says that dreaming (a term referring to the back-and-forth process of brainstorming in the mind) opens the door to creativity and allows the imagination to invent something wonderful. It happens when your mind drifts to take you to a place you've never been so you can come back and tell readers about it. Possibly this is where writers got such a bad rap with those who see us daydreaming constantly. Little do they realize that, until a writer has brainstormed adequately, she won't have a story to tell.

Another really popular novelist said that for her next book, she was going to hold it inside her until it was like a piece of fruit on a branch bowing almost to the ground it was so ripe. Isn't that an incredible picture of how a story can grow in our minds until it absolutely has to be written? That's exactly as it should be (though you can do the same for an idea that's not ready--it'll just be a *lot* harder). Ideally, don't start your story until you have a lot to work with. The productive writer starts with a solid story that's ready to drop into her hands like ripe fruit.

I recommend creating story folders for every book idea you have no matter how sparse your ideas are for it. Whenever you have an idea about this story, write notes about it and tuck them into the appropriate folder. By the time you're ready to begin outlining on a particular story, ideally you'll have a nice stack of notes to get started with.

The Ways

Brainstorming is the very ambition, focus, and joy necessary to planning and completing a project. Both inspiration and productivity flow from this exercise, and brainstorming should never truly stop from the beginning of a project to the end. Brainstorming is so often what turns an average story into an extraordinarily memorable one. It's the magical element every writer marvels about in the process of completing a book. When I'm working on a project, I try to brainstorm day and night, whatever I do, wherever I am, whenever I possibly can. Dreaming about your story infuses you with the inner resources to write with that coveted magical element.

Something every author covets is the ability to sit down to a blank screen or page and begin to work immediately. The secret to doing that is brainstorming! When you brainstorm constantly and productively during both the outlining and writing processes, you'll always be fully prepared to begin writing without agonizing over the starting sentences or paragraph. Brainstorming has the amazing side effect of forcing a writer to move from Point A to Point B and to continue on from there. Having given you a few sparks, it requires you to connect the dots in order to get those elements to fit together logically and cohesively. Brainstorming keeps your writing so fresh, you don't have to worry about getting stuck at any point.

Without adequate brainstorming, a writer has no motivation for fantasizing about every aspect of the story she desperately wants to write. The process of writing will be dry, and she'll likely never make it past chapter three.

In *First Draft Outline,* I recommended that authors start brainstorming days, weeks, months, or even *years* before beginning tangible work on a story. By doing this, you create the building blocks for your story over time; this type of strong planning produces cohesion in your work. Brainstorm enough, and when you sit down to start the project, it'll be like turning on a movie and writing fast to keep up with everything you see.

In *First Draft Outline,* I offered several suggestions for using brainstorming to light a fire under your muse. If you ever need help dreaming about your story, some of those suggestions might help you get started.

Oh, that writers could have the joy of brainstorming forever! Unfortunately, life many times gets in the way, especially if, in keeping the momentum of a career going, you sell too many books on proposal, which prevents you from having a lot of time to brainstorm through your many projects. I know I'm not the only writer who longs for the endless hours spent daydreaming on a single project. When did life turn into something in which every moment has to be filled doing something instead of letting the mind blissfully wander? Sigh.

Do everything you can to keep your brainstorming fire lit, even if it means selling less to give yourself more time to keep the joy of story building alive.

The Means

One of the tricks of a builder's trade is to storyboard or design and construct a collage of the house he plans to build. During the storyboarding process, the builder clears an office wall and divides it into two sections: one side for the interior design/build package, and another for the exterior design/build package. The builder creates himself a visual to use while making decisions. He might hang pictures, colors and samples, sketches, newspaper excerpts, magazine pages, and photographs on this storyboard. While he works, he adds and deletes from his aesthetic collage on a daily, weekly, or monthly basis, changing things in order to improve the house style. This method is considered art with a purpose.

Building a story folder is similar to this, and I discussed this process in-depth in *First Draft Outline*. Either purchase a large, multi-sectioned pocket or accordion folder, or create a special hanging file section for a single story project, with separate folders for each aspect of your story. These will hold your story ideas. Begin by writing the working title of the story on the front of the folder or on the section tab, then insert your research, and transfer any notes you write (including any outlining and writing you've already done) into this folder. What you'll include in your story folder will depend on what you need. You might have handwritten or typed notes about the story (possibly divided into story sections, or simply free-form). You might also have character worksheets for each main character in a character section, and you might have setting and plot sections. Of course you can do all of this on your computer in separate files as well. Remember to save copies of everything on a disk or flash drive!

Ideally, you'll have a story folder for all of the "big" story ideas you have, and over a period of years, you'll jot down notes about the story and insert them into the folder. I recommend that you start brainstorming on upcoming projects *years* in advance if you can. When it's time to work on that project, I'm raring to go. I have a ton of ideas and the motivation to get them down and that carries me through the outlining. Because I've always got multiple books going at one time--each one in a different stage of the process--I'm constantly brainstorming on these projects in the back of my mind. That's so crucial to the overall strength of your stories and for the momentum of your career.

I keep all of my story folders in one cabinet, which I call my story cupboard. Keep all of your big story ideas percolating on a low flame until it's time to work on that particular project. When you need to, make a note and insert it into the folder.

STAGE 2: RESEARCHING

Just as a builder will identify, gather, and absorb as much research about lots, house styles, floor plans, etc., as he can before he begins building, a writer needs to identify, gather, and absorb research to write a particular story. Research is a layer of the story, and we can divide the research process into four parts:

1. Identifying
2. Gathering
3. Reading
4. Using

1. Identifying

Before you begin the actual research, you should attempt to identify what you need to research for your story. You can do this by creating a handwritten list of everything it's necessary to research. Essentially, you're creating a list of topics you must know about in order to write your story. For instance, you may need to research your characters' careers so you've got a clear idea of what's done and why, overall and day-to-day. You may need to interview people in a certain profession or area of expertise, or research the places your characters live in or travel to. You may need to research clothing, etc., for the time period your book is set in. You might need to research specific trees or animals indigenous to an area, historical events, or state laws. If your book is a mystery or suspense, you may need to research police procedures. If you don't feel you have enough knowledge of a subject to write about it easily, it needs to go on your research list.

On the whole, in the preliminary stages of research, try to limit your research to what you know is absolutely required, not things you aren't sure about exploring. If you do want to explore, do it well in advance to see if the topic is something you want for your story. If you find out early enough that it's not right for your particular project, you can abandon the research whenever you want. Once the required research is done, you can usually find time between stages in a project to explore those "maybe" items.

A simple listing of topics on a sheet of paper is all you need for the identification step.

2. Gathering

Once you've identified *what* you need to research, you can begin gathering your materials. Over the years, I've found that the internet seems to have a good amount of what I need when I research, but I still need to purchase or check out books for many projects.

3. Reading

Ideally, give yourself time to do the bulk of your reading research *between* projects. For authors who generally spend nine months out of every given year researching, and for those authors with extremely complex plots, this may sound impossible, but it can be done with enough planning and discipline.

As you'll see in the coming chapters, you'll set a project aside between each stage of development. This gives you lots of free time when research can be done on various upcoming projects. During this time, you can do your reading in a much more relaxed way without worrying about an impending deadline you might not meet if you don't put your nose firmly to the grindstone.

4. Using

As I said, research is a layer of story building. But research is also a form of brainstorming. While you're reading, you're thinking of ways you plan to use the material you're researching. Research will give you the knowledge you need in order to plan a story. It will also give you story ideas. That's why it's so important to do your research *before* you begin a project--not during. This isn't to say that you won't need to do some follow-up research when you realize your outline or first draft has taken a turn you hadn't planned for.

For *The Fifteenth Letter*, the third book in the Falcon's Bend police procedural series I write with Chris Spindler, quite a bit of research was necessary on bank robberies (examples and the legal aspects), maps, and various other topics. I kept separate files on my computer for the bank robbery information and the maps. I created separate sections in each of those files so I could group the information in such a way that it would be easy to use when it came time to outline the book.

So, over a period of time prior to outlining the book, I identified, gathered, and read the research material while simultaneously figuring out how to use all of the information within the story. The research formed the basis for character development, an appropriate setting, and much of the plot, fitting them together naturally. When it came time to prepare an outline for the book, I consolidated all of the information on my computer, then printed it and put it in a binder with section dividers. Whenever I needed information, this easy reference allowed me to flip right to what was needed, without endless searching.

You'll know you've done your research well when you can write about everything in your story intelligently, without questioning anything, and when your research becomes an integral part of the book.

This is the time to open the story folder for the project and begin the outlining.

STAGE 3: STORY BLUEPRINTING

Blueprints are copies of mechanical or other types of technical drawings. Drawing or sketching is the universal language used by engineers, technicians, and skilled craftsmen. These sketches need to convey all the necessary information needed to create or assemble an item. To be more specific, blueprints show the construction details of buildings, machines, ships, and the like.

A story blueprint serves much the same purpose. It's essentially a guideline the writer uses to create and assemble a story. Many times, blueprints of certain aspects of writing are referred to as *sketches*, such as character or plot sketches.

Whatever form of blueprint an author chooses to use (specific options are discussed a little later), it needs to show the details *behind* the finished product--details that many times are invisible in the end, like tension and mood, but that need to be identified and developed and made cohesive with the other elements of the story even before writing begins.

No reputable builder--and certainly no successful one--would even consider building a house without a blueprint. Working without one would cause unending problems. Imagine a novice builder without a formal plan, without the crucial experience to do the work. (Remember the one I talked about in the introduction?) Working without a blueprint of some sort, he'll end up with a finished product that the big bad wolf will have no trouble felling with a few wisely placed huffs and puffs. Ask nearly anyone, and he'll tell you that the mere idea of someone building a house without a blueprint is downright laughable.

Unfortunately, the idea of an author writing a story without some sort of plan is acceptable, even encouraged, and prevalent. Don't get me wrong, those authors who have been through the process of writing a book many, many times *have* a blueprint regardless of whether it's formally written down or not. Their own experience in the process is guiding them. An author who's written nothing, or only a few books and works without plans in one form or another to get her started, may end up with unstable, disjointed stories that reviewers love to rip to shreds.

Anyone can throw up walls, cover them with paint, put in a

floor and carpet, add some comfortable furniture, and then settle back believing the work is done. But imagine when problems crop up, as they did in the true story I told you in the introduction. Hard weather sets in. Cracks form and deepen. Pipes burst. Power is needed, but only part of the wiring was laid in or it was improperly done. Now only intermittent surges come, or nothing at all. This builder would have no choice at this point but to rip out the walls and floor to fix or replace the wiring. If he needs water (and who doesn't) but he didn't bother with the plumbing or what he did is a mess, he'll have no end of trouble.

Just as wiring and plumbing need to be put in and the rest of the house built around it, a story needs the proper foundation, framework, and internal workings to be strong. Choosing the right elements before the first draft is begun will also prevent endless rewrites and non-cohesive stories.

In book writing, preliminary sketches and formatted outlines like the ones you'll be creating contain all the detailed construction information necessary for you to begin working on a daily basis, from the start of the project to the finish.

What you'll find in the upcoming pages is a capsulated version of many of the things I talked about at length in *First Draft Outline.* While *First Draft Outline* provides more in-depth outlining details, the material in the following sections provides you with everything you need to complete a scene-by-scene outline, which will ultimately feed into the creation of your Story Plan Checklist (discussed in the next chapter).

(If you'd like to see examples of all the preliminary sketches, worksheets, and the rest of this outlining process filled out, pick up a copy of *First Draft Outline* and the *First Draft Outline Bonus Companion Booklet.*)

Preliminary Sketches

So, you've started a story folder and you've held the story inside it until now--when it's ripe to begin the process of preliminary sketching. You can do the steps in any order or all at the same time, filling out as much as you can on one and going on to the next. Sketching will help you envision the separate components that make up your story. Namely, research, characters, settings, plots, and scene summary notes. Think about these as the puzzle pieces that make up your story. Later, when you start your scene-by-scene outline, they'll also help you fill in the gaps in your story puzzle.

Preliminary sketches are a layer of story building, one your book will be missing if you skip, and they consist of character, setting and plot sketches, and free-form scene notes. What you create during this time will later be incorporated into your formatted outline.

Constant brainstorming is the most important part of writing an outline or a book and should begin long before you start work on a story. During this time, you should be jotting down notes about your ideas as they come to you and storing them in individual project folders.

Remember as you're going through each step of the preliminary sketching that this is for your own use--the rich imagery, textured sentences, clever turns of phrase all come later. The goal right now is to get started.

Character Sketches

You can find a blank character worksheet in Appendix B as well as in the *Cohesive Story Building Bonus Companion Booklet*. Use this or another worksheet that you like to do this, or write everything free-form if that works better for you. Write down everything that comes to you, no matter how trivial. The sketch will help you think about the depths of your characters. Remember to give *all* your main characters (including the villain) internal and external conflicts. This will bring your characters to life.

Setting Sketches

Fill out the setting worksheet in Appendix B or in the *Cohesive Story Building Bonus Companion Booklet*, any other you prefer, or free-form write in any way that gets you thinking about the story's setting details.

Plot Sketch

Begin filling out a plot breakdown worksheet in Appendix B or the *Cohesive Story Building Bonus Companion Booklet.* Alternately, free-form detail what's included below for this step. Like a tapestry, every story is woven of threads that become invisible within the overall design. By familiarizing yourself with story threads (long- and short-term plot and subplot points) and being aware of them as you work, you can learn to knit story threads skillfully into your own book. All of these threads work together to form your plot sketch. Remember, at this stage you probably won't be able to fill in all of these sections, but it's still important to start thinking about them. Simply write in whatever you can for each section and remember you can go back and add more later. One sentence is enough to begin with. Let's explore each thread:

- **Story Goal (Thread #1):** In all genres of fiction, the story goal is the catalyst of the book--the reason why the characters are there, the reason why the story evolves, the reason why the reader opens the book, starts and keeps reading. All other threads and characters are involved in achieving the story goal.

- **Romance Thread (optional):** In a romance story, the most important part of the book is the relationship between the hero and the heroine. This long-term thread is as important as the story goal, and it continues from the beginning of the story until it ties up with the happily-ever-after theme. It should be in every or almost every scene of the book, and should be knitted in seamlessly with all other plot threads. Anything that happens affects the romance, just as the romance will have influence over the other plot aspects.

  When you're using romance as a long-term thread, you want to keep it foremost in your mind, which is why it has its own section on the plot sketch worksheet. In genres outside romance, this thread is a subplot thread instead of a long-term thread, and, since it's not a dominating aspect of the plot. If you include a minor subplot of romance in your book, remember that this thread needs a beginning, middle, and satisfactory resolution just as all other threads do. If your book isn't a romance or doesn't include a long-term romance thread, you don't need to do anything with this section of the worksheet.

- **Subplot Threads:** Subplots function as secondary plots. They typically contrast or run parallel to the main plot. These threads should work working in harmony to effectively develop both character and plot. Each will depend on the others as the book comes to a close.

  Subplots can range from health conditions and financial worries to physical or mental conclusions a character must reach: returning home after a family member dies, moving out of an apartment, changing careers. In all cases, it should be clear to readers how the subplots connect with the main story goal.

  How many of these subplot threads you include depends on the length and complexity of your story. There is no standard number. Just remember that the more main characters, conflicts and pages you have, the more subplot threads you'll end up with. Remember that you will have to give regular attention to all of your subplots. Even with a complex plot line, you never want to leave *any* of your threads for too long. You want to create tension, not forgetfulness and frustration in the reader. You also want your threads to mesh to the point that you've created a net your characters won't easily find their way out of.

  The subplot section on your plot sketch worksheet may prove to be the hardest for you to fill out simply because most stories have several subplots working together with the story goal. For now, write what comes to you, even if it's only a few words under each subplot number. Don't worry about putting the threads in order of importance. Please also note that the story goal is the number 1 story thread. Therefore, your subplot list will begin with #2.

- **Plot Tension:** In all genres, plot tension is essential. This kind of tension is anything that brings the reader to fever pitch of anticipation. A story without plot tension leaves the reader uninvolved and unemotional. We'll go over the importance of and ways of increasing tension in-depth later.

- **Romantic/Sexual Tension (optional):** In a romance story, romantic/sexual tension is essential. You want to start this tension as early in the story as you possibly can. If you don't start the suspense promptly and keep it intense, the reader will be disappointed--or worse, embarrassed--during moments she should be temporarily relieved or exalted. Later in this book, I'll give you tips on creating this effectively.

- **Release:** A release is an easement of plot or romantic tension. In a mystery, a release might take the form of a resolution to one aspect of the main problem. In a romantic or sexual thread or subplot, a release could be a kiss, lovemaking, or a declaration of feelings. The final words in a story should also produce a "finale" release that satisfies the readers and makes them long to revisit the story again, even if only in their minds. More about this in later chapters.

- **Downtime:** Downtime is a form of release, but as it happens during a time of incredible tension, it should be one of the most poignant scenes (or *scenes*) in your book. During downtime, which comes at the end of the middle section of the book, the main character may step back from the action and reflect on what happily-ever-after could have been (if not for all the obstacles put in his way). The main character may also believe for a time that the story goal is unachievable, and he may seem to give up the fight. Never for one moment, however, will the main character feel a sense of satisfaction or contentedness about this new course of action. Your character will be utterly tormented at every turn.

The reader is lead to an even higher level of anticipation because of downtime. In a romance, this is a glimpse of the hero and heroine living happily ever after--a sensual or emotional scene(s), or a stolen moment in a chaotic time. In any other genre, downtime is a temporary respite from the extreme tension the plot is creating--a bittersweet moment of some sort.

Following downtime, your character will form a new plan of action. This will be his final, desperate attempt to fulfill the story goal, and the ground won't feel at all solid as he moves forward. In some cases, your character will come to the decision to act because the stakes of the conflict are again raised--danger is near, and he must move forward whether he wants to or not. This episode will provide the motivation to propel the story to the next level.

Downtime is absolutely essential, though a lot of action/adventure/suspense authors neglect it. What they don't realize is that, if you don't give your reader a chance to breathe between high-intensity action scenes, you'll lose her, whether for a few hours when she quits reading the book to recover...or indefinitely. More about that later.

In nearly every situation, downtimes must be followed with a black moment. Downtime releases the tension for a short period, and that tension must be built back up quickly or you risk losing your reader.

- **Black Moment:** The black moment in the story is commonly referred to as the climax of the book. The worst of all horrors is happening, and the characters (as well as the readers) are now thoroughly convinced the future will never be happy. The black moment, which occurs in the first part of the end section of the book (when tension is at its highest) leaves the reader and the characters wondering whether evil will overcome good.

  If you're writing a romance story, you'll have two black moments--one black moment for the story goal and one for the romance thread. The black moment for the romance thread usually occurs in the end section of the book, just after the story goal has been resolved satisfactorily. Most genres have only one black moment--for the story goal.

- **Resolution:** The resolution of a story comes after the climax, when the story's main problems have been resolved. This is your chance to tie up any loose ends and provide satisfying conclusions for your subplot threads. Tying up these loose ends is crucial to leaving the reader satisfied. A satisfactory resolution doesn't allow the reader to wonder about dangling plot threads or to feel cheated--you, as the writer, must fulfill the underlying promise of a logical, acceptable conclusion, even if it isn't a happy one.

- **Aftereffects of Resolution (optional):** An aftereffect of a resolution may come in the form of an emotional reaction or an event that carries the story goal or a subplot thread beyond its conclusion. In other words, the thread may continue even after it's been resolved. Very few writers include aftereffects of resolution, though they're used frequently in horror movies.

As you're puzzling out your sketches, keep these threads in

mind--they'll come up again and again. Once you've added detail and depth to your outline and developed your story, the threads should become almost invisible, just like the skeleton beneath your skin. Go into as much detail as possible on your plot sketch, but keep in mind that your first pass will be light on details. Don't worry! It will grow significantly.

Scene Summary Notes

Once you've gotten started on your character, setting, and plot sketches, start writing scene notes in the form of a summary essay, describing the images and specific details you already have in mind for any beginning, middle, or end scenes. You can use any blank sheet of paper for this. Summarizing specific scenes of a story will allow you to begin collating the story in a stronger way. In essence, your scene summary outline notes will cover the opening scene of your book and moves forward scene by scene through the story as these ideas come to you. Try to cover the beginning of the book in a linear (chronological) fashion as far as you can go.

Inevitably, as you're working on a brand new story, you'll hit a snag in the scene summary notes where you don't know what should happen for many scenes in a row you may still have additional ideas about what will happen later in the story. These can include anything that doesn't fit chronologically just yet but will be somewhere in the middle section of the book. These notes could be about elements or threads you're unsure of or vague ideas you want to remember to explore later. Writing down such information is vital because it widens your perspective.

Writing down end scenes is simply brainstorming non-linear scenes in your outline that you think will go in the last section of the book. They won't fit into your outline in chronological order just yet. Because you'll want to remember them in as much detail as possible so you'll be able to drop them into the outline exactly where they're needed later, you should write them down now. End scenes are very important to building the structure of your outline and eventually your story. The more pieces we can create for our story puzzle, the easier it'll be to put them together in the right order when it's time.

With the preliminary sketches started, we've built a strong foundation for what's to come, and, soon we'll be able to create a formatted (final) outline that's usable in writing your book. Go back over everything you've accomplished often, layering and strengthening where you can, and brainstorming continuously.

The Formatted Outline

As you now know, putting together an outline is much like putting together a puzzle, except in this case you're not only assembling the pieces--you're *creating* them. You've already created several of your puzzle pieces with your preliminary sketches. We're now going to talk about creating a formatted outline.

The primary goal of this step is to consolidate all of the information you've worked so hard to develop thus far. Combining information from the sketches you've filled out into a single document has a number of benefits:

- Because you're still working on your outline, the process of consolidating all your sketches and scene notes, into one main document will help you flesh out your outline even further. During this consolidation process, you'll be able to see the holes in your plot. You'll know in a glance what still needs work, where the pacing is slow, where you need to drop in a clue or increase the tension.
- Going over the outline scene scene-for-scene as the story progresses will help encourage your mind to brainstorm and your outline is more likely to begin snowballing, which is a marvelous one-thing-leads-to-another effect that speeds up the whole creative process.
- Providing yourself with a snapshot of the entire book allows you to revise and fine-tune as much as you need to.
- Having everything you need in one place helps you stay focused when you start to actually write the book

and keeps you from getting side-tracked by small details. You won't have to interrupt the flow of your writing to find the information you need as you work on a particular scene.

Formatted Outline Capsules

The first step in combining all your information is completing formatted outline capsules (detailed below with a blank worksheet in Appendix B and in the bonus companion booklet) for each scene. These brief scene summaries help you organize your information by scene and allow you to start thinking about your information in an organized, linear manner.

Let's go over these categories that make up the capsule so you have a clear understanding of what to include in each space. If you're not sure about a particular detail, you can put a question mark in that area for now. Also, much of this information is necessary for consistency. You may not actually use it in your outline or even your story. For instance, the day and time may be simply for your own use. If you don't want to include each section, use the ones that are most effective for you.

- **Day:** Jot down either a specific date or just the day the scene takes place.
- **Chapter and Scene #:** A chapter or a series of asterisks are visual indicators tell the reader that one scene has ended and a new one is beginning. In this section of the formatted outline capsule, you would include the chapter number, followed by the scene number within that chapter: "chapter 4, scene 3" for instance.
- **Point-of-View (POV) Character:** List the scene's main character.
- **Additional Characters:** List any other important characters who are in this particular scene.
- **Location:** You can put a location without specifics, or you can put the location and details about that location here.

- **Approximate Time:** Include the time of day when the scene takes place.
- **Draft of Scene:** Sketch out what happens in this scene. (You may not be able to put much in this section on your first pass, but ultimately you will flesh it out fully.)

Keep in mind that you'll be going over these capsules several times while you outline your story, so your first pass doesn't need to be too detailed. For example, your initial might look something like this:

Day: February 12th
Chapter and Scene #: Chapter 1
POV character: Angela Lewis
Additional characters: Kiowa Mackenzie
Location: Lubbock International Airport
Approximate time: 10 a.m.
Draft of scene: Keri and her cousin Joshua in Baggage Claim. She's not feeling good. She didn't sleep last night, couldn't eat before her flight, tried to read on the plane to keep herself from thinking too much--all of which have increased her susceptibility to the airsickness she's now experiencing.

Either insert a page break after each scene capsule or use a fresh piece of paper to allow space for expansion of the scene draft. This will always help you to visually note what still needs to be done in your outline.

Incorporating Outline Information Into Your Scene Capsules

Next up, you'll need to incorporate portions of your research, character, setting and plot sketches, and your scene summary notes into your formatted outline capsules. It's best to start at the beginning of your story and, working chronologically, go as far as you can in expanding all the initial capsules using your beginning scene summary notes. Incorporating from scene summary notes that fall somewhere in the middle of a book is a bit harder because many times you won't be sure where they should go, or even *if* they should go. Make a guess where you think certain events might go. If you're not sure if they progress the story, include them for now. Once you're done with the outline, you should know whether or not they should stay or go.

Incorporating end scenes won't be as difficult because most of them will fall in the last section of the book, so you just have to put them at the end of your document in the appropriate order. You'll be able to switch the order of any of the scenes easily later, so don't worry too much about putting everything from your scene summary notes in exact right place.

Incorporating character sketches isn't as easy as dropping a scene into its chronological place, so that task will be a bit trickier for you. However, because much of your individual formatted outline capsules are in a progressive (or linear) format, you should be able to see the best places to intersperse your character sketch information. Writing sensory descriptions of your characters and their behavior gives your readers the ability to move and use their senses right along with your characters. Put these descriptions directly in your outline.

Similarly, most of the important setting sketches come at the beginning of the book, because that's where the setting is first introduced, so many of your early scene capsules should include setting information. You'll also establish setting for the reader with every new scene, so be sure to include all necessary setting information into each scene capsule. Follow the principle of including what you need where you need it, even if you ultimately don't use all or some of the information when you write the first draft based on the outline.

Whether or not to include research directly into your outline is your call, but I do recommend that you try to if your research isn't extensive. Put any specific research directly into the scenes you'll need it to write intelligently. Remember, you don't want anything to distract from your work by having to go on a search elsewhere. Put what you need where you need it, and you'll be able to focus when it comes time to write this book. If your research will increase the size of your outline immensely, instead of putting the research itself into the outline, label and paginate each piece of research then put research labels and page numbers into the outline so you can easily find what you need when you're writing the scenes that need this information.

Below, you'll see a brief example of a story capsule filled in for one of my novels:

Outline Capsule Example from
The Deep, Book 3: Woodcutter's Grim Series
by Karen Wiesner

Chapter and Scene: Prologue
POV Character: Cheyenne Welsh
Day/Time: 1994, 20 years ago, October when the weather is cold and rainy
Location: Woodcutter's Grim, Wisconsin **[Setting description: Chey considers it a portal of hell]**
Draft of scene: Chey is 15. Her mother is ill again and she's supposed to be watching her 5-year old sister Dulcie, but James (neighbor and boyfriend) **[Character description: soft brown hair cut close with rugged, blunt sideburns that make his face look chiseled from stone; hint of mustache and a line of hair along his strong, forceful jaw; deep brown eyes]** came around earlier, asking to see her and so she'd gone off with him to his family farm.

Now Dulcie is nowhere to be found. The two of them start searching outside frantically. James says they have to call her dad, but she's terrified to do that. They notice his car is in the garage--strange. He's hardly ever at home on the weekends. He's usually at the university where he teaches cultural anthropology.

The door of the basement opens--the door her father returned from Africa this past summer and replaced with this steel one--and put massive bolt locks on it to keep them out. Chey had known he'd brought back something from his travels, something he didn't want any of them to see. Something alive...*Die diep.* Her grandfather and father's obsession. He's dressed strangely...

[Research: *Banganga* harness the powers of the dead by creating a portable container. Once this *nkisi* is built, the *banganga* return to the village covered in paint and behaving in a strange manner.]

Notice this example contains pieces of my preliminary sketching--character and setting descriptions and even some research.

Starting at the beginning of your story and working chronologically, go as far as you can to fill in scene capsules. Basically, it's like you're writing a story--but your point here is to get down whatever should happen in this scene to progress the story. The difference is that you don't need to write well. This draft of scene is for your own use and no one else will see it. Just set up the structure of the story scene by scene as if you're writing a detailed description of every scene in a movie--only this one is in your own head.

One of the hardest parts of writing a book is laying down the foundation of character, setting and plot plus all the research necessary to make the story authentic and believable. All the multi-faced aspects of each of these needs to be started from the very first scene and dribbled out throughout the course of the book. But because much of your outline will now be in a progressive (or linear) format, you should be able to see the best places to intersperse this information. So, as you introduce characters and have them interacting with other characters, drop in short physical descriptions. Include some information about their personalities, external and internal conflicts, goals and motivations in the progressive scenes. Do the same for setting, plot and research.

Remember, outlines can and should contain anything that helps you see the story more clearly. That means including dialogue, descriptions, introspection, tension, and "for author's eyes only" notes. Drop these in as you go, as it seems to make sense, and don't worry too much about being brilliant. It's okay to include simple directions to yourself that you'll use when you're writing a fully-realized draft of the scene. The more fleshed out your outline, the easier it'll be for you to write the book--and each scene in it--when the time comes.

Generally, you can get pretty far at the beginning and through some of the middle as you outline each scene because you're discovering your story yourself and you may have quite a bit to go on already. If you're not sure about a scene, how many you should have, where in the outline or what should go into it, insert a blank capsule onto a new page and keep going. You'll be able to switch the order of the scenes easily later, especially if you're working on the computer, so this early in, don't worry too much about putting scenes in exactly the right place or order. Wait until you've got a better handle on the basic framework of the story.

At this point, your outline should be shaping up very nicely. You'll probably see a lot of holes, but you'll also see a solid progression. Continue brainstorming to fill out the remaining holes in your outline. Remember that each scene you write has to advance the story. Each scene must add to the one before and work to move the characters and plot forward. Your formatted outline acts as a road map: You can see the path you should take, and you can place your scenes accordingly. It's much easier to pace your story when it's in outline form than it would be if you just started writing the story. With an outline sketching out each scene in detail, you can tell at a linear glance (or two) whether each scene pushes the plot to a tight conclusion. Once you complete the formatted outline, any scene that seems to slow or halt progress--or that simply doesn't belong--can be moved or cut before the actual writing of the book begins.

Also remember that your story should grow. It's normal, natural and necessary for it to do that constantly throughout the outlining as well as during the writing. Your original premise may take a lot into account--the very things you'll be exploring and learning as you outline--but it should also go far beyond your original premise.

When you've gone as far as you can from the start of the book to the finish, take a look at your outline from top to bottom again. Flesh out wherever you can. You might want to print your outline and spend a day or two going over it, trying to fill in the holes where there are missing puzzle pieces. During this process, you'll be able to see the holes in your story in terms of scenes that need to be added and fleshed out and any areas that don't have enough spark to sustain the scene. You'll see where the pacing is slow, where you need to drop in a clue or increase the tension. Going over the outline scene-for-scene as the story progresses will help encourage your mind to brainstorm and your outline is more likely to begin snowballing, which is a marvelous one-thing-leads-to-another effect that speeds up the whole creative process.

For some people who have trouble writing an outline from start to finish, try outlining as far as you can go. Then write the first scene as you outlined it. If it gets your ideas flowing again, outline as far as you can once more. If or when you stall, write the next scene as you outlined it. I think you'll find that your outline will grow as you outline and write in tandem. Eventually, you'll get to the point where you can outline your book from start to finish without writing any part of the true draft during the outlining. That's the ultimate goal you're striving for with this method. You can revise the outline as much as you need to in order to fine-tune your story.

I honestly don't think it's possible to overthink *anything* when you're outlining. You never know where it may lead. During the outlining stage of a project, I often find myself waking up in the middle of the night with a new "lead" because my mind is constantly at work untying all the knots in the story.

With your first-draft outline is complete, you should be able to see just how easy each scene will be to write when it comes time because *it's all there*--just waiting for you, the author, to turn those scenes into something magical and exciting. The outline you prepare ideally months before you write the book will allow you to produce final copy material the first time around.

The Simple Falsework Sketch Approach

As used in house-building, the term *falsework* refers to temporary supports of timber or steel that are sometimes required in the erection of difficult or important structures. When falsework is required on an elaborate scale, general and detailed drawings guide construction. For simple falsework, field sketches may be all that is needed.

I mention this here because many writers opt to use a very simple story sketch, which is basically a jumping-off point that gets them immersed in their story. Once they've established the premise, they'll write without a formal guide (beyond their muse, of course) or constant brainstorming. However, when progress is impeded, they may need to create more sketches--general or detailed--in order to get them moving forward again.

What Works Best? You Decide

There are arguments for and against both types of outlining. I stand by my oft-mentioned stance that there's no *wrong* way to write a book, but there are very *ineffective* ways. Certainly, not using any type of guide before beginning a project is the most ineffective means available to any author. After all, if your vision of a story is muddled or lost in some foggy moor, you may never home in on it. What do you do then?

A writer who does little or no pre-writing on a story starts with an idea--an idea that may or may not be terribly well-developed in her head. Generally, there's a little bit of brainstorming involved in this process, and then one day the author sits down and just starts writing. Chances are, the first three chapters will come easy, because these are the ones she can see very clearly and will have no trouble getting down. After that, things become foggy, and she may find that she's often writing blindly, following any road she manages to happen onto in the haze. Now, if this author is a crash-and-burn type who doesn't need to eat, sleep, or leave the house, she could conceivably finish this meandering book in a short amount of time--maybe a month or two, possibly less unless she's really lost. But let's face it: Most of us *do* need to eat, sleep, and leave the house occasionally, not to mention pay some attention to our family. A draft of a story, therefore, typically takes anywhere from four months to a year or more to write, depending on how many road signs become clear in this writer's wandering style of writing.

What does this author do now that she has that first draft?

Well, now she starts the *hard* part of this whole writing process. She got the easy part out of the way and left herself with the torturous work of untangling, organizing, reshaping, revising, and polishing up three hundred or more disjointed pages.

Many an author who employs this method of working may need to do *multiple* drafts or revisions to get to an editor-quality manuscript that is consistent and mostly coherent. Also consider that most authors obsess over every word, before they write it, while they write, and after they write it. They're revising pretty much all of the time! How many days of writing are lost because the author sat down and started revising, editing and/or polishing scenes she wrote previously instead of writing was she intended to? The worst part is that, the only way to know whether a book is solid is to *finish* a full draft and evaluate its strength from top to bottom only then. Until that first full draft is complete, revising, editing and polishing (which should be relegated to the final steps in writing a book) are wasted efforts. Why pretty up an unfinished, possibly seriously flawed manuscript? I'd venture a guess that writers like this do 100 percent more work than they really need to. It's never productive to plunge into a story and write endless pages that either get discarded or have to be laboriously re-worked.

Now, let's look at how the process of writing a book should be in the ideal: The author will have spent a considerable amount of time--months, maybe even years--brainstorming on a particular idea for a story. She may have also written quite a few notes on this idea, and they'll be bulging from her story folder. Now it's time put it all together. She outlines her story in the way that makes the most sense of her ideas and that will allow her to begin writing immediately afterward. Her outline is probably approximately a quarter of the size of her completed story will end up being, and it includes every single one of her story threads, unfurled with the correct pacing and the necessary tension from start to finish. All of those story threads open, develop, and conclude logically, and, best of all, they're wonderfully cohesive. Because of this guide she's created for herself, she never has to face a sagging middle, a loss of tension, a poorly constructed story thread, or weak characterization, because she addresses all of those problems during the outlining process. Like a builder does when she's working on a building project, the writer revises *her blueprint* until it's completely solid. Only then does she dare start the actual work.

This efficient author writes her first draft. With "Chapter One" at the top of her page, she uses her outline to decide what needs to be in that particular scene. She writes the second chapter, again based on her outline...and so on. As she's working, her outline is expanding considerably, taking on layers of richness, complexity, depth, and cohesion. She fleshes out the scenes with characterization, dialogue, introspection, action, descriptions, and appropriate tension in all its wondrous forms. (When she's done with the outline, she'll also use a Story Plan Checklist to verify that her story is as solid as she thinks it is, but more on that in the next chapter.)

This author worked out the kinks in her story in the outline stage and ensured that the writing and revision of her book would be the *easy* parts of the process. She did her hard work first, so she won't have to rip her story apart in order to get in the solid foundation she should have been building on right from the start. Nor will she need to duplicate any part of the process with numerous drafts.

A first draft developed through the use of an outline or some other sort of guide will be much more polished than the first draft that most authors create off the top of their heads. That's something few would dispute. In fact, this kind of first draft is close to a painstakingly crafted manuscript that's been through many drafts and revisions.

An outline has the dual purpose of creating a firm foundation for a story as well as putting the hard work of writing where it belongs--at the beginning a project. If you work out the kinks in the story at the get-go *in the outline*, you'll ensure that the writing and revising were the easy parts. Best of all, what you ended up with will be solid, requiring only minor editing and polishing to make it publishable. The outline should be the story foundation that can support the framework you build onto it afterwards. Until you have that solid foundation, don't move into writing the first draft of the book.

How does all this work in the real world? In my world, I always outline a book scene by scene before I write it. I work chronologically through this outline. When I can no longer work chronologically, I insert a few blank pages, and I skip around, working on scenes that I know will come in at some later point in the book, and so the middle and end of the book begin to gain structure. As I work, all my sketches get expanded on considerably, taking on layers of richness, complexity and depth. I keep working like this until my outline contains every single scene I'll have in the book. I should mention that when I first started doing this, I used a process I call "outlining and writing in tandem" which I talked about earlier and basically meant outlining as far as I could go scene by scene in the book. When I hit a roadblock, I would start *writing* the book's first scene. Sometimes writing that scene showed me what should happen next in my *outline*. In that case, I returned to outlining the book as far as I could go from there again. If I hit a roadblock, I'd write the next scene in the book. I always returned to the outlining, if I could, as soon as I wrote a scene because the process of writing expanded the idea in my mind and gave me ideas for how to progress the story from the point I was in outlining it. My goal, of course, was to finish outlining the book long before I finished writing it. I don't need to do that anymore but I did when I first started this method and it worked beautifully.

Something I want you to notice is that this isn't simply an outline. This is unmistakably the first *draft* of my book because it is my book...condensed. An outline like this is so complete it contains every single one of my characters and setting developments along with plot threads, unfurled with the correct pacing and the necessary tension from start to logical finish. Because it's an outline, it doesn't even need to be my best writing!

Once my outline is complete and contains every single scene in the book, I set the outline aside. Later, I come back to it and read it all over, filling in any holes, fleshing out the scenes with dialogue, introspection, action, descriptions, whatever. Basically,

I *revise* the outline in the same way I would a first draft in writing.

Now I can set aside (preferably for months) this solid structure that I'll later use to write the book, knowing I'll never again have to face a sagging middle, deflated tension, a poorly constructed plot thread or weak characterization because all those serious problems have been fixed in the outline stage.

In general, a regular full-length story can be approximately 400 manuscript pages. A "first draft" outline usually ends up being approximately a quarter of the size of the completed book. Do you want to know how many drafts an editor-quality story that started with an outline like the one created through this method should take? One. Why only one draft? Because you'll do all the hard work of writing this book *first* with the complete outline (and the Story Plan Checklist to verify its strength), and you'll get the difficult stuff out of the way, making the actual writing of the story simplicity itself.

Also, most authors don't and won't spend endless time revising the words and sentence structure, whatever, in an outline, since they're the only ones who'll see it. That makes for a lot less obsession over every word and sentence, and puts the revision where it should be in the logical order of writing a book--at the end. Revising 100 pages of an outline will certainly be much easier than revising 400 manuscript pages! Writing your manuscript based on an outline this complete might almost make you feel guilty, like you're cheating, because the writing process should be simplicity itself.

Also, because the story is so solid in the outline, revision of the actual draft amounts to very little work. When I finish that, I have a critique partner go over the book, and that's followed with a final edit and polish (which means reading the book off the computer--where I'll catch more typos). That completes the project and gives me confidence that it's ready to go to my editor. Most of my editorial revisions are minor commonsense suggestions to refine word usage and smooth out the flow of sentences. I can't remember the last time an editor pointed out a structural issue in one of my books.

Now, before we go any further, let's talk about something that most authors who don't like to use an outline say: That they fear using an outline will kill their enthusiasm for writing the book or that their creativity will be hampered or caged by the outline. Nothing could be further from the truth. I've *never* felt stifled by an outline. Just the opposite, in fact. The outline frees me to explore every aspect of a book--without risk. It allows my ideas (and my characters) to come to life on their own and grow. Use your outline to explore *any* angle you want. If new characters crop up, wonderful! Include them. If they're not right for the story, getting rid of them won't take you much time at all. Explore a new story thread--follow wherever it takes you. If it's a logical thread, keep it. If it's not, delete it. You'll only lose a little time, and your story will be stronger for it. If you realize halfway through or even *all* the way through outlining a book that some of your ideas aren't working, it's just a matter of deleting the offensive scenes and starting again in a new direction. This is a change that probably won't take longer than a few days to make in the much shorter outline (instead of the months or even years it might take to identify and correct a full draft of a book created without an outline).

When I was working on the outline for *Until It's Gone*, the fifth book in my Wounded Warriors Series, after a period of about a week, I completed scene-drafting up to the final scenes in the book. It was then that I ran into problems, because I was starting to see I had a secondary character playing a major role he didn't fit in, and that my main plot thread wasn't working the way I'd hoped it would. I spent a good amount of time brainstorming in different directions that would make the story stronger. Ultimately, I had to cut maybe two dozen scenes I'd already outlined--not the major problem it sounds, since everything around these scenes was good.

The next day, I deleted the unworkable scenes from the story file on my computer, keeping a printout of them in case I needed them later. Then I started laying in my new story threads and getting down the groundwork for the revised role of the character in question. By the end of that day, I had the outline back to the same point I'd had it the day before--only now the story worked beautifully. The following day, I continued going over my outline, filling in with new ideas that fit the revised portions. The end of the book came together easily because the rest of the story now meshed.

I lost only a day or two backtracking by deleting bad ideas and exploring new, stronger ideas. If I'd skipped the outline and gone directly to writing the book, I would have spent at least a month (probably a great deal longer) getting three-quarters of a 70,000-word book written and *then* having to delete most of it because it wasn't strong enough. Endless pages would have been scrapped in a revision that would have reshaped most of the book from scratch. Exploring new angles, characters, and concepts *while* outlining allows you to avoid spending countless hours laboring and only then finding out these don't work.

Working the kinks out of a story *within the outline* is productivity in the ideal, and it's within every writer's grasp. The clearer a writer's vision of the story before the actual writing, the more fleshed out, cohesive, and solid the story will be once it makes it to paper. Remember, your blueprint is just one of *many* layers of your story. If you're jumping directly into the writing of any story, you're missing so many layers that will have to be tacked on awkwardly or laboriously overhauled and reshaped during multiple revisions...revisions that ultimately may not fix the foundational problems your story has. Working from preliminary sketches and an outline, you'll be expanding and layering with every stage that follows, including the creation of a Story Plan Checklist. How cohesive your character, setting, and plot elements are will become obvious while you're writing your first draft.

When I sit down to write the book months after I've outlined it, I work from my scene-by-scene, "first-draft" outline and always know what's going to happen in the story on a daily basis. This is not to say that the book doesn't come to life, grow and flesh out more deeply and vividly as I write. It does immeasurably! So there goes the argument that writing an outline will kill your enthusiasm for the book. If anything, it becomes even more exciting because you're taking the structure of your story and making it breathtakingly powerful, layered, cohesive, and beautiful with your distinguished prose.

I want to challenge those who say an outline kills your enthusiasm for writing the book to try this method anyway--a couple of times if you're willing. You really do have to experience this to understand it, but, when I write a book based on a "first draft" outline, pure magic happens because I watch the skeleton--the framework of the book contained in my outline--putting on flesh. Becoming a walking, talking, *breathing* story right before my very eyes. If anything, it's more exciting this way--and a whole lot easier!

STAGE 4: SETTING THE STORY BLUEPRINT ASIDE

We talked a little about how, in an ideal situation, a writer goes through twelve stages to get a finished book. You no doubt noticed that several of those steps are about "setting the story aside". A few words about why that's so crucial: I believe a book is best if you give it time to breathe between these stages. Letting your projects sit for a couple of weeks--or even months--in-between stages will provide you with a completely fresh perspective. All writers get too close to their stories. Distance gives you objectivity and the ability to read your own work so you can progress further with it.

Another reason for setting projects aside between stages is that writers always reach a point where their motivation runs out, and they may simply want to get away from the story as fast as they can. Who wants to write a book you've just spent weeks or even months outlining? Nobody wants to revise a book he's spent weeks or months writing. With every single book, I get to rock bottom and I'm convinced that if I ever see the manuscript again, I'll tear it to shreds. Setting it aside between the various stages the project goes through really gives me back my motivation for it. I'm always amazed at how much better I can face the project again when I haven't seen it for a couple weeks or even months. I fall in love with it again. The next stage in the process becomes easier, too, and that helps my writing to be much better.

Working in stages is the absolutely height of productivity in that regard.

Also, the more books I have contracted, the more I seem to *need* these breaks in-between the stages of each project I do. If I put it on a back burner for an extended period of time (as long as I can possibly allow and still meet my deadlines), amazing things happen over a low flame! By the time I return to it, I find myself bursting with new ways to fix any problems I couldn't resolve when I was too close to, and sick of, the project.

Another reason for working in stages is that I'm able to start brainstorming on upcoming projects sometimes *years* in advance. Because I've always got multiple books going at one time--each one in a different stage of the process--I'm constantly brainstorming on these projects in the back of my mind. That's so crucial to the overall strength and layering of your stories and for the momentum of your career.

The most important reason for working in stages is because putting a project on a back burner for an extended period of time will allow you to see more of the connections that make a story cohesive in terms of knitting characters seamlessly to plot-situations and setting. Each step is a layer that's added to the book, a layer that makes it stronger, richer, and more cohesive.

To set your project aside between stages, return everything to your story folder (whether that's on your computer with a hard copy in some form or a physical folder). For as long as you possibly can, put this book on a shelf and forget it. Get to work on something else so you won't think about this project, or take some well-deserved R&R to help the soil in your brain become fertile again (and get some research done on a future project, if you're so inclined).

***

The first layer of a story is created when you plan for and lay the foundation. Through the stages of brainstorming, researching, story blueprinting, and letting it rest, you'll create an extremely strong initial layer--one capable of supporting everything you build on it afterward. Next, we'll go in-depth with the second layer and build the framework of your story with a first draft that contains utterly cohesive character, setting, and plot elements.

LAYER II, PART A
Building on the Foundation

Once a builder has laid down a solid foundation, framers come in to build interior and exterior walls, floors, and ceilings. Roof, windows, sheathing, and siding are usually installed next, protecting the home from the elements while the electrical, plumbing, and ventilation systems are roughed in and installed. Drywall is put up and prepared for painting, and cabinets and interior trim are installed. It's here, with the framework, that a house becomes solid, so it won't fall over with the first wind (or big bad wolf) that blows in.

In writing, there are similar layering steps involved in building the framework of a story through completing a Story Plan Checklist and in writing the first draft with both outline and Story Plan Checklist merged. In the introduction, we talked about the stages necessary, including:

1. Completing the Story Plan Checklist
2. Evaluating the blueprint
3. Writing the first draft
4. Creating a punch list

It's in these crucial stages that a story gains its cohesive molecular force.

STAGE 1: BUILDING A COHESIVE STORY WITH A STORY PLAN CHECKLIST

Most builders/homeowners spend a lot of time dreaming about their ideal house, but there comes a time when they have to wake up to the reality of building by analyzing what they expect from a house and whether the plans they've selected will meet their needs. Architects argue that it's better to build from the inside out.

This is where a home plan checklist comes in handy. This list assembles the key considerations to keep in mind when deciding on a plan, including what are called exterior (relating primarily to the outside of a house and its environment) and interior monologues. (The word *monologue*, in building, refers to a single facet of overall composition on the inside or outside of a house, such as flooring material or aspects of landscaping.) This same home plan checklist can be used even when considering remodeling or building onto an existing home.

Writers spend a lot of time dreaming about their ideal story. Eventually they have to face reality and analyze whether the story will work. Authors, too, usually build from the inside out--in other words, they know what they want at the heart of their stories and they build around that.

This is where a Story Plan Checklist becomes essential, because it targets the key considerations necessary when building a cohesive story that readers will find unforgettable. A Story Plan Checklist has basic external (a story's exterior elements) and internal (the interior elements in the story) monologues. *Monologue*, in writing, refers to internal or external workings of a story.

On a Story Plan Checklist, external monologues target those things relating to the story's external elements, like character overviews, occupational skills and settings. One way of looking at this section is as the outer shell of your story. This is where you identify your main characters and describe the essence of who they are, what they do, and where they live. External monologues need to be done for each main character but they carry over through each segment of the story (beginning, middle and end) so you'll only do them once.

Internal monologues are the inner workings of your characters--essentially, emotional complexities brought about by conflicts. Internal monologues need to evolve and expand resolve multiple times throughout the course of a story as conflicts intensify and characters grow and develop in response, and eventually they have to resolve. In general, these are all composed individually in free-form summaries, but they need to form cohesively.

The Story Plan Checklist is the means in which you can ensure cohesion between character, setting, and plot. This checklist connects all the dots between characters and settings, internal and external conflicts, and goals and motivations that must evolve from the start of a story to the end, thereby guaranteeing the cohesion all stories require. Like we said in the introduction, the checklist isn't necessarily used to craft scenes the same way an outline is, but used together, your story will really be something amazing. We'll talk more about this later.

I'm going to assume that you completed the scene-by-scene outline for your story in Layer I and that you're ready to create your Story Plan Checklist.

In its most simplified form, a Story Plan Checklist includes free-form summaries covering each of the following:

PART I: THE BASICS
Working Title:
Working Genre(s):
Working POV Specification:
High-Concept Blurb:
Story Sparks:
Estimated Length of Book/Number of Sparks:

PART II: EXTERNAL MONOLOGUES
Identifying the Main Character(s):
Character Introductions:
Description (Outside POV):
Description (Self POV):
Occupational Skills:
Enhancement/Contrast:
Symbolic Element:
Setting Descriptions:

PART III: INTERNAL MONOLOGUES
Character Conflicts (Internal):
Evolving Goals and Motivations:

Plot Conflicts (External):

As we said, Parts I and II of this checklist are done once. Later, we'll break the internal monologues out a bit more to allow for the beginning, middle, and ending sequences required for each story spark (a plot invigorator, which we'll discuss shortly).

I call this list a Story Plan Checklist not only because of its correlation with a home plan checklist, but because if you haven't considered each of these areas, written something solid about them, then checked them off one by one, your story may not be fully fleshed out and cohesive enough to fuse irrevocably. Sooner or later, the basic structure will begin to fall apart.

A note for clarification: The Story Plan Checklist you'll find for your own use in Appendix C is slightly different from the one we're going to work through step by step in this chapter. I had to present the checklist items in a slightly different order here to facilitate discussion. We need to talk about story sparks before we can assign an estimated number of them, and so forth. You do *not* need to work in the order presented in this book with your own checklist. Feel free to mix the items in whatever way makes the most sense to you--or in whatever order the ideas come to you--and check off that area when you finish it. Each time I've used the Story Plan Checklist myself, I've found that I *don't* follow the order listed above. I work steadily on the one area I'm inspired to get going on at the time. When I finish that, I check it off, then look through the list and see what I'm inspired to develop next. Later, you may revise your completed Story Plan Checklist to reflect a more chronological order, especially if, as we're going to discuss in Layer IV, you plan to turn your Story Plan Checklist into a killer synopsis you can submit to a publisher or agent.

A few additional notices before we begin: Don't forget that your major goal in using the Story Plan Checklist is to come up with *cohesive* ideas for character, setting, and plot, so you won't just be brainstorming random ideas and putting them together. You need to make each of the items on your checklist cohesive, finding organic ways to link all the elements. I'll be reminding you of this throughout the process to keep you focused and on task with your goal in filling out the checklist.

Next, your checklist only needs include what you require to make the necessary cohesive connections in your story. Don't duplicate what you may have already done with your sketches and outline. For example, in your preliminary sketching, you might have completed numerous character sketches. That's *not* the same thing we're doing here. As we said, the point of the character overviews on the Story Plan Checklist is to make your characters cohesive with your plots and settings. You're not filling out another set of character sketches here. But keep in mind that this checklist is for your own use. If you want to combine or add anything to it, that's your choice. Whatever helps you.

For an average novel (75,000 words) that you've already outlined, a Story Plan Checklist will usually end up being about five to ten pages long, at most. A longer story might be double that, but not necessarily. What really adds to the length of a Story Plan Checklist is how many characters are complicating the story. If you have a lot of characters (and *Harry Potter and the Chamber of Secrets* does, as you'll see in Appendix D), and all of them are important enough to have their own external and internal monologues, your checklist will be decidedly longer.

Your Story Plan Checklist may read very much like an incredibly well-developed synopsis, and should give you a very strong idea of all the major points in the book--including the resolutions. Remember, this checklist is for your own use, so you don't have to use your best writing, nor do you even have to be concerned with switching between past and present tenses (until you're turning the checklist into a synopsis anyway). As long as the Story Plan Checklist helps you understand your characters, settings, and plots in a rich, cohesive, and logical way, it's fulfilling its purpose.

Throughout this chapter, I'll offer an example of each step in the checklist process using Agatha Christie's classic cozy mystery *Death on the Nile*. I can't stress enough the importance of seeing the development of a cohesive story plan from start to finish. Though I can only guess how Dame Christie went about the preliminary work of developing this novel, and naturally it's cheating a little to use a book that's already completed and rock solid, the example Story Plan Checklist should give you a very good idea how to craft your own--before you ever write a word of it.

I also want to note that I can only use what's presented in the published work of other authors for my examples of Story Plan Checklists here and in Appendix D. The checklist examples may seem sparse on details in some sections; because *Death on the Nile* and the other bestsellers I use as examples aren't my stories, I can't make up material to fit into each item on the checklist. I can only use what I found in the book, and, in some cases, there wasn't much to find. In *Death on the Nile*, I could only guess at internal conflicts, but they may not be entirely accurate, 1) because this story doesn't have a lot of deep internal conflict depth, and 2) because my own experiences influence how I view the characters. If the author didn't provide, say, setting descriptions, I can't put much (if anything) in the setting description section of the Story Plan Checklist example. Also, most of the characters (even minor ones) in, say, *The Friday Night Knitting Club*, another book I discuss in Appendix D, were given point-of-view scenes at one time or another, yet some of these POV characters didn't have fully fleshed-out internal monologues throughout each story spark. Either the author had the information and it didn't make its way into the book, it was cut before publication, or the author (or editor) goofed. If sections of the Story Plan Checklist aren't filled out, there's a good chance the story has a few plot threads that aren't as cohesive as they could be and, therefore, might be contributing to incomplete resolutions.

If you find a character (or anything else) isn't properly developed from start of story to end of story on your own checklist, you can do more work in that area. Blank or sparse sections are invitations to do more work. That's why you're doing the hard word before you write the book! So you don't have loose ends; illogical or even unfinished, unsatisfactory resolutions; or characters, settings, and plots that aren't cohesive.

On the opposite spectrum, the example Story Plan Checklists I've provided include *much* more information than you'll include on your own for the reason that these examples need to make sense to readers. On your own checklists, you'll add only what you need to make sense of your story. You won't be duplicating what you've already done with your sketches or outline. For example, if you are already doing some sort of other character sketch, you'd really just be duplicating your work by including more than a simple paragraph for this item on the Story Plan Checklist. In fact, if you've already completed your outline, you will and should find your Story Plan Checklist short and easy to fill out. You probably don't need more than a sentence or two for your character introductions and descriptions. The rest of the information on the checklist is really looking for something more or different than your outline probably includes, but, again, we'll talk about that more later.

Also important for you to understand is why some Story Plan Checklists include a lot of main and secondary characters and why others hardly include any at all. For instance, in the *Dead Drop* example included in Appendix D, there are only two main characters--hero and heroine--on the list, and only one of the secondary characters made it on the Story Plan Checklist. In certain genre stories, like romance, *only* the characters who go through each internal monologue cycle (including internal conflicts, goals and motivations, and external conflicts) may be included on the checklist. If you do add secondary characters, remember that their internal and external monologues will be revealed through the main-character internal monologue cycles.

How do you know which characters to include on your Story Plan Checklist? I use three criteria:

1. If a character has internal monologue cycles (i.e., beginning, middle and end), then that character definitely needs to be included.
2. If you put a simple designation for the character (like "Mike, Perry's FBI partner"), and that's all that's needed to explain the character's role in the story, you don't need to include that character at all on the checklist. You can if you want to, of course, since it's for your own use.
3. If there's a lot of background on the character that

needs to be told even though the character won't have internal monologue cycles that go through beginning, middle and end, it's your choice whether to include them on the checklist. Any secondary character can be included but won't necessarily have cycles that follow through the entire book.

Secondary characters fill specific roles and perform specific, necessary tasks in a story. This is no way implies or assumes that these characters are irrelevant. One way to express this is to consider the secondary characters' internal monologues as short term, while the main characters' will all be long term. If you just don't know for sure at this point, go ahead and add any character (main or secondary) on the checklist. By trying to fill out their internal monologue cycles, you'll inevitably discover whether the character has enough material to warrant including them. If you look at the examples included in Appendix D, I think you'll get a clear idea why certain characters were included in detail and why others weren't.

To further clarify the sections of the Story Plan Checklist, I'll also use examples from popular fiction as well as movies (as movies tend to be better known and easier to visualize) in this chapter. In Layer IV, we'll turn the Story Plan Checklist for one my books into a tight synopsis, included in Appendix G.

PART I: THE BASICS OF A STORY PLAN CHECKLIST

While you're in the beginning stages of forming a cohesive story plan, sit down and figure out some of the working details (which may change throughout the process). These include what follows.

Title and Genre Specification

First, come up with a working title. All you need here is something to use to reference the project (and you may have already created this during your *First Draft Outline* sketching and outlining).

While you don't want to lock in your genre too early, since stories evolve in unpredictable ways, get started with genre specification. For now, list all the genres this story *could* fit in.

For *Death on the Nile*, the preliminaries of the Story Plan Checklist would look something like this:

<u>Title:</u>
Death on the Nile by Agatha Christie
<u>Genre:</u>
Cozy Mystery

POV Specification

Now, start thinking about what point of view you want to use for this book. It's very important to start your Story Plan Checklist thinking about this because who your main characters are will play a huge part in your characterization, and subsequently, each of the areas you'll be summarizing on your checklist. Most stories spark with a character, who may end up becoming your main character. If you're a romance writer, your romance stories will most likely spark with both a hero and a heroine, and therefore you'll want both of their viewpoints. If you write complicated suspense stories, you'll have many characters with their own viewpoints.

Though most writers know the various types of point of view, let's briefly sum them up:

- ***First Person:*** This is the "I" POV. Everything is seen through this character's eyes, as if he's talking to someone about himself. This can either be a very intimate story, or a limiting one, depending on the skill of the author.
- ***Third Person:*** This story is told by "he" or "she", or by more than one person, such as in a romance with both hero and heroine leading viewpoint scenes. Naturally, you could also use this viewpoint for a villain, or, in a

longer, more complex book, with many different characters in play. Not only can you go into all main characters' heads in this viewpoint, but you can see the characters from the outside, from the POV of other main characters. I strongly caution against hopping from one head to the next within a single scene, though. While this was a popular thing to do in the past, it's become a no-no and for very good reason. (We'll talk more about this when we discuss creating intimacy with our characters.) Stay in one character's head for the full duration of a scene. Never jump into another's--even if that character is allowed viewpoint in the story--in a scene that starts in a different character's head. The third-person viewpoint is the one most often used, and it really does offer authors a good amount of freedom to tell their stories.

There are other viewpoints (second person, such as stories told entirely through letters of some form, and hybrid points of view) but they're not generally recommended.

Your best bet for deciding which character's viewpoint to use: In any scene, stick to the viewpoint of the character with the most at stake, the one with the most to lose or gain.

For *Death on the Nile*, the Story Plan Checklist would list:

POV Specification:
Most of the main and even some of the secondary characters have third-person POV scenes.

High-Concept Blurb

The high-concept blurb is a tantalizing sentence--or sentences (no more than a short paragraph with up to four sentences; one or two is ideal)--that sums up your entire story, as well as the conflicts, goals, and motivations of the character(s). No easy task. Here's a simplified explanation of what your sentence needs to contain:

A character **(who)** wants **(what)** a goal because he's motivated **(why)**, but he faces conflict **(why not)**.

Or you can simply fill in the blanks--whichever works best for you:

____________ **(name of character)** wants ____________ **(goal to be achieved)** because ____________ **(motivation for acting)**, but who faces _______________ **(conflict standing in the way)**.

Fill this out for all your *main* characters as you would for a back cover blurb and in a synopsis. As with a basic synopsis, secondary characters probably won't be included. Ideally, you would want to weave all the long-term plot threads into the high concept blurb--as concisely as possible.

Remember, your high concept blurb is completely for your own use when you're working on your Story Plan Checklist so don't get too bogged down trying to perfect something brilliant. That said, you *do* want to look ahead because when you start turning your completed checklist into a synopsis (which we'll discuss later), you will need to lock this down.

For *Death on the Nile*, we have this high-concept blurb:

High-Concept Blurb:

While on holiday, the famous, retired detective Hercule Poirot **(who)** is aboard the SS *Karnak*, his keen little gray cells in need of stimulation. **(what)** Poirot sees that every woman on board envies Linnet Ridgeway for her beauty as a rich society bride on her honeymoon. Poirot also observes with worry how Linnet thoughtlessly stole her new husband, Simon Doyle, from her best friend. **(conflict)** Can the detective prevent Linnet from becoming an irresistible incentive to murder? **(motivation)**

Story Sparks

At this point in the checklist, we've established the basics of the story, and we're ready for the beginning spark--so crucial to drawing a reader's interest!--followed by the initial external and internal monologues on the Story Plan Checklist. Here, you'll begin the cohesive development of your story. Most authors do start strong because the idea that initially fascinates them guides them through this first portion of the sequence naturally. Let's talk more about the many facets of story sparks.

A story spark is something intriguing that ignites a story scenario and carries it along toward fruition. It's that "aha!" moment that a writer has when he thinks up something that completely captures his imagination so he has to see how it unfurls and concludes. I daresay there's not a writer alive who hasn't come up with one idea that blows the mind. However, most don't realize that a story *has* to have more than one of these sparks to sustain it. A story spark must infuse and re-infuse the story, and a new one must be injected at certain points in order to support the length and complexity of your story.

Most novels up to 75,000 words have three story sparks: one for the beginning, one for the middle, and one for the ending (we'll look at the total number of sparks a story should include in just a bit). The beginning story spark sets up the conflict. The middle story spark (or possibly more than one middle story spark) complicates the situation. Finally, the ending story spark resolves the conflict and the situation. Short stories, flash fiction, and novellas usually have only one or two sparks (beginning and ending). All of these sparks absolutely must be cohesive to ensure a solid story.

We've all heard writers say that at some point their story seems to "sag" (usually in the middle) and they need to shake things up again. This should actually be called the spark injection point. The suggestion most often given on how to get the story flowing again is to throw a dead body into the plot. That might not work for every story (it'd become cliché and boring if *everyone* did that), but the underlying principle is an excellent one. A story that's dragging is a wake-up call for any author.

What is "sag"? Usually, nothing more than a deflated story crying out for another spark (or sparks) to enliven it. You need only take what you've already developed with your initial spark and throw in some shocking, intriguing scenario that'll have your characters running at full-speed again and will progress the story. This is what keeps the reader panting along beside you.

Personally, I wouldn't define sparks so much as plot points but as story invigorators. Sparks should affect all long-term story threads. You can't invigorate one long-term plot thread without invigorating the rest of your long-term plot threads. If you can, your story isn't cohesive.

Let me put this in another way: You'll most likely have several long-term plot threads running through your book. If you're writing a romance, that will be one of the long-term threads. If you have a mystery or suspense plot running along that thread, that's another long-term thread. Both of these are long-term threads and need to have new sparks injected periodically in order to invigorate the plot, ratchet up the tension, and carry the next 10- or 20,000 words (depending on the overall length of your story). The romance *has* to affect the mystery or it's not a cohesive story, and vice versa. You can't have the mystery progressing while the romance stagnates behind it. These long-term threads progress together, and they have to do that in ways that make perfect sense with your story.

All your long-term threads will be included in each story spark because all the long-term threads will need to be invigorated at various points throughout the book. That's something that should be deliberate on your part, though you'll want the development of your story to be natural and not forced in any way.

What's the difference between story sparks and plot conflicts? Not a whole lot, so it doesn't matter if you combine or overlap these. To fall into a whole new metaphor here (sorry), the difference between a story spark and external plot conflict is similar to the differences between a guitar and a bass guitar. Both are guitars, both are essential to the strength of a song, but guitars tend to be more melodious and in-your-face. The bass guitar is in the background, carrying the song. Similarly, a story spark enters the story with a lot of fireworks and gets a lot of attention. The development of the story is kicked up to another notch and sends the story off and running. External elements may not be as showy, but they're just as important because they allow the story to grow and develop as they run along the foundation of your story. You'll have a final external plot conflict resolution at the end of every story.

Near the end of the book, you need another spark to *enlighten* the situation for the final course. The final spark doesn't exist solely to enliven the plot, though it probably will inadvertently. Soon after the third spark, you'll reach a point where all of your character and plot conflicts need to tie up logically.

Here's the beginning story spark for *Death on the Nile* (which, incidentally, has three story sparks, which we'll cover in this chapter: one at the beginning, one in the middle, and one at the end):

Beginning Story Spark:

While dining at a restaurant, Hercule Poirot overhears a heated discussion between a couple obviously in love. Poirot worries that the woman, Jacqueline de Bellefort, loves her beau, Simon Doyle, too much. When next Poirot meets Jacqueline, they're on a ship, and Simon has married Jacqueline's former best friend, Linnet Ridgeway. Jacqueline ruthlessly stalks the couple on their honeymoon.

I can easily guess that this was the concept that intrigued Christie--and her fans, once the novel was published. Every part of the story that follows grows naturally out of the main, intriguing spark.

Estimated Length of Book/Number of Sparks

Your estimate of the length of the book should decide the number of sparks you'll need to carry the story. Remember, most stories up to 75,000 words will probably need only three sparks--one at the beginning, one at the middle, and one at the end--though you're certainly free to include more if you don't mind your book running longer.

The more sparks you include, the longer and more complex your book will be. There's little way around that, so plan accordingly; but don't consider it the end of the world if your "little" idea evolves into something big and beautiful.

With that in mind, a story over 75,000 words may have more than three basic story sparks, especially in the middle, since a longer story needs complexity to sustain it. A middle story spark can appear anywhere after the beginning one--before the end--though it usually does appear somewhere toward the halfway mark of the book.

To give you a basic idea of how many sparks you'll need for novels, you can figure that if you have an estimated 250 (double-spaced) words per page:

- up to 75,000 words = 300 pages **(3 sparks)**
- 90,000 words = 360 pages **(4 sparks)**
- 100,000 or more words = 400 pages **(5+ sparks)**

If you think your story will need more sparks, estimate how many you'll need for your length. You might also want to make a note about *where* you want to place the extra spark(s). In general, you really want extra sparks to come in the beginning or middle of the book.

There's a tendency for authors to include too much backstory and action in the beginning, and you don't want your story to be overdone from the get-go--starting with focused action and backstory is the best way to do it, then dribble more in when the story is capable of accepting it in the middle. A reader should never feel lost or completely in the dark, nor should she ever be able to see a clear path to the end of the book. Give her just enough that she can see a small square of light in front of her on the path toward the end. She should be side-by-side with your characters, not running ahead or lagging behind. Remember that because it's crucial to how much you as the author give at any one time.

The end of a book won't need more than one spark, since you're winding down at that point and you'll be focused on enlightening the reader and tying everything up rather than on introducing new ideas. Remember the obvious: More story sparks *will* prolong one or more story threads.

How often should story sparks come? Well, let's say you estimate you'll have three story sparks and 75,000 words. The first will come right in the beginning within the first few chapters, the second will come around the halfway mark of the book (around 40- to 55,000 words in) with the last just near the end at maybe 75- to 80,000 words in. A more complex book may have sparks coming approximately every 15,000 to 20,000 words into the book. However, the final two sparks will probably come quickly, back-to-back with each other (possibly 10,000 words apart) to sustain the suspense--though of course the fourth spark is intended to *enliven*, while the fifth should *enlighten*.

For *Death on the Nile*, we have:

Estimated Length of Book/Number of Sparks:
54,000 words/3 story sparks

Weaving Together Part I of Your Story Plan Checklist

As you can already tell, a Story Plan Checklist provides for natural growth. Many times, authors go gung-ho on an initial spark for three or four chapters, then they have no idea where to go with the story. The checklist takes into account every single area you need to think about to develop a cohesive story.

The strongest stories are the ones in which *every* part of the story--the characters' strengths and weaknesses, goals and motivations; the main story goal and subplots; even suspense--becomes cohesive and fits together organically.

We've all read stories in which the parts don't merge naturally. Maybe we didn't notice a specific problem, but we knew *something* was off, that something lacked logic or didn't quite fit with the rest of the story, and it frustrated us. There's a chance you never finished reading the story, or that you threw it against the nearest wall.

The books that you absolutely cannot put down without losing a little of your sanity, the stories that stay with you every minute of the time you're reading them and for years afterward, are the ones in which every aspect is so intricately connected that separating the threads is impossible.

Cohesion starts with the first spontaneous spark of a story in your head. Characters must blend naturally with the setting you've placed them in, just as plot must become an organic part of your character and setting. If a story doesn't work, it could very well be because your character, setting, and plot elements aren't blending naturally.

It could also be that your story isn't following one of the cardinal rules of writing: Everything that happens at the beginning of the book must be linked to something that happens later on.

In every story, the writer has to meet a basic challenge in order to create a successful book. This challenge almost always follows this course (where you see the arrow, substitute the words *leads to*):

Character → Event → Conflict → Backstory → Goals → Motivations → Choice → Resolution

I love how Debra Dixon puts this challenge in its simplest form in *Goal, Motivation & Conflict*:

- Who = character
- What = goal
- Why = motivation
- Why not = conflict

She goes on to say that "A character wants a goal *because* he is motivated, *but* he faces conflict."

PART II: EXTERNAL MONOLOGUES OF A STORY PLAN CHECKLIST

A Story Plan Checklist targets the key considerations necessary when building a cohesive story, and includes in free-form summaries those things relating to the story's external elements that develop and grow cohesively.

In your quest to form a cohesive story plan, sit down and figure out the working details (which may--*should*--evolve throughout the progression of the story). These include what follows.

PART II: EXTERNAL MONOLOGUES
Identifying the Main Character(s):
Character Introductions:
Description (Outside POV):
Description (Self POV):
Occupational Skills:
Enhancement/Contrast:
Symbolic Element:
Setting Descriptions:

We talked earlier of the external monologues as the outer shell of your story. This is where you identify your main characters and describe the essence of who they are, what they do, and where they live. Keep in mind that the core of a character won't change--and shouldn't. Think of your principles, the morals, the fundamentals of who you are and what you build your life on. For the most part, these areas of you remain unchanging, though you of course grow as an individual as you experience life. In fiction, a character can't be a chameleon, altering his makeup to fit his situation. When a character constantly changes his core self, he's not realistic or even likeable. He's wishy-washy and all over the place, which makes it impossible for readers to ever truly get to know him and they'll forever question his goals and motivations as a result. They simply won't care enough to keep reading.

The external monologues need to be done for each main character but they carry over through each segment of the story (beginning, middle and end) so you'll only do them once.

Most writers know the obvious when it comes to characterization. You need to make readers like your characters by showing them *why* they should care. You need to make readers root for your characters, even when those characters are steeped in the past, pain, and emotional baggage. Readers should see the potential hero in a character despite his oh-so-human flaws. Readers should respect characters for their choices (maybe not right away, but soon enough to warrant cheering at the end when they win), instead of constantly questioning characters' choices and growing frustrated with them--possibly to the point that they quit reading the book. Readers need to understand characters in order to be able to forgive them for the silly or even terrible decisions they might have made in the past. It almost goes without saying (but I feel it needs to be said anyway) that this sympathy factor from readers is essential to the overall success of your story, and it's what distinguishes a hero from a villain. (Later in this chapter, we'll talk about this more.)

In real life, you can get to know some people easily. With others, it may take you years and an incredible amount of effort to truly get to know them and understand who they are. You learn never to trust first impressions, since a cruel mother may disguise herself with the face of an angel. A heart of gold may hide beneath a gruff exterior.

Characters are just the same. Some come to life with the first story spark and flesh themselves out continuously through the pre- and draft-writing stages. Other characters refuse to come out of hiding so easily. In some ways, these characters are hiding from the writer, so it becomes that much harder for the writer to get to know them and bring them to life for readers. These characters have barriers the author absolutely must break through in order to bring them to life.

A lot of authors ask, *How do I know whether my characters are coming to life?* The assumption is that, if a character is walking, talking, and moving through each scene in the book, she must be coming to life. Real, living characters and merely lifelike characters are two completely different things, especially in this age, when it's so easy to manipulate images and facts. Real, living characters are what you're striving for, because only these characters allow the readers to understand what lies behind the face they present within the story. Readers will see personality, deep issues and conflicts, goals and motivations, and amazingly natural growth. Life*like* characters are merely cardboard, and most readers will see right through the careful façade you constructed, because there's clearly nothing behind it--no personality, no growth, no true internal conflict or goals and motivations.

If you *don't* have to ask whether your characters are coming to life, it's probably because your story is reeling through your mind in full color. As a writer, you should wake up with your characters in the morning and go to bed with them at night. In any given situation, you should know exactly what they'd be thinking and saying and doing. You see them growing and developing as they work through their conflicts, and you have a solid idea about what motivates them in any situation. It goes without saying in this best of all scenarios that your characters *are* living and breathing through you. If your critique partners, publisher, agent, and readers feel the same way, consider yourself blessed.

It's harder to define when--and especially *why*--some characters don't come to life. However, in most instances, the characters are cardboard because the author hasn't developed them (given them the crucial breath of life, as it were) enough to allow them to live and breathe. You as the writer need to create solid personalities, conflicts, goals and motivations and, of course, development in characters throughout the story. But keep in mind that both author and character need to share control of development. An author should never be so controlling that the character is too stifled by rigidity to come to life, nor can an author allow the character to run amok in a story in ways that simply don't fit. The author should give his character enough freedom to be able to emerge and develop naturally and enough discipline to keep the story logical and cohesive.

Some telltale clues that your characters are adamantly hiding from you:

1. **The main character runs out of the scene the instant things get heavy.** Now, you can surely explain this behavior by making it part of the character's personality from that point on. But if you know deep down it's not a personality trait, that you as the author truly don't know what your character would and should do

in this situation, then your character is hiding from you.

2. **You, as a writer, head-hop between characters because you have no idea what's going on in the POV character's head.** If you're writing in third-person POV, you may have two or three POV characters within the book. However, you should only have one of those characters as the *main* POV character in each *scene*. Head-hopping in a single scene is an avoidance mechanism that indicates the basic problem of lack of character development. Some authors claim to use head-hopping in a scene as a means of getting to know both POV characters at the same time. Maybe that's valid (but, hey, isn't that what effective dialogue and introspection are for?), although nearly all cases of head-hopping simply confuse the reader. One minute he's comfortably resting in one character's mind, hopefully discovering nuggets and emotions that make this character likeable and understandable to him, and the next he's abruptly thrust into someone else's head and thoughts. I encourage you to picture this scenario in your mind because it'll prove how discombobulating it is for a reader to be forced to head-hop in a single scene. After a while, this reader will start dreading the leap back and forth (kind of like a Ping-Pong ball would dread a match if it were alive). At the beginning of each scene, the reader has to orient himself to the setting, action, and characters. The writer disrupts the established scene whenever he head-hops between characters within that single scene.

3. **You replace your main character's authentic, gut-wrenching emotions with uncharacteristic and illogical actions inconsistent with what you previously set up as part the character's personality.** In some way or other, you force a shocking situation into

the plot that lays a particular character flat. Instead of having a character consider what's happening, and possibly his part in it, you have him do something that makes absolutely no sense for the character or to the reader.

For instance, I've read a lot of unpublished books in which a responsible, sentimental heroine is grieving, feeling sorry for herself, or in such dire emotional straits that she has no clue how to extricate herself from the situation. As if it solves her problem, she acts completely out of character and sleeps with the first guy she sees. As anyone who's read a chick-lit novel knows, she always regrets it, but by then the damage is done, and the writer spends the rest of the story trying to get her out of the mess she made by acting uncharacteristically irresponsible.

In this case, plot and characters will feel very unnatural to the reader. Hence, the story will become artificial and probably won't be loved by readers. The author of a story like this has gotten it into his head that the character's behavior has to be justified, and he creates his own means to defend the direction all of this is going. Again, the character's behavior could be passed off as a personality flaw the writer fully intends and keeps going with, or the author could face the fact that the character is desperately trying to hide from him, and instead reach for more cohesive story elements to bring the character out.

Characters need to be *real*, likeable (or at least sympathetic), and consistent, in identifiable situations, making logical choices. In moments of duress (and that's what fiction is--conflict!), a character's mask drops and the reader comes to know the character's true nature by how he reacts. That's why it's so important not to set up a character one way and then have him react in another.

4. **Secondary characters become more interesting than main characters.** If your main characters aren't interesting enough to carry the plot you've set for them, but the secondary characters are, then you definitely need to do more work in developing your true main characters (whoever they may be). Or switch the roles accordingly.

5. **You allow resolutions to stem from symbolism, events, or other people.** In other words, the character never truly solves his own problem. This is sometimes referred to as "coincidence resolution". While you can have a plot that begins this way, the coincidence must fade to be replaced with very clear choices, purpose, and action. Something similar to the coincidence resolution is deus ex machina--"god from a machine". This device introduces a resolution brought about by something outside of the story, something cataclysmic or even supernatural that's not cohesive with the rest of the story--basically, anything illogical introduced at the end of the story to resolve a central conflict. In fiction, true change and growth should come from strength within, just as it does in real life. You can't wrap up a story with an act of nature, something symbolic that parallels a character's conflict but isn't actually part of it, or in a stranger-to-the-rescue type of event--it won't be believable or fair to the reader, who's spent the entire book waiting to see your character reach the goal of self-fulfillment and success.

   When readers finish a book, they should close it believing that it ended the only way it possibly could have.

6. **You place your characters in situations or settings that just don't fit them.** If there isn't cohesion between character, setting, and plot, your story simply won't work. The character's conflicts, goals and moti-

> vations must match the situation he faces in order for him to be believable. Search for the situation and setting that brings your character to life, since characters generally search out the setting that most fits their personalities.
>
> In some cases, the setting must *enhance* the conflict, and in this case, the setting may not be one the character would choose for himself. Force him into intimate situations that break the barriers that allow him to hide. Reshape his personality, if necessary, by sketching and re-sketching him with strengths and weaknesses, goals and motivations that provide organic ways for him to emerge and grow. His setting must allow for this to happen. This is truly where cohesion comes in.

In *Creating Character Emotions*, Ann Hood stressed the importance of making character emotions in any situation effective and honest in such a way that readers will ask, "How did you know what it was like to...?" Fill in the blank. How did you know what it was like to have cancer? Lose a child? Be trapped in an unreachable place with no hope of escape? A realistic character will remind someone somewhere of his own experience--this reader will feel like your character went through exactly the same thing he did. Even if you've never experienced the situation you're putting your character through, you need to draw on your own emotions from similar situations to capture the experience. (After all, the only experiences you've gone through intimately are your own.)

The layering process from brainstorming, preliminary sketches, outlining, writing, revising, and editing and polishing will help you create characters that live vividly beyond the static page. If there isn't cohesion between character, setting, and plot, your story simply won't work. The character's conflicts, goals and motivations have to match the situations (the conflicts) he faces in order for him to be believable. Search for the situations and settings that bring your character to life. This is truly where cohesion comes in. Develop characters from the inside out, and they'll walk right off the pages.

Identifying the Main Character(s)

If you have no idea who your main characters are, chances are that this particular story needs a lot more brainstorming, not to mention preliminary sketching and an outline. Even if your story is more plot- than character-oriented, brainstorming on your characters the way character-oriented writers do until you can fully envision them, filling out character sketches, and writing out a Story Plan Checklist will help immensely.

I also highly suggest cutting pictures out of magazines of people who resemble your characters. Having a fuzzy mental picture of a character doesn't make you feel you know him as well as you should. If you can picture your characters clearly, actually see them, chances are you'll write about them in a more intimate, comfortable way. For me, having those pictures is like a brainstorming infusion each time I look at them. I desperately want to know what makes that person tick! My characterization development becomes deeper through the tangible visual.

In this section of the Story Plan Checklist, simply list the names of the characters you've identified as your main characters. While a complex book will have more primary and secondary characters (in fact, that seems to be a trend I'm not sure I can get on board with, considering how difficult it is to keep up with ten plus POV characters in a single book!), most 75,000- to 90,000-word stories have, at least in terms of main characters, a hero, a heroine, and/or a villain.

One thing that's extremely important to note for authors of all genres, especially for less experienced writers, is the point of introducing characters in a story. A character can be main, secondary, or even minor, but *all* characters must be important to the story. A character who fits the role and achieves the goal you set for him, however small, is an important character. If not, why include him at all? All important characters should be introduced in the beginning and middle of a book (in most genres, introduction is done in the beginning, but suspense and mainstream books may also introduce in the middle). It's unfair to the reader, not to mention to your story, to introduce a new character late, thereby all but ensuring that his development will be decidedly meager. Introducing important characters in the latter part of the story isn't generally recommended.

There's only one situation in which I would consider the introduction of a new character at the end of a book valid (and, even then, it would have to be done skillfully to work). You might introduce a new character at the end of a book in order to set up for the *next* book in a series. By necessity, this introduction must be brief and intriguing without being overwhelming. The fact is, the new character is important only because of his role in the *next* book. The sole purpose of this introduction is meant to give the reader a small, tantalizing taste that will whet his appetite for what comes next.

In *Death on the Nile*, Christie has a profusion of characters, most of whom are well developed. In general, there are four main characters in this novel--just three in the middle and end sections, as one of them dies early on. Only the main characters have internal monologues completed throughout each story spark. With the middle story spark, a host of secondary characters is introduced. While their initial conflicts and motivations and goals are covered in this section--as they're important to the plot--the main characters take over after that point, providing the resolutions of all subplots. To avoid confusion, I'll introduce these secondary characters in the middle story spark.

<u>Main Character Identification:</u>
Hercule Poirot, Linnet Ridgeway-Doyle, Jacqueline de Bellefort, and Simon Doyle

Character Introductions

The introduction of a character in the Story Plan Checklist is a springboard into finding out more about him. It's like meeting someone for the first time. You say your name and a few pertinent details about yourself.

In the Story Plan Checklist, you list a name, the character's role in the story, and an overview of his personality. Don't duplicate what you've done in your character sketches. Remember what we talked about earlier concerning how to know whether to include a character on the checklist. Go back over that section if you need refreshing. Also, don't worry about including occupation and setting information here, nor internal conflicts and goals and motivations (if you end up including them, it's fine, of course). We'll cover all of those later.

Keep in mind with your overviews that your goal is to outfit your characters with the tools they need to succeed against the conflicts they'll be facing. You have to set the stage from the beginning for those to be believable. Don't try to pull a fast one by expecting the reader to believe, for instance, that a man who can barely get out of bed in the morning and who's afraid of his own shadow can suddenly knock down walls and take on an armed man with nothing more than a rubber band and a rock. Remember, when David fought Goliath, he'd already killed a lion with his bare hands.

Each of your main characters will have particular skills that are shaped specifically for the characters and plot, and that's really what you're introducing in this section of the checklist. Some of these could and should be carefully selected occupational skills, but most will go far deeper than that.

For instance, in the fourth book of my Incognito Series, *Dead Drop*, the heroine has had the experience of losing the man she loved to a covert government organization. She's an FBI agent, and she's spent years fruitlessly searching for this man. When the same organization approaches her son for recruitment, her experiences in the past kick in and provide her with the personality traits, conflicts, goals and motivations that are necessary to prevent the same tragedy from happening again--and that may also help her now find the man she still loves.

In another instance, the heroine of my inspirational gothic romance, *The Bloodmoon Curse*, has miscarried frequently, and this has naturally devastated her. So when she's asked to care for three orphaned children, she's led by all-too-fresh past conflicts, the goal to end suffering for these children, and the motivation of also finding the means to heal her own pain. You see how these personality traits and the roles the characters fill within the stories are shaped specifically for them? The whole of the character's makeup must be cohesive with the story you've placed him in.

Feel free to compose something for character introductions for your secondary and minor characters, too (especially if they fit the three criteria for including them listed earlier), but the main characters are the ones who absolutely must be fleshed out in order to create a truly cohesive story.

In *Death on the Nile*, the introductions are as follows:

Main Character Introductions:

- ***Hercule Poirot:*** Retired detective on holiday.
- ***Linnet Ridgeway-Doyle:*** Twenty-year-old heiress rumored to be the richest girl in all of England.
- ***Jacqueline de Bellefort:*** An old school friend of Linnet's.
- ***Simon Doyle:*** Formerly Jacqueline's fiancé, now Linnet's husband.

Character Descriptions From Outside Viewpoints

If you're using a third-person POV, chances are that your main characters will be described by other characters. Although this kind of description can include physical appearances, it should always incorporate *impressions* made by your characters upon the ones around them. You can (but don't have to, since the checklist is only for your own use) describe the main characters from *each* individual viewpoint in the book. Or your summary can simply encompass the most basic impressions without ascribing them to the person offering them, such as the descriptions here from *Death on the Nile*:

Description (Outside POV):

- ***Poirot:*** A small, round man with an egg-shaped head, Poirot dresses impeccably in all weather. His intelligence and sympathy draw those around him to confide in him their deepest, darkest secrets. Poirot loves to have the last word.
- ***Linnet:*** Described as a "beneficent tyrant", Linnet is the girl who has everything, or can get it simply because she wants it. She has complete assurance in herself, displayed by a natural habit of command.
- ***Jacqueline:*** Hot-blooded with an ungovernable temper, Jacqueline is known to get extremely worked up over things. Once, she stabbed a boy with a penknife for teasing a dog.
- ***Simon:*** Boyish, simple, and charming in his appeal, though weak, Simon is filled with male impatience and annoyance, taking nothing seriously and instead playing games and refusing to grow up.

Already, we're building some strong characterization. Let's add another layer to it.

Character Descriptions From Self Viewpoint

Very few people describe themselves the same way others describe them. That makes it even more important for main characters to describe themselves, since the reader gets a strong sense of who your players really are with both outside and self-descriptions. In essence, these are like mini first-person profiles. The characters talk about themselves, and sometimes also give their impressions of the other characters.

For obvious reasons, providing self POV descriptions was difficult to do for an already published, well-known book, but here's what I came up with for *Death on the Nile*, based on impressions I got from the novel:

<u>Description (Self POV):</u>

- ***Poirot:*** It's been observed by my peers that my investigative methods are characterized by the active pursuit of the psychology of the murderer, noting minute details and Freudian slips by asking a series of seemingly pointless questions. I enjoy finishing each case with a dramatic, ordered summary. I am indeed "the greatest mind in Europe".

- ***Linnet:*** I'm fanatic about my possession of Wode Hall, my kingdom to rule as I, the queen, see fit. I truly believe I don't have an enemy in the world--ironic, I suppose, to those who have had the opportunity to view me up close and personal.
- ***Jacqueline:*** I admit it--I'm excitable, mad, tragic and frightened somctimes of my own overwhelming love and obsession with Simon Doyle.
- ***Simon:*** I'm a cad for my behavior with Jacqueline--there's no doubt about that. But I'm an Englishman and I believe in restraint and propriety--and I also feel a woman should be owned by a man, *never* the other way around.

Character Occupational Skills

The *First Draft Outline* method, as well as other book-writing approaches that consist of character worksheets, includes at least one section about occupational skills. Few go in-depth, even though occupation or hobbies can define us as individuals. (The older I get, the more I am convinced this is true.)

Especially in a work of fiction, what the characters do is pivotal to their personalities, their motivations--just about everything hinges on these interests, hobbies, or jobs. In nearly every book, what the character does (in terms of a job, a career, or even just a hobby or specialty interest) for a living gives him the necessary skills to deal with the conflicts he's facing through the story.

To build the form of cohesion we've been talking about, the skills the character is equipped with should be directly related to either his internal or external conflicts. In the best-case scenario, is his skills will connect to both in some way. Best-selling author Sandra Brown has said aptly something to the affect that if the hero's a firefighter, then the heroine had better be an arsonist. Cohesion between the characters' occupations and the conflict is *that* essential. (J. Madison Davis adds that anything not naturally relevant becomes "an odd appendage, glued onto the story like a clock stuck into the belly of a *Venus de Milo*".)

If the character doesn't have a nine-to-five job per se, that fact says something about his character. In her Silhouette Intimate Moments release *A Dangerous Man*, Marilyn Pappano presents a hero who's a retired Army master sergeant. The skills Rory Hawkes learned in the military figure very profoundly in the plot of the novel. If Pappano had made him, say, a restaurant owner, or even an accountant, the plot would have fallen apart, or gone in a direction that simply would not have been anywhere near as effective. Occupation fused with the character, setting, and plot in this story, and nothing else would have worked quite as well.

The occupations Christie chose for her main characters in *Death on the Nile* are very appropriate and cohesive with the overall plot:

Occupational Skills:

- ***Poirot:*** The brilliant Belgian detective, a retired police officer known for his deductive reasoning and his immense mustache, has had a long and glorious career. Though now retired from his life of crime-detection, he finds himself time and again forced to employ his infamous "little grey cells" to solve a dazzling array of complex whodunnits. At this time, Poirot is a man of leisure. Having made the 'economies in his time', he has the means to enjoy a life of idleness.
- ***Linnet:*** Shrewd heiress of a vast estate left to her by her grandfather.
- ***Jacqueline:*** A penniless secretary, proud as the devil and unwilling to let anyone help her.
- ***Simon:*** For the last five years, Simon has been in the city in a stuffy office. He grew up poor on an estate and has had business training. When the business he works for downsizes, his job is cut out.

In a story that has more than one main character (like a hero and heroine in a romance book), the other main character should also have an occupation that creates the same level of cohesion as that of the first character. Pappano's heroine in *A Dangerous Man* is a lawyer in a corrupt small town. Her father, the district attorney, had tried to fight the corruption, and he'd been killed in the process. You can really see the level of cohesion in all this, since a small-town lawyer would have little chance of going up against a corrupt system all on her own. With the backing of a retired master sergeant, she's got a shot at winning.

The basis of my romantic action/adventure suspense novel *Dead Drop* was a man inducted against his will *because of his occupational skills*; he was told lies that drove him to become a machine instead of a man as their operative. In this book, I needed to have a heroine with the skills and strength to find the man she loved, to stand up to an organization that prizes its anonymity above all else, and to get the hero out when the time came. As I said earlier, I decided on an occupation as a FBI agent for her because it was a logical, fitting choice for her role and character within the story.

Any main character who doesn't have an occupation or skills that suit his internal conflicts and plot conflicts can't be truly cohesive. But that doesn't mean that a character's occupation has to be predictable. In real life, you can find cops who are unpredictably ruthless and greedy. You can just as easily find doctors and nurses who don't really care about patients. It may work for your story to find a way to make the unpredictable fit. To be cohesive doesn't mean to be predictable.

Enhancement/Contrast

If you want to create a truly unique character--and what writer doesn't?--the best way to do so is by providing his personality with enhancements and contrasts. Enhancements are the subtle, balanced, or extreme elements that complement what the writer has already established as characteristic traits for that character. Enhancements are personality traits that make that character uniquely larger than life. A writer can't create a truly ordinary joe because he would be boring to read. But, in the fictional world, an author may present a hero who at first glance seems ordinary. But there must be something about him that makes him stand apart. This something may not be revealed until later, when his quality is tested.

A contrast, which can also be subtle, balanced, or extreme, is an element that is in opposition to what the writer has already established as characteristic traits for that character. A contrast in a personality is one of the best and most often used ways of making a character rise memorably to the spotlight. Few readers want to know a hero who advertises "Hero for Hire--Inquire Within" on a sign outside his office. The hero who's optimistic to a fault, whiter than snow, and perfect in every way is dull.

Flawed (but likeable!) characters are the ones readers root for, because a character without flaws or fears is a character without conflicts. Readers know that true courage is facing what you fear most, pursuing your goals and not giving up even when there's little chance of success. Readers go crazy for a rough and raw, imperfect hero with more baggage (of the emotional kind) than a pampered socialite. An eternal pessimist, he wants nothing to do with the title, let alone the job. He's only forced into it by an oft-buried sense of nobility, or because something or someone he cares about deeply is in danger.

Readers want baffling contrasts. They want to see a high school dropout spouting Byronic poetry. A bleeding heart paired with an unmovable hero. The wounded warrior rescuing a stray dog. The uptight virgin wearing six-inch stiletto heels. They want to watch a character rebuild and rediscover his dignity, his self-respect, his inner moral compass.

A character who's so hard and jaded he almost seems untouchable will need a soft contrast--something that makes readers like and sympathize with him, forgive him. Readers must in some way be touched by what's beneath his mask.

A hardened cop who's seen the worst there is in his fellow man, yet who never fails to visit the chronically ill children in the hospital makes a poignant impact on readers. The contrast proves not only that he's human, but that there's still vulnerability buried deep inside him that will surely rise to the surface in other ways, given time and opportunity.

An emotionally guarded, straitlaced woman, perhaps cold in her manner to co-workers who don't know her well, sitting in the shadows of a smoky Jazz bar and closing her eyes, swaying while she listens to the sensual trumpet, is a woman who's obviously not as uptight as she wants her fellow employees to believe. *Her sensual vulnerability breaks free in the dark of a nightclub--where else might it show?* the reader will wonder. What makes her feel she ever has to hide? The reader wants to know more.

Think of some of the most unique characters in history, on the big screen and in literature. Indiana Jones, dashing adventurer and ambitious scholar, is truly a study in contrasts. He'll enter any dangerous situation to retrieve an artifact, yet he's terrified of snakes. Everything about him *fits him*. All the things that make up his personality enhance his character and make him unforgettable.

Take the character of Westley in William Goldman's unforgettable *The Princess Bride*. An acquiescing farm boy quietly in love with his mistress goes off to seek his fortune to make himself worthy of winning her hand in marriage. He comes back a notorious, invincible pirate who kidnaps her, then repeatedly rescues her even after he's dead...or only mostly dead. He's charming, tenacious, forgiving, and an unshakeable believer in true love. Pair him with a princess who's not sure of anything but who comes around in the end, and two loveable rogues, and this is a story that has utterly cohesive building blocks from start to finish.

Think of Heathcliff, the dark, tortured hero in Emily Brontë's classic, *Wuthering Heights*. He is an unwanted orphan who, in contrast to his emotionless, humble beginnings, becomes violently obsessed with Catherine, the daughter of his benefactor, to the grave. Everything about him is extreme, and it enhances him in a way that makes him stand out (perhaps not positively but nevertheless irrevocably) in a sea of ordinary men.

Éowyn, the daughter of Rohan, in *Lord of the Rings*. A caretaker by nature, and yet not content to stand by while the men of Rohan ride off to war. She puts on battle armor and marches to war beside them. Soft, vulnerable, and yet the very warrior who defeats the immortal Witch King.

In *Death on the Nile*, Jacqueline is poor, Linnet is rich. Jacqueline is hot-headed, Linnet is careful. In direct contrast to Simon Doyle's insistence that a man must never be "owned" by a woman, he allows his new bride Linnet to control nearly his every move.

All of these characters have enhancements and contrasts that make them breathtakingly memorable.

Employing Commonalities and Contrasts With Other Main Characters, Love Interests, Secondary Characters, and Villains

Another way to develop a main character is by introducing another main, secondary, or minor character (love interest, family, friend, or villain) who either enhances or contrasts with his personality.

You'll see the saving-herself-for-marriage woman paired with a slutty best friend. The street-smart guy with the 4.0 GPA buddy. The happily married accountant with 2.5 kids living vicariously through his footloose, unfettered college buddy who's been to every corner of the globe on one hair-raising adventure after the other. The friend-rivals who have everything in common, constantly trying to one-up each other.

The brilliant Sherlock Holmes had his bumbling Dr. Watson. In the same vein, Holmes' arch enemy, Moriarty, is his equal in every regard, and therefore the rivalry enhances the legendary detective's character. A worthy opponent's agenda always threatens to swallow up anyone who crosses his path--and that creates endless and cohesive conflict!

Hercule Poirot had his ignorant-of-the-little-grey-cells-approach Captain Hastings. In *The Emperor's New Groove*, Yzma, the emperor's fired advisor, tried to take over the kingdom with her loveably stupid big oaf Kronk. Bambi learned about life from take-a-bite-out-of-life-from-the-flower-not-the-greens Thumper. Even Harry Potter has his best friends: Ron Weasley, poor and a little jealous; and Hermione Granger, too smart for her own good.

In the *Moonlighting* television series with Cybill Shepherd and Bruce Willis, Maddie was the former model, straitlaced, by-the-book detective partnered with the off-the-cuff, refuses-to-follow-the rules, does-it-his-own-way David--a man who inevitably succeeded. Together, they contrasted and enhanced each other, creating an undeniably irresistible tension in their union.

In *Death on the Nile*, Christie employed this technique for some of her major characters:

Enhancement/Contrast:

- ***Poirot:*** none in this novel
- ***Linnet and Jacqueline:*** Jacqueline and Linnet are exact opposites: Jacqueline is poor; Linnet is rich. Jacqueline is hot-headed and impulsive; Linnet is careful and deliberate. Linnet is light where Jacqueline is dark. Linnet is the picture of sophistication, attracting attention everywhere she goes, while Jacqueline scrapes by, barely noticeable to those around her.
- ***Simon:*** Simon's character belies the reality of his situation when he makes a point of saying he doesn't like to be owned by a woman, yet that's exactly what he becomes as Linnet's husband. Linnet holds all the purse strings, and Simon becomes her "Prince Consort".

As a general rule, a character who is an extremist in any regard (whether hard, obsessive, ruthless, etc.) will need someone or something to soften him. In a character who's more balanced, an enhancement or contrast may be more subtle, but should be just as effective. Whatever you do, choose characteristics that will be necessary at some point in the book, that don't hit the reader over the head, and that advance each story element.

Think of an aggressive reporter who faints at the sight of blood in a suspense, or a creature-feature enthusiast encountering the real thing in a paranormal. Unique characteristics put a spin on the norm, surprising readers and keeping them intrigued.

Symbolic Element

Another effective means of developing character is to give him some sort of symbolic element that defines him, defines the situation he's in, or does both. These symbols are sometimes called by the musical term *leitmotif.* In the world of writing, we use them to associate characters, objects, events, and emotion. Each appearance makes them more intense and meaningful.

Whether you make symbolic elements subtle or well defined, they take on layers of meaning each time they're mentioned, becoming an integral part of the story. As a general rule, each character should have only one associated symbolic element, but if you have two total in the book, one of them should be subtle while the other is well defined. The point is to enhance or contrast, not take over the story so the symbol becomes the focal point when you have no desire for it to be.

The symbol can certainly be tangible, in the form of something that defines the character, setting, and plot in some way--a piano, pet, flower, key, map, or necklace.

But it doesn't *have* to be. It can be a trait or mannerism the character uses frequently that says something about him and/or develops the character, setting, and plot in some way. It could also be a hobby, vice, or a character disability or disfigurement, like a scar.

This tangible or intangible symbol must be cohesive and not thrown in just for the fun of it. In one way or another, it has to enhance or contrast and thereby develop the character, setting, and plot in deeper ways.

In my inspirational women's fiction *Wayward Angels,* the heroine has many unique personality traits that, at first, just seem off-the wall. She makes up a personality and history for a cat featured in the story. Readers learn from this that she's reticent about talking about her own past and, by making up a history for the cat, she can tell the hero about herself. The cat's history is actually her own, and she's revealing pieces of herself when she speaks through the pet. This oddity is the heroine's symbolic element, and hints at something deeper than what the reader sees on the surface. Each time the symbol is mentioned, it takes on more meaning and advances the plot. In the course of the story, the reader eventually learns that the heroine is bipolar and this oddity is indicative of her unwillingness to accept her condition.

In the same book, I wanted to subtly show how the hero has left behind the things that led to his downfall in the past. Several times, it's mentioned that the only colors in his house are black and white (this is true even of the shelter for troubled boys he runs), and there are absolutely no decorations to be seen. He shrugs this off by saying he's never had much time to do any decorating or fixing up. However, this unwillingness becomes a very evident indicator to the reader that the hero has a black-and-white fear in his life--the fear of letting color back in and the trouble that came with it before. This lack of color is a symbol with deep character, setting, and plot connotations.

In my novel *Dead Drop*, my hero's more-machine-than-man personality required a symbolic element that contrasted in softness: The character's ability to play elaborate classical pieces on the piano. Before he was inducted in the covert government organization, this balanced his scientific side with a touch of the artistic, and lent romanticism. Now he's a man hard as granite, and he needs the softness of music. As an operative whose life is his work, he owns a grand piano, yet never plays it because to do so would resurrect memories of a life stolen from him. The first time he plays the piano after the heroine enters his life again is the signal that the defenses and guards he's constructed for himself are beginning to crumble.

The heroine in that book also had a symbolic element that showed the romantic side of her personality--*and* enhanced and progressed the plot in pivotal ways. Her love of growing roses--particularly lush, blackish-red blossoms in a hybrid tea rose called Ink Spots--is her symbolic element. It's in her rose garden that the hero makes "dead drops" to keep in touch with her after they come together again, and it's this same type of rose that reunites them in the end.

As I said, a symbol may very well be a tangible symbolic element. In the first Indiana Jones movie, the heroine Marion had carried around a sentimental artifact for years. She wore it around her neck as a means to remember her father, who'd given it to her. Later, she finds out that this artifact is the headpiece of the Staff of Ra that Indiana Jones needs to discover a long-buried vault containing the Ark of the Covenant. This kind of symbol is used a lot in fiction because it so effectively adds character, setting, *and* plot enhancement.

In *Death on the Nile*, note that Poirot and Simon don't have symbolic elements but I've included their names just to help track all the characters--remember that no one will see your checklist except you so include as many details as you need to:

Symbolic Element:

- ***Poirot:*** none in this novel
- ***Linnet:*** A string of exquisitely matched pearls worth about fifty thousand pounds. She wears them all the time and, once on the ship, leaves them on her bedside table at night.
- ***Jacqueline:*** A small, pearl-handled pistol--a dainty toy that looks too foolish to be real--that Jacqueline carries around in her little silk handbag. She shows Poirot the gun, telling him she's a good shot. She bought it after Linnet stole Simon from her, meaning to kill one or both of them, though she couldn't decide which.
- ***Simon:*** none

I had a problem writing the third novel in my Wounded Warriors Series. *Dark Mirror* (originally titled *Mirror Mirror*) was romantic paranormal psychological thriller. This book continued to elude my best efforts to create something wonderful, suspenseful, and cohesive. My first draft of the book was so bad, I refused to send it to my publisher, even if it meant keeping my fans waiting on that third book in my Wounded Warriors Series. I made a long list of notes on all that I thought was wrong with the book (believe me, it was a huge document!), then I put the book in my story cupboard for three months in order to get the story brewing on a low flame again. At that time, I came up with another unworkable outline.

Feeling increasingly desperate, I put the story aside, terrified I'd never finished a book that had already been promoted as "coming soon". More months went by, during which I had a series of creative percolations that made me rethink the direction of the book. I reshaped all my characters, consciously trying to flesh them out in ways that related to the plot much more than they had in the past.

However, it wasn't until I realized something so obvious, I feel silly about it now that I finally knew why my previous drafts hadn't worked. The heroine wasn't directly involved in the resolution of the plot. How could this character achieve her full potential if other characters solved her problems for her? How could the story be cohesive if the character had nothing to do with the wrapping up of the plot?

My second realization was that I had to make the plot fit more naturally with my main character's struggle not to accept her gift of clairvoyance by pushing it away and feeling ashamed for it. She needed to *use* her gift in order to solve her problems. Also, her setting, and how it related to the villain, needed more cohesion.

I also acknowledged that my little hint earlier in the book that the villain was terrified of dogs was the key (the heroine's symbolic element!) to having her save the day. Also, I decided that the final "glue" in making my story cohesive was to make the hero and the heroine's pasts merge and parallel. Everything fell into place then.

You see the challenges I had with the book. I had to make the heroine's gift of clairvoyance and her beloved dog mesh with the villain's terrifying curse of clairvoyance and his fear of dogs. All of these things had to fit with the hero and heroine's pasts, which intersected in ways neither of them ever dreamed. The setting of all the characters also needed to fit.

I wasn't sure I'd fully succeeded in this task until a reviewer said of the book, "An excellent psychic thriller that will have you holding your breath until your lungs ache. The author uses her writing gift to connect both Gwen and Dylan's pasts with a dark, menacing force and tangles a web so strong that readers will not want to stop reading."

Build in symbols to make your plot, setting, and characters a trinity. The nice thing about incorporating cohesive symbols is that, though it's ideal to do this *before* you begin writing the book, it's never too late to come up with this kind of story enhancement. After I finished the outline for the sixth book in my Incognito Series, *Renegade's Rose*, I felt unsatisfied with the story for various reasons that weren't major but could be easily fixed. Through the completion of a Story Plan Checklist, I realized that I needed a tangible symbolic element to connect the hero's past to his present. What I came up with drew *all* the elements of the story together cohesively.

Setting Descriptions

Before a writer even begins putting words on paper, he has a vision of something--a character, a setting, a conflict. Research and refining help him bring that vision to full, realistic color and make his characters, settings, and plot more realistic. If carefully chosen and developed, these elements fuse into a cohesive whole.

Readers rarely start a story with a vision. It's up to the writer to paint the picture for them, giving just enough for readers to begin their own vision. As Stephen King says so eloquently in *On Writing*, "Description begins in the writer's imagination, but should finish in the reader's."

Just as writers have to get to know their characters before they start the story, they should get to know their scenes, since each will have its own setting and mood. To get to know scenes, writers do research and form descriptions that they later intersperse where most effective in the story. Your setting is a basis for building your story. To develop cohesion, the settings need to be appropriate to the situations you're putting these characters in, allowing all three to flourish. While many stories have settings that are fine for the character and plot, I'm sure you can come up with dozens where the author could have spent more time making the setting extraordinary--so the reader actually wants to visit it again in another book--instead of simply getting the job done.

The importance of creating a setting cohesive with character and plot can be illustrated by imagining different settings for classic novels. What if *Moby-Dick*, instead of being set at sea, had been set in, say, a lighthouse? Captain Ahab (a man who's never been on anything bigger than a sailboat) boasts around town about how he'll get the whale. *Moby-Dick* wouldn't have been the novel that's become so well known if the setting had been anywhere else but where the author put it.

The Lord of the Rings would have been drastically different (and so disappointing!) if it'd been set in America instead of fictional Middle Earth. If the *Amityville Horror* had taken place, in, say, a department store, some of the horror would have fizzled. If Harry Potter went to the local public school (or St. Brutus's Secure Center for Incurably Criminal Boys, like Aunt Marge wants to hear) instead of the private, magical boarding school Hogwarts, the series may have been radically altered. Setting has a huge impact on the overall readability of any story. What a difference a vividly memorable, cohesive setting makes to so many books we consider popular!

If your setting doesn't match the other elements, you'll work harder at creating fitting characters and plots. Additionally, you'll find it hard to create the appropriate mood. In any case, you'll have to find a skillful way to play against the contrast of setting. My advice is to make a setting *more than* fit your characters and plot--make that setting come *alive* in the reader's mind. Make them want to visit and re-visit it. Heck, make your readers want to live there indefinitely!

While the setting should *enhance* the characters and conflict, that's not to say that a contrasting setting won't also be perfectly cohesive in your story. In other words, the setting may not be one the character would choose for himself. Put him into situations that mesh with the other elements in the story. Good settings *should* convey characteristics and plot elements.

Describe the setting in such a way that it not only becomes evident to you how the characters and plot fit there but supercharges your whole story. What does the setting reveal about the character's personality? What in the setting means the most to him? How will this setting create the stage for conflict and suspense? How can you make it so real, your reader will believe the place actual exists?

The setting information you'll include in your Story Plan Checklist isn't necessarily the kind of setting information you would list on worksheets for the *First Draft Outline* method or another like it. What you're doing with the Story Plan Checklist is matching your settings to your characters and the plot.

You can use the setting section of your Story Plan Checklist to describe all the settings in the book and how they evolve--even if these settings aren't introduced in the beginning of the story. However, feel free to drop in settings in as they appear in the book, rather than putting them all under the External Monologues. You may do this when there are many important settings in the book (as opposed to one important setting, as most books have), so none of them get lost against the other settings. Do it whichever way makes the most sense to you and your particular project. There are very few rules here, beyond making the checklist work as effectively as you can make it.

While *Death on the Nile* has many minor settings, below I've described the one where the majority of the action takes place, very appropriately and cohesively, and which is therefore the most important.

Setting Descriptions:

Aboard the small steamer ship, SS *Karnak*, on a seven-day journey to the Second Cataract and back. As the boat isn't full, most of the passengers have accommodations on the promenade deck. The entire forward part of this deck is occupied by an observation saloon, all glass-enclosed, where the passengers can sit and watch the river unfold before them. On the deck below are a smoking room and a small drawing room. The deck below that is the dining saloon.

You'll notice that Agatha Christie often set her novels in places where the cast of characters can't escape, while also limiting the number who could have committed the crime. This greatly increases tension and also focuses the plot on these particular characters, allowing the reader to participate in unraveling the mystery in a closed setting, where the surprises will be highly logical ones that stem from the trinity of characters, setting, and plot.

In my novel *Dead Drop*, when the heroine, Perry, locates the front headquarters of the covert government organization that inducted the man she loves, I gave descriptions that only added to the intrigue and cohesion of character, setting, and plot in this story:

Network/ETI Setting Descriptions:

Nothing about the ETI skyscraper made a viewer think "secret" or "covert". The innocuous-looking building rose high above the group. Did high-level employees live there? Perry wondered if there was an underground compound as well. The blueprints certainly didn't indicate anything like that, but the schematics they filed *wouldn't* be accurate if this was the location of a covert agency. Any entrances inside the ETI Chicago branching down to the compound below would be so well concealed, they'd be all but invisible. People without clearance wouldn't be allowed within a hundred feet of the entrances without alerting security.

Notice in this example that even Perry's skills as an FBI agent are brought in. She's thinking like an agent, not a civilian.

The heroine's own home adequately describes her setting and fits her sophisticated, sensual personality to a T:

Perry's Setting Descriptions:

Perry lives in a picturesque neighborhood just outside the city. Instead of traffic and sirens at midnight, she hears crickets and the wind's breath. She owns a 1923-era Craftsman-style home, surrounded by fragrant woods and the explosively lush, colorful garden she loves babying throughout the year (the very garden the hero later leaves "dead drops" in to keep in contact with her, the garden with the roses she'd been planting the day they met). The interior of the house boasts knotty pine walls stained a warm honey; beamed, twenty-foot ceilings; and expansive rooms filled with plump, oversized chairs, generous tables, and a profusion of pillows and throws that help create the informal coziness she prizes. In the living room is the polished Bösendorfer piano the hero used to play every night.

Pieces of the character (some of them painful) and plot details are woven into this setting. Like we said, good setting descriptions *should* convey characteristics and plot elements--otherwise they're general information without a strong, cohesive purpose.

PART III: INTERNAL MONOLOGUES OF A STORY PLAN CHECKLIST

On a Story Plan Checklist, internal monologues target those things relating to the story's internal conflicts. These are written out in free-form summaries.

In this step, the crucial need for cohesive character, setting, and plot becomes boldly evident because now we're deep delving into your main character's internal workings. This is truly the heart of your story. Life is conflict, and fiction even more so. Without conflict, you don't have a story. But if your conflict is only external and not internal as well, why should any reader care to read the story?

For each story spark your story has, you'll check off one of each of the following steps for all the major characters. As I said earlier, this is optional for secondary and minor characters:

PART III: INTERNAL MONOLOGUES
Character Conflicts (Internal):
Evolving Goals and Motivations:
Plot Conflicts (External):

Character Conflicts (Internal)

Character internal conflicts are emotional problems brought about by *external* conflicts that make a character reluctant to achieve a goal because of his own roadblocks. They keeping him from learning a life lesson and making the choice to act.

In fiction, internal conflicts are usually why external conflicts can't be resolved. Simply put, the character can't reach his goal until he faces the conflict. (Sounds a bit like not getting dessert until the vegetables are eaten, and this is pretty accurate.) The audience must be able to identify with the internal and external conflicts the character faces in order to be involved and to care about the outcome. Character growth throughout the story is key to a satisfactory resolution.

In *Creating Characters*, Dwight V. Swain talks about giving the main character drive, which basically entails devising something for him to care about; fitting him with suitable goals, always keeping in mind the direction you want him to go in; threatening that goal; and finally establishing reasons for him to continue fighting against the threat on the road to reaching his goal.

Keep in mind that clearly defined conflicts are ones that won't hit your reader over the head or frustrate him. If you as the writer don't quite understand the conflicts in your story, your instinct will be to compensate by bombarding the story with unfocused ideas. The reader won't find it any easier to sort through them and identify the true conflict than you will. Unclearly defined conflicts usually lead to the reader putting down a book and never picking it up again.

Also, conflicts can easily overwhelm the reader if you have too many (especially too soon or at a single time) or if you're unrelenting in driving them forward. I absolutely adore J. Madison Davis's take on this in *Novelist's Essential Guide to Creating Plot*: "Even the greatest excitement and most spectacular events can become wearying if they are relentless. I remember hearing one disgruntled moviegoer whisper to his wife sometime around the third hour of *Titanic*, 'When is this dang boat gonna sink, fer pity's sake?' The writer who has one unremittingly, relentlessly exciting scene following another can wear the reader out. Too much shouting makes us deaf, and shouting even louder after that will not be heard because of the deafness". Too many conflicts (especially at the beginning and end of a book) and failing to allow the reader to breathe between action sequences *{is anyone else thinking about Dan Brown's Robert Langdon series novels here?}* equate to too much shouting that can deafen your reader. We'll talk more about the critical importance of release and downtime a bit later.

Your first story spark will usually suggest what the character's conflicts are, and they're almost always based on someone or something threatening what the character cares about passionately. In some instances, a loved one is in jeopardy, or something the character wants, needs, or desires above all is at risk of being lost. It's your job as the writer to give the character incentives not to give up until everyone is safe and has what he was fighting for.

Internal conflicts are different from external, but they're related causally--the best definition of concept I've heard is: "Can't have one without the other." Internal and external conflicts depend on each other, and therefore they need to be cohesive. Internal conflicts are all about characters, and external conflicts are all about plot. But keep this in mind, lest confusion creep in: Both internal and external plots belong to the main character(s). After all, if both didn't affect him in some profound way, they wouldn't be conflicts for him and therefore wouldn't even be part of his story.

Think of it this way, everyone has a passionate hot button: Cruelty to animals, breast cancer, child abuse. You fill in the blank with yours. But not everyone has the strength of passion for your particular hot button. We're all individuals that way because we usually put our passion into something that has touched us deeply in our lives. If your mother died of breast cancer, you'll want to see that particular disease cured. It's your hot button. This doesn't mean you don't sympathize and care deeply about other causes, even if you're not quite as passionate about them as you are about the ones that affect you most. What it does mean is that if something critical happens in the area of your passion, you're probably going to step up to the plate and fight for what you believe in.

You're telling a story about your particular characters, and they have hot buttons, too. Since it's their story, their hot buttons will naturally be their conflicts. All of these conflicts must parallel, intersect, and collide for a story to be truly cohesive.

So, though the external plot conflicts may stem from an outside force or situation, they nevertheless belong to the main character as much as his internal problems do. Like I said, if he didn't care deeply about the external plot, it wouldn't be his story.

In the action/adventure movie *Die Hard 2: Die Harder,* the rough and gruff main character, John McClane (played by Bruce Willis) is a cop at the airport on Christmas. He's off duty, but begins to sense trouble is afoot in what seems like the busiest place on earth--and things are looking to get worse before the day is through. The airport cops don't share his uneasiness--they've got their own worries to handle. Though McClane is very reluctant to get involved, his inner integrity won't allow him to stand by. He checks it out, figuring he'll let the airport police handle anything that's amiss.

His gut instinct is dead-on. Terrorists take over the airport. This shouldn't be his problem, but it becomes so because: (1) the airport cops refuse to do their jobs; and (2) these terrorists have pushed McClane's hot button. A year before on Christmas, McClane single-handedly took down a band of terrorists at the Nakatomi building, where his wife worked. Terrorists, particularly those who threaten his wife, are undoubtedly McClane's hot button, his external plot conflict.

Enter his cohesive internal character conflict--his wife is currently on one of the planes circling overhead, a plane that is unable to land because of the terrorist attack paralyzing the airport and is rapidly running out of fuel. Not only have these terrorists hit John's hot button, they've made it very personal, and there's no way he can sit back and consider this not his problem.

Let's go over the sometimes subtle distinction between character (internal) and plot (external) conflicts with some examples from best-selling books.

In all of the Harry Potter books, young wizard Harry constantly battles his internal conflict. His parents are dead and he's been forced to live with his detestable and magic-hating aunt, uncle, and cousin. That's a simplification, of course, of a complex situation. In all the Harry Potter books, the external plot conflict is Harry coming to terms with his accidental relationship to Voldemort, who killed his parents, and how his contact with this person affected him inside and out. (See the Story Plan Checklist for Book 2 in the series, *Harry Potter and the Chamber of Secrets,* in Appendix D, and you'll agree that this external plot conflict is evident there just as it was in the first and all subsequent books.)

In *Dances With Wolves,* Lieutenant John Dunbar has nearly lost his life in the war, and his sense of purpose and self-worth has wavered, although his sense of adventure and sense of duty are intact. Feeling like he doesn't belong where he is, he ventures into dangerous Indian Country, where he finds his purpose, his self-worth, and comes to learn that he belongs to and loves the new culture he finds. These encompass his internal and external conflicts. Plot and character conflicts in this story center around the Indians he encounters, which both threaten him physically and heal his soul, showing him both the ugly and honorable sides of his fellow white men.

In all of these examples, you see how the internal and external conflicts differ--one's outside, one's inside--how they parallel, intersect, and collide, and how you can't really have one without the other.

Balancing Necessary Human Flaws With Heroisms

What makes a reader root for a character? Sympathy. At times, even empathy. Everyone has flaws. Everyone sins. Everyone falls short of the ideal. A protagonist's flaws and sins draw a reader's sympathy because the reader is likely to identify with a problem everyone struggles with, and this makes the character flesh and blood in the reader's mind.

However, the sympathy has to be balanced with heroisms--noble traits--in order for the main character to truly be a "hero" in the reader's eyes. When we talk about nobility, we think of excellent, redeeming moral qualities, honor, and motives. A character without nobility is generally considered the story's villain, or antagonist. Keep in mind that a lot of writers, usually inexperienced ones, have a tendency to create protagonists without heroism, and this makes them unlikable.

As mentioned earlier, the only difference between a hero and a villain, from a reader's standpoint, is *forgiveness*. Both characters are human (unless you're writing a paranormal) and both have a unique combination of redeeming, weak, or evil traits, and both should be filled with polarities of good and bad. This makes them real to the reader. The difference lies in variations on the basic equation governing reader response to the character:

Character's Flaws → Reader's Response →
Character's Behavior → Reader's Response

With a hero, the equation will follow this course:

Character's Flaws → Reader's Understanding →
Character's Growth → Reader's Forgiveness

With a villain, the equation will follow this course:

Character's Flaws → Reader's Understanding →
Character's Lack of Growth → Reader Withholds Forgiveness

If your hero isn't particularly likeable, try putting him into the hero equation above--is he acting more like a villain? Then you know what you need to fix in his character.

A hero's crimes need to be balanced by the reader's understanding of what he did and why he did it. In many fictional cases, the crime is a noble one, or the character redeems himself through his current and future actions. All through the hero's outward conviction carrying him on what may seem like a self-destructive course, he'll give away hidden pieces of himself that contradict his crime. The reader will sense a dual conflict, understand that something terrible has happened, is happening, and may happen again to this character he's rooting for, and, despite any semblance of wrongdoing or ruthlessness on the hero's part, the reader will feel sympathy for this realistic character. The reader bestows forgiveness on the hero because, throughout the course of the story, the hero grieves, repents, mends his ways, and performs gallant deeds worthy of the reader's applause. Dwight V. Swain says that "only the character who cares about something, finds something important, is worth bothering with".

In the same way, a villain should have a complex, identifiable reason for his crime. But his reason is rarely noble, nor can it be justified. He should never be evil through-and-through (unless you're writing a paranormal and the villain isn't human). The most effective villain is the one who rouses almost as much sympathy as he does revulsion in the reader. However, the villain never repents and, in fact, goes on to commit even worse crimes. The reader can't go beyond his own sense of morality to forgive this character, no matter how sympathetic he may be toward him, because the character shows no evidence of growth, no indication of nobility. Intrigue us though the villain may, we can't accept his goals.

Plot conflicts need to be urgent enough to require immediate or pretty close attention. But if your internal and external conflicts go in a straight line, with no off-shoots to complicate it, no failures when the hero makes an effort to solve his problems, your reader will grow bored with the story and less intrigued by the character. Additionally, intensity of conflicts should continue to rise in the middle of a story and that's why story sparks need to be injected periodically keep the story alive.

In *Death on the Nile*, the main characters' beginning internal and external conflicts worked together, creating what appeared to be a no-win situation. Let's start with internal conflicts:

Beginning Sequence Character Internal Conflicts:

- ***Poirot:*** Though retired now as a detective, Poirot perpetually longs to have a perplexing riddle to put his little grey cells to work on.
- ***Linnet:*** Linnet remembers the queer, blurred note of earnest

in Jacqueline's voice when she spoke of her mad love for Simon. Linnet herself never felt that way about anyone and she believes this is a flaw in herself she must rectify. And she does when she meets Simon, who makes her feel frightfully, frightfully happy. She worries also that she'll lose her inheritance if she marries a man she can't control. With Simon, she remains the queen of her kingdom and no one will ever take it away.

- ***Jacqueline:*** Jacqueline is proud and has always refused to take anything from her rich friend. However, her love for Simon is so great that she goes against her pride and asks Linnet to give Simon a job as a land agent on her estate. When Linnet sets her sights on Simon herself, Jacqueline loses Simon. She's unable to forgive this double betrayal.
- ***Simon:*** Simon is embarrassed by his treatment of Jacqueline, but he's also protective of Linnet, especially when Jacqueline begins stalking them and terrorizing Linnet with her unrelenting presence at every turn.

Evolving Goals and Motivations

Goals are what the character wants, needs, or desires above all else. Motivation is what gives him drive and purpose to achieve those goals. Goals must be urgent enough for the character to go through hardship and self-sacrifice.

Multiple goals collide and impact the characters, forcing tough choices. Focused on the goal, the character is pushed toward it by believable, emotional, and compelling motivations that won't let him quit. Because he cares deeply about the outcome, his anxiety is doubled. The intensity of his anxiety pressures him to make choices and changes, thereby creating worry and awe in the reader.

Beginning goals and motivations don't generally *change* so much as they become *refined* to the increasing intensity of the conflicts (though this must be clarified when looking at complex books, especially mystery ones that must include red herrings and foils to keep the reader guessing). Your character's goals and motivations will certainly evolve each time you introduce a new story spark, since he's modifying or reshaping his actions based on the course his conflicts are dictating. It's your job as the writer to give the character incentives not to give up until he has what he's fighting for. In other words, to equip him with appropriate conflicts, goals and motivations.

Remember we talked about how, if your character's internal and external conflicts don't match his unchanging character overview, his goals and motivations won't make any sense to the readers. This is where you'll really see this become evident. So be sure your goal in filling out the checklist here is to make everything cohesive.

In *Death on the Nile*, many of the characters have hidden goals and motivations. However, on the surface, the characters' beginning goals and motivations were:

Beginning Sequence Evolving Goals and Motivations:

- ***Poirot:*** Poirot moves from being a cautious observer who sees that Linnet is victimized by Jacqueline's dogging presence during a time she should be blissfully enjoying her newlywed status (and he believes deep down that there's more than annoyance and fear in her manner), to agreeing to speak to Jacqueline on Linnet's behalf concerning her efforts to poison everything for her former best friend and fiancé. His detective instincts are telling him that Jacqueline's actions are the first steps toward opening her heart to evil. He believes that by talking to Jacqueline and Linnet both, he can prevent something drastic from happening.
- ***Linnet:*** Linnet's goal was to have Simon. Now that she's done that, her motivation is to get Jacqueline to go away quietly. After all, these things happen. Better to break an engagement than for three people to suffer needlessly, she reasons logically. She speaks of sorrow over the hardship Jacqueline has had to face, but insists guilt has no place here. Poirot's insinuations offend her. She made a choice, she didn't hesitate because all Linnet's life, she's had whatever she wants, has had everything she's ever wanted--why should she have to settle

now? Linnet insists that Jacqueline is acting unwomanly and undignified, but, deep down, Linnet's inner conviction tells her that her friend has right on her side. About this dark truth, Linnet refuses to be honest with herself.

- ***Jacqueline:*** Jacqueline's entire life was bound up in one person--Simon Doyle. Like the rich man who stole the poor man's one ewe in the Bible, Linnet stole Jacqueline's love. Linnet was her best friend, and Jacqueline trusted her. But Linnet has never denied herself anything and felt she shouldn't have to even when it came to the man Jacqueline loved...*loves*. Jacqueline compares herself to the moon. When Linnet, the sun, came out, Simon couldn't see her any more. He was too dazzled. And though she believes Simon will always love her, she also believes he now hates her--perhaps as much as she hates him and her former best friend.
- ***Simon:*** Simon is furious that Jacqueline won't accept events (and he feels lucky that he escaped her clutches, considering the lengths she's willing to go when scorned). His must protect Linnet from Jacqueline's terrorizing, but he abhors running away as if he and Linnet have done something wrong.

Plot Conflicts (External)

Previously, we talked a little about the difference between plot (external) and character (internal) conflicts. Plot (external) conflict is the central tangible or outer problem standing squarely in the character's way that must be faced and solved by that character. The character wants to restore the stability that was taken from him by the external conflict, and this produces his desire to act. However, a character's internal conflicts will create an agonizing tug of war with the plot conflicts. He has to make tough choices that come down to whether or not he should face, act on, and solve the problem.

Plot conflicts must be so urgent as to require immediate attention. The audience must be able to identify with both the internal and external conflicts the character faces in order to be involved enough to care about the outcome of the story. Plot conflicts work hand-in-glove with character conflicts. You can't have one without the other, and they become more intense and focused the longer the characters struggle. The stakes are raised, choices are limited, failure and loss are inevitable. In *Novelist's Essential Guide to Creating Plot,* J. Madison Davis defines plot "like a cone that characters are moving through from the wide end to the narrow. It closes in the farther along they go".

In *Die Hard* 2, the pilot of John's wife's plane is aware that if he doesn't land immediately, they'll plummet to their deaths. The problem with landing is that the terrorists still have control of the airport, and they've closed down all the runways except the one they need for their own getaway. There are no lighted landing strips, so any landing is dangerous because it'll be done blindly. Without a choice, the pilot announces to the tower he's making an emergency landing, and, of course, McClane hears it. If he doesn't act this instant, his wife will die and the terrorists will escape. The cone has closed to the point that he has almost no room to maneuver. The suspense is nearly more than the viewer can bear--he loves it!

You see all through this that every time John tried to fight back, he was thwarted and something worse happened. The problem kept escalating. Each "escalation" (or story spark injection) was an off-shoot that complicated the situation and upped the ante until the end, when resolution and enlightenment came. All of McClane's goals and motivations (his strength and heart) come down to stopping the terrorists, and this action, in turn, provides his wife's plane with the lighted strip the plane needs to land. This perfectly fits all the external and internal conflicts, and it's in his character overview to do exactly what he did from start to finish and did with his own unique flair.

We said earlier that a story spark is that intriguing something that ignites the story and progresses it toward culmination. In other words, this is your plot--the external conflicts in the story. Each story has to have more than one of these sparks to sustain it (generally 3 sparks for a 70,000 word novel--one for beginning, one for middle, and one for end). Once a spark fizzles out, another must infuse the story, and new ones need to be injected in order to support the length and complexity of your story.

So, on this section of the checklist, you'll include your story spark. You'll do this for each story spark--generally, the beginning one, the middle one, and the end one. For each story spark your story has, you'll check off one of each of the following steps for all the major characters. As I said earlier, this is optional for secondary and minor characters.

In *Death on the Nile*, we've established what the characters are facing. But now a situation is introduced that inevitably changes the stability of many lives. I've included the beginning story spark for your reference, along with the beginning external plot conflicts the characters face:

Beginning Story Spark:

While dining at a restaurant, Hercule Poirot overhears a heated discussion between a couple obviously in love. Poirot worries that the woman, Jacqueline de Bellefort, loves her beau, Simon Doyle, too much. When next Poirot meets Jacqueline, they're on a ship, and Simon has married Jacqueline's former best friend, Linnet Ridgeway. Jacqueline ruthlessly stalks the couple on their honeymoon.

Beginning Sequence External Plot Conflicts:

When Poirot suggests Linnet hire a personal bodyguard, she says that Simon is absurdly sensitive about money. He'd see it as a needless expense and a threat to his masculinity. So she must continue to live in the fear that she's unsafe, surrounded by enemies who hate her. Refusing to act for Linnet, as she asks him to, but agreeing to talk to Jacqueline about her stalking, Poirot does what he can to prevent something worse from occurring. But he doesn't believe he'll succeed.

When Poirot goes to her, Jacqueline refuses to bury her dead, give up the past, and face a new future. Even if what's done is done and bitterness won't undo it, even if she's suffering and this will only prolong it, Jacqueline simply can't turn away from her journey down the dark river of revenge. Jacqueline pulls out her gun and says that she wants to kill one of them, or both, but waiting is more fun. There's nothing Linnet can do about her presence--imagine, the powerful Linnet Ridgeway is helpless! All Jacqueline has to do is wait for the right moment. She's not afraid of death--what has she got to lose after all? But Poirot reminds her that there's a moment of choice--the same choice Linnet had--to stay her hand and let evil pass by, or to reach out and take its hand. Once the latter happens, the act is committed and there can be no second chance at choice. Poirot attempts to persuade Jacqueline to abandon a course of action that promises disaster to everyone...to no avail.

Linnet agrees to Simon's plan of taking a cruise on the Nile aboard the SS *Karnak* while he lays a false trail to shake Jacqueline. He explains his plans to Poirot, who proclaims that it won't help; Simon and his new bride won't see the end of this matter so easily.

Tension and Suspense

Tension and suspense can be described as the sensation of uncertainty and anticipation in the reader. Without them, your reader is uninterested and uninvolved in your story--cardinal sins where any work of fiction is concerned.

Tension is any type of awareness that brings the story to the fever pitch of anticipation. Tension must begin at the start of the story and must be kept intense throughout to prevent your reader from being disappointed or bored.

A romance book has another kind of tension: sexual. Sexual tension in a romance story is obligatory, although books in other genres may also develop the same tension between romantic interests. It's like cake and frosting. Take away one, and what's the point? Sexual tension must begin at the start of the story and must be kept intense throughout to prevent your reader from being disappointed--or worse, embarrassed--during moments at which she should be temporarily relieved or exalted. (See the tips at the end of this section on how to create enough sexual tension to lead to a glorious love scene either hinted at or written with the bedroom door open.)

Keep in mind that all genres generally feature a mild or heavy romantic relationship, and therefore authors have no excuse not to develop romantic and sexual tension between the characters involved. Logically, since books of all genres--not just mysteries and thrillers--must employ suspense, then by the same reasoning all genres that include a degree of romance should have the same degree of sexual tension.

While many writers probably don't see a difference between tension and suspense, in the structure of a story I believe tension is the milder of the two. Tension is anxiety, where suspense is agony. So tension could be considered the positive form of the two, because there's an element of hope in it. With suspense, there's danger, and it's generally because something dreadful is coming.

Think of the movie *While You Were Sleeping*. There's no real *danger* in this romantic comedy, outside of the fact that the heroine might marry the wrong guy. The film crackles with hopeful tension--the viewer worries because she desperately wants Lucy to end up with Jack, not his good-looking but mimbo brother, Peter. What's at stake is happily-ever-after for two wonderful people. Viewers feel tension, not suspense.

The danger in the Aliens movie series is of the global-annihilation sort. Viewers are held in agonizing suspense, knowing that if these creatures escape and multiply, the worst thing imaginable will happen--and the viewer dreads it. What's at stake is total elimination of the entire human race. No happily-ever-after for anyone.

Both tension and suspense are tricky to achieve and sustain. In each, you're bringing your audience to the snapping point, and then and only then giving them what they want--*temporarily*. The tricky, sticky part is that you're withholding a resolution that the audience desperately wants. If you keep it out of reach too long, you'll lose your audience. If you give them too much of what they want too soon, they'll have no reason to stick around.

Tension and suspense are absolutely necessary in *every* story, and both must be cohesive with the other elements in your story.

Release and Downtime

In *First Draft Outline,* I describe release as any temporary easement of either romantic/sexual tension or plot tension. Some of the many forms release can take are a kiss, the resolution of a red herring or a clue that seems to solve part of the mystery, or an answer that leads the character closer to getting what he wants. Release, like tension, is part of the causal chain of events essential to reaching resolution. It has to make sense in that chain and become part of its natural progression.

Downtime is a form of release, but it's more intense and, like the climax, it happens only once during the course of a story, during a time of incredible tension. This is the bleakest portion of the story, when all hope has seemingly been lost. The obstacles standing in the way are too numerous, too monumental, too impossible. The main character takes release from the action to reflect on what's happened and what could have been, and, by all appearances, he seems to give up the fight. During downtime, the character now has a glimpse of the happily-ever-after he's convinced has slipped from his fingers. This is a temporary respite from the extreme suspense. Characters--and readers!--need this desperately. If you don't include it, the reader will get so exhausted from the fast pace, she won't care how the book ends. She's too tired to care.

Following downtime, the black moment, as the climax of downtime, comes. The character has no choice but to act at this point. Remember John McClane in *Die Hard 2: Die Harder*? He felt he'd expended all viable options to save his wife and stop the terrorists. He's depressed, brought to his lowest point, and he reflects on all that's happened and what he's about to lose (this is the downtime). But then the pilot brings a swift end to all dithering when he takes the chance of blindly landing the plane--at exactly the same time the terrorists are attempting to make their getaway (black moment). At that point, John has absolutely no choice but to find a way to succeed. This provides the momentum for the final showdown.

Here again, I see a difference between release and downtime. Like tension, release is the milder of the two. Release is temporary relief from *anxiety*, while downtime is temporary relief from *agony*. Release could be considered the positive form of the two because there's an element of hope in it. With downtime, the character believes he's lost everything, danger's on its way back, and he's convinced there's no stopping it. The ultimate dread is produced, because few people can relax when they know everything they ever wanted is about to go down the toilet. That naturally produces restlessness, recklessness, and intense edginess.

Release and downtime are absolutely necessary in *every* story, and you'll soon see that these two, like all other plot elements, must be cohesive with the rest of your story.

Tip Sheet: Producing Killer Sexual Tension and Love Scenes in Any Story

1. **Let your characters decide the level of intimacy they share.** Rarely will an author write a book that requires a level of sensuality he's not comfortable with, because he'll automatically choose characters that fit his own comfort level. Remember, despite where popular opinion is leaning these days, there really *isn't* a fine line between romance and pornography. Romance has an equal balance between sexuality and emotional bonding. Pornography has sex with little or no bonding before, during or after the purely physical act.
2. **Make love scenes realistic instead of hokey or overly sentimental.** When you're writing a character, you're exploring those illogical, contradictory, good-and-evil people and their relationships. You need all of those traits to make a character three-dimensional. You make your love scenes real by making your *characters* real. A fully fleshed-out character will make readers look at the world around them and the people in it in brand new ways. And a fully developed character will certainly make readers want to find out what turns her on.
3. **Use exaggerated awareness.** In romantic fiction, you take for granted that this couple was destined, meant to be, fated,

designed specifically for each other. That may or may not be true for other genres, but I'd vote that any story with a fair amount of space devoted to the development of a romantic relationship will have readers rooting for those two crazy kids to spend forever together. Therefore, every single look, touch, and sense is larger than life between them. The sexual tension must reach the breaking point and satisfy the reader (and characters) only temporarily until happily-ever-after. When the hero touches the heroine, even accidentally, the reader should see sparks igniting between them. When he looks at her, a profound feeling should come over the characters and the reader. The emotional impact needs to be conveyed through their every encounter. Don't skimp on this just because you're not writing a romance book. Remember, if your logic as a writer tells you that suspense is essential for every genre, then your logic should also tell you that every story with a romantic relationship (even if it's not the spotlight thread) needs to feature realistic, palpable sexual tension. Anything else is sheer laziness, or an inability on the author's part to admit he has a writing weakness he either can't or won't overcome.

4. **Start sexual tension from the get-go.** Exaggerated awareness between your hero and heroine needs to begin immediately, the first time they come together in your story, and it needs to increase in depth with each subsequent meeting. There are only two possible reasons for a reader to *not* want a love scene to take place: (1) the reader picked up a spicy book by mistake; or (2) the writer didn't set the stage for love scenes early or well. If there's no tension between a couple, no exaggerated awareness, a love scene is going to shock and embarrass the reader as much as it will the characters. This is what I see in a lot of books written by authors who want to include a romantic relationship for the main character (because they know it increases character depth, conflicts, and makes the story stronger), but who aren't skilled at writing romance. The scenes are nothing short of awkward or downright embarrassing. These authors need to hone their skills

instead of justifying their lack by dismissing romantic genres as frivolous. If for no other reason, these authors need to do learn to write romance skillfully because readers hate awkward, embarrassing love scenes, scenes made that way by a clumsy writer. When a hero and heroine finally come together for a kiss, an intimate touch, or lovemaking, the reader should exult. He should be panting for consummation, ready to claw tooth and nail to see that these two characters have a clear path to the bedroom and aren't interrupted while there! And, most of all, the *reader* must be satisfied when all is said and done.

5. **Never use purple prose or silly euphemisms for body parts or reactions.** Use words that are appropriate to the characters and the tone you've set for the story. No author would want to find out that the local book club passed around her book, laughing uproariously about your hero's throbbing member bobbing like a flag pole before it enters the heroine's love nest. Soon the lovers are soaring on a comet, going higher and higher in one another's arms until they explode and finally float back to earth, replete as two turtledoves. The key to writing a great love scene is to not get mired in either the emotional or the physical aspects for too long. Don't let your characters get so swept away, they're riding on a cloud of the author's purple prose rather than on the emotions of the most intimate form of bonding imaginable. At the same time, don't let your characters get so involved in the physical act that it becomes, quite disappointingly, mere sex. Remember the difference between romance and pornography, and write accordingly.
6. **Set the scene and the mood for yourself and your characters.** Take note of scents, sights, tastes, sounds, and textures. Light scented candles, peel an orange, play sensual music, put silk or lace or velvet against your own skin. Dab your spouse's cologne on yourself. Put on his jacket (guys, please don't put on your spouse's lacy nightgown, though it's perfectly sexy to have it near enough to touch and smell). Do not for any reason other than an emergency answer the doorbell or the phone

while you're writing your love scene!

7. **Use the genre you're writing to the advantage of your love scenes.** Imagine the sensuality of a love scene in a horror story, where the heroine both fears and is helplessly attracted to the mysterious, potentially dangerous hero. The heroine would be aware of the temperature of the room, the coldness, and the abrupt way she warms when the hero appears in the doorway. She recognizes that shift of tension within and *without* her own body. She acknowledges her palpable fear and excitement, warring with each other. She notices the shadows of the room, the shadows on his face, on his body; the moonlight spilling across the stone floor. She breathes deeply of the hero's intoxicating scent, primal and raw. She starts at the slightest sound and hears her own heartbeat and bated breath in the eerie absence of sound that follows. His voice both unnerves her and catapults her to excitement. Try using danger in a love scene in your mystery, or suspense in your romance story love scene. In this unique way, genre can be used to help develop your love scenes.
8. **Use your characters' backgrounds and experiences in your love scenes.** While you probably won't use words or phrases that make you uncomfortable, your characters will help you choose the appropriate words *they* would use in a love scene. For instance, when writing a love scene between musicians, try using musical references. If your heroine is a dancer, have her seduce your hero with the sensual movements of her body while he helplessly watches. If your hero is a mechanic or rides a motorcycle, he'll think in terms of revved engines, power, ultimate freedom. These images are evocative in his love scene.
9. **Choose your point of view very carefully.** I've heard many authors advise writing every love scene in both the heroine and hero's POVs. Remember all the reasons I listed for why head-hopping in a single scene is never good. You don't want to take any chance at all of confusing and annoying your reader. Your point with a love scene is to deepen the connection, and you can't do that by showing both characters' reactions to

every little thing in alternation (talk about overkill). Use introspection or dialogue in the next scene with the other POV character--you'll both heighten the intrigue and maintain the deep connection you established previously. Also, make the next love scene from the alternate POV.

10. **Write love scenes chronologically.** I've heard writers say they make notes of where love scenes should fit in while they're writing, then write all the love scenes last, after the first draft is completed. My opinion? I've never seen this go-where-I'm-inspired, chaotic way of writing work effectively. Keep in mind that each sensual scene should be an off-shoot, a layering of the characters' conflicts, goals and motivations, showing their growth toward each other and their tug of war not to take what they want more than anything. If you just drop something as pivotal as a love scene in later, you lose the mood, the momentum, and the cohesion from one scene to the next. Writing chronologically, everything will fall into place in an emotion-filled, cohesive way. The progression and tension will increase without taking the reader out of the book to wonder if the scene actually fits.
11. **Focus on a certain aspect of a character that intrigues the opposite character.** This characteristic enhances the awareness building in the story and makes it more powerful. Make your hero obsessed with the heroine's mouth--it's the first thing he noticed about her when they met, and he can't stop noticing it whenever they come together afterward. Imagine when he first kisses it. Wow! Fantasy become reality. There's nothing more potent for the characters or the reader.
12. **Use dialogue within a scene of sensual awareness to heighten the erotic edge immeasurably.** A few words (even if they're nothing sexual) can prompt immeasurable excitement. In a scene like this, nothing even vaguely sexual is said, and yet the tension will be palpable.
13. **Don't be afraid of humor, even in an introspective or dramatic book.** Tenderness can sometimes cross the line into sentimental. Depending on the situation or characters you've created, humor could provide release and, in the pro-

cess, give the reader a magical glimpse into the depth and three-dimensionality of your characters.

14. **Increase both physical and emotional intimacy.** Another thing I've heard both editors and writers say is, "You have to raise the stakes with each sexual encounter," be it with a look, a touch, a kiss, or lovemaking. My opinion? The stakes involved in a romance are emotional *and* physical. When you raise the stakes from encounter to encounter, you're increasing physical *and* emotional intimacy. If you're not, you're not writing a romance (and then you don't need to worry about this too much). Emphasize the physical (and that's becoming more and more prevalent with erotica taking over the marketplace), but never at the expense of the emotional. Books that don't emphasize the emotional on the same scale as the physical are disappointing because they cast the reader in the role of a voyeur watching two people go at it like dogs when little or no emotional ties connect them. Chances are, if a reader chooses romance over pornography, it's for the emotional ties involved in lovemaking. Equalize physical and emotional intimacies as if you're weighing them on a balance. Love scenes need to employ a wonderful combination of raw physical need and breathtaking emotional intimacy. If an author can make readers want her hero so bad they're all over their husbands that night, she's truly created three-dimensional characters that a real person can interact and become emotionally involved with.
15. **Don't write love scenes for the sake of sex or simply to fill pages.** Romance readers choose romance over pornography because they want heartfelt, romantic sex that leads to bonding, not empty sexual encounters with just anyone that lead to nothing. The heart of every romance is the emotional bond between the hero and heroine. Even if you're not writing romance per se, your book may have a large romantic element because of the main characters' relationship. That emotional bond is what you'll probably leave the reader with in the end. It's a reward for a job well done. Everything else becomes a layer of the emotional bond. Don't lose sight of that as you

write love scenes. Make each one count, make them reveal something pivotal, make them advance the plot, and make them *necessary* to building the emotional bond into something unbreakable. Love scenes should be as crucial to the characters and plot of a story as any other element. If you can take a love scene completely out without affecting the story in any way, you've probably got an extraneous scene on your hands. Treat it the way you would any other scene without a point. Cut it ruthlessly and don't look back.

16. **Remember, less can be more.** You can't write out every love scene in detail, and sometimes a very short scene can sum up a loving encounter better than two to five pages of graphic detail. Reader imagination will take over, and they'll have a full heart, wet eyes, and maybe even the urge to light a cigarette to savor the moment. They'll forget that they've read words instead of experiencing one of the most emotional, exciting bonding moments of their life.

Alternating Tension With Release

Tension goes with release like frosting goes with cake, and the two must complement one another perfectly. Sexual tension is an exaggerated awareness that may lead to an enjoyable release. You wouldn't follow sexual awareness with a slap instead of a kiss. Nor would you have a hero find some other woman to relieve himself with when the reader desperately wants to see him with the heroine. (This might happen outside of the romance genre, but romance readers would inundate a publisher with outcries of betrayal if something like this happened in a romance.) If tension and release don't blend, you produce disappointment instead of temporary relief.

Let's discuss an example of the tango between tension and release from the romantic comedy movie *French Kiss*, with Kate (played by Meg Ryan) and Luc (played by Kevin Kline):

Kate has gone against her every natural instinct and gotten on a plane to Paris to go to her fiancé, Charlie, who's fallen in love with and become engaged to some Parisian goddess. **[tension]** On what she'd expected to be the most traumatic experience of her life, Kate instead meets the coarse Frenchman, Luc, a thief with a potential heart of gold, on the flight. She has a lively discussion with him, taking the focus off her fear of flying, and he promises to drive her to Charlie's hotel. **[release]** Luc has put a necklace he's stolen into her bag, since she'll breeze through the check-point and he won't, and he plans to take back his stolen goods once they reach the hotel.

Circumstances prevent this. Kate arrives at the hotel in a taxi, and the manager refuses to tell her Charlie's room number. Horror of horrors, she sees her fiancé with the vixen. She faints, during which time her bags are stolen. **[tension]** Luc arrives and, lo, he happens to know the thief who took Kate's luggage. Kate is facing Murphy's Law continuously, yet she's getting away from the more immediate problem of having her passport, credit cards, and vitamins stolen in order to get to know her eventual hero, who's trying to get his necklace back while telling her he's helping her win Charlie back.

On the train heading toward the place where Charlie will be meeting his new fiancée's parents, Kate and Luc share a kiss (some question about who started it!) while she's sleeping. Luc had been attempting to go through her bag to get his necklace, but this kiss completely befuddles him. The wonders of Kate are captivating him, and he's redeeming himself in the viewer's eyes. **[release]** While Kate and Luc continue their attempts to lure Charlie's heart back where it belongs, they're falling in love with each other.

You can see from this example that tension and release go through a dance together, one step after the other, a sense of hopeful anticipation pervading. These steps match. They're logical and cohesive. It would make no sense at all if Luc put his necklace in someone else's bag, if he didn't know the thief who stole Kate's bags, or if, in the course of the film, he fell in love with Charlie's new fiancée instead of Kate.

If story tension and release moments don't blend, your reader will have one of those dreaded moments where he'll close the book forever.

Alternating Suspense With Downtime

As we discussed earlier, downtime takes place at the end of the middle section of a book and is always followed by the black moment. Suspense is agonizing dread of what's to come.

Let's use *French Kiss* again to find our downtime, suspense, and black moment examples, since these three need to do a complicated leap-frog near the end of a book:

Kate and Luc devise an elaborate ploy to get Charlie back. She'll confront Charlie and show him that she's over him...partially due to Luc's ministrations. Charlie and his fiancée are stunned--and made wary--by her calm, cool attitude. She proposes that she and Charlie go out to dinner and work out the details of "breaking up". Kate and Luc's plan is that Charlie will have realized by this time that he's made a huge mistake, and Kate will have her man back where he belongs--this time on a leash.

Kate is stunningly beautiful to Luc that night, and he finds himself rethinking everything he wants while he gives her last-minute advice on how to reel Charlie back. Kate also finds herself uncertain--does she even want Charlie back? Her feelings for Luc are confusing to say the least. Why do his arms feel so right around her? **[suspense]** But she goes through with dinner with Charlie, figuring, *What else is there to do?* There's something between her and Luc, but neither have admitted it. She knows Luc is a thief (he's told her the necklace belonged to his grandmother and he plans to sell it to get the money to buy a vineyard--a very worthy goal that appeals to Kate more and more), and she's agreed to take the necklace to the jeweler Cartier for him the next morning...at which time the two will part for their separate lives. She'll go home with Charlie, they'll get married and use her impressive nest egg to buy the house of their dreams. Yet Kate no longer feels like this is what she wants out of life. The reason why she doesn't is obvious--she's in love with Luc, the man who, at the beginning of the movie, equated true love with the silly notions of a little girl.

Meanwhile, Luc is keeping up his end of the plan by distracting Charlie's jilted fiancée, and the goddess is more than willing to strike back at Charlie and make him jealous. In the heat of passion, it's Kate's name that escapes Luc's lips. But, after the next morning, he'll never see her again. Even with the promise of his very own vineyard, somehow he finds himself unhappy with the outlook of his future. **[downtime]** Kate and Luc have planned well, and Charlie wants to come back to her. But she now knows she doesn't want him back. She wants Luc, and she sees no way for them to be together. **[suspense]** The next morning, Kate makes a last bid for happiness. She trades her nest egg for the necklace, which she gives to the police, and allows Luc to think Cartier has given him the money for the necklace. They part forever, destined never to be happy because neither is willing to step out and take a risk. **[black moment--the greatest suspense]**

You can see from this example that downtime, suspense, and the black moment leap-frog each other, a sense of absolute dread pervading (as much as is possible in a romantic comedy anyway). Remarkably fitting in this story is that the viewer roots for Kate when she follows Charlie with the purpose to get him back and continues to root for her when she decides she doesn't want him after all; and Luc becomes a loveable character despite the fact that he's a thief--one who never gets his due, beyond a punch in the mouth from his brother.

Everything that happens is logical and cohesive. It would make no sense at all if Kate fell on her knees before Charlie and begged him to come back to her; if, when Charlie admits he wants to come back to her, they fly back home, buy their dream house and live happily ever after. No one would be happy if Luc was apprehended by the police and spent the future he should be spending on his vineyard with Kate in jail instead. The story couldn't have ended on the black moment with Kate and Luc truly going their separate ways. Logically and cohesively, only the happy resolution of Luc finding out that Kate had given him her nest egg, and him running to her side to tell her she can't leave him--ever--because he'll never stop wanting her, could satisfy the viewer. The only resolution the viewer will accept is that Kate and Luc put down roots and live on their vineyard happily ever after.

In the same way, only with a cohesive logic in the build-up of downtime, suspense, and black moment, and with an equally meshed logical resolution, will your reader be left satisfied and smiling upon closing the book.

This in no way, however, means that you can't throw a twist in at the end of your story--provided that it fits logically and cohesively with what you've already set up in the beginning and middle of the book. We'll talk more about twists in the end sequence of the Story Plan Checklist since that's generally when (though doesn't necessarily have to be) when twists come into play.

Tip Sheet: Creating Tension and Suspense in Any Story

1. **Use doubt to create suspense.** The unknown is the "it" factor when creating suspenseful stories--and stories must indeed be suspenseful or your readers will have nothing to stick around for. If you can truly make your characters (and readers) believe that the main character will never reach his goals, you'll have succeeded in creating a book that absolutely can't be put down. Involving the reader means making sure that your story is cohesive enough to draw him inexplicably in, right where you want him. A cohesive story will never allow the reader to become too comfortable.

2. **Let mood and senses create the atmosphere you need for suspense.** Remember that mood is a carefully constructed means of building suspense. Essentially, it's a springboard with limited purpose. In order to sustain it, you must involve the reader. Prepare for it with cohesive characters, setting, and plot, then use all of the senses to build the appropriate tone. You wouldn't want a slapstick tone in a drama any more

than you'd want a sensual tone in playful story intended for children. Mood (or tone) is a carefully constructed means to build tension and suspense, and the mood almost always fits the genre, though of course the mood of an individual scene is more changeable. Science fiction generally has an adventurous tone. Suspense has a tense mood. Gothic has a heavy feel of foreboding. The most effective way to capture mood is to use the senses. Where are the characters in your scene; what are they seeing, touching, smelling, hearing, tasting, feeling (the little-acknowledged sixth sense)? What emotions are they dealing with? If you want to create a sensual atmosphere, describe the scent of a candle burning, the touch of silk against bare skin, the strains of romantic music playing, or a heroine's reaction to the appearance of her lover. If you want to set the mood for danger, make the character tangibly aware of the temperature (cold--goose bumps on skin); the lighting (darkness or shadows); a revolting smell; a sudden sound or the eerie *absence* of sound. If you want to create a tone for character shock, have him in the middle of a bite of what had previously been a delicious meal. With this mood, the food becomes sawdust in his mouth, the taste unnoticeable or unappetizing, and he chokes when he finally attempts to swallow it. This example from my inspirational romantic gothic, *The Bloodmoon Curse*, incorporates the senses, developing the setting, character, and the plot:

"Come with me," the woman said in a nervous, hushed tone. She didn't wait for Amberlyn's acquiescence. She started back down the hall without her. Amberlyn shot to her feet and ran after the woman.

The smell of excessive mildew and dust, the kind only extreme age could bring, filled her nostrils immediately. Even with the lantern, the halls they walked through absorbed no light. Amberlyn could see only that the woman leading her wore her hair back in a severe bun, over which a hair net had been placed. She was extremely thin, about Amberlyn's height. Her long black dress with an apron, similar to an old-fashioned maid in bygone days, swished as she scurried ahead like a frightened mouse.

Amberlyn practically ran to keep up with her and nearly crashed into her back when the maid suddenly stopped before a cavernous room lit by candles in a wide chandelier. Priceless old gothic furniture filled the room. Panels of lovingly stained wood lined every surface, including the walls, ceilings and floor. A stone fireplace took up almost all of the opposite side of the room. The bleeding moon carving on the knocker had also been carved into both sides of the arched fireplace. Amberlyn opened her mouth in awe at the structure. If a roaring fire hadn't been already going in it, she could have walked inside of it several feet across without bending over.

With better lighting, the room might have been described as exquisite, but, even with the dozens of candles burning, shadows cast crooked tendrils over the whole of its breadth, making it frightful instead of warm and inviting.

"Miss Kat will be along shortly. Wait here, please."

The maid disappeared like a silent wraith down another hallway. Amberlyn had no time to inquire about a bathroom, and the thought of going off on her own in the dark house wasn't pleasant. This room, too, gave her the creeps. The low lighting and the flicker of the candles resembled fingers reaching toward her, pulling back only on gasps of fresh oxygen.

She moved into the chair nearest the fire. Her wet socks and shirt made her shiver again. Glancing around to make sure she was alone, she reached under her shirt and pulled out the cotton nursing pads. She tossed them into the fire, which snapped and sputtered in protest but incinerated them in an instant. Her skin felt awful, sticky and stiff with drying sweat and milk. She knew she must look and smell awful, too.

At least fifteen long minutes later, she heard strange noises--a tapping, followed by a slow dragging or shuffling sound. Amberlyn felt the hair on the back of her neck stiffen as she tried to imagine the source of the sound. The noises didn't resemble footsteps, not normal ones anyway. They came louder, closer, from the hall on the side nearest the fireplace. ...

Use sense descriptions at their most potent times. This kind of description brings the reader directly into the story. You give him something tangible in your vision. He moves and uses his senses right along with your characters. Create a natural means to blend all the elements of your story.

3. **Contrast to keep readers on edge.** Pair a pessimistic hero with a bleeding heart heroine. Paint the image of a beautiful rose growing steadfastly in a desolate landfill. Develop character personalities and backstories, settings, and plots that make these contrasts blend together naturally.

4. **Pace your story to keep it flowing smoothly, even as tensions run high.** Don't rush to pick up story threads. Keep the reader guessing. Draw out scenes involving rescues and explanations, and offer readers unsatisfactory alternatives to the problems your characters face. Cohesion is crucial when pacing your story, since organic mingling will create the need for (and enable) pacing that matches. Imagine that you introduce into your plot a time element. If the hero doesn't act by a certain time, the worst horror he can imagine will happen. Pacing picks up considerably. Now imagine that this hero is given a glimpse of his happily-ever-after, but he no longer believes he can succeed. After all, he's tried everything and failed. The pacing will naturally slow down because he's at the bottom. Suddenly, conflict arises and the hero has absolutely no choice but to act. He finds a way to save what he cares about most. The pace picks up again. All of this works causally with your characters, setting, and plot.

5. **Foreshadow by hinting at what is to come, not by answering the crucial questions of a story.** Foreshadowing needs to be built into a story in advance. A writer can't foreshadow something he doesn't know will happen. Properly developed foreshadowing brings together all the elements in your story. In *Conflict, Action & Suspense*, William Noble calls foreshadow-

ing "a fine technique for developing suspense and extending action because it offers a *possibility* that will pick at the reader". If your reader cares about your characters, he'll pick up on foreshadowing immediately and every time it's touched afterward. It'll worry him to no end. And that means he'll be involved and hanging on every word.

6. **Use flashbacks to slow down the action and/or provide missing details, hidden motivation, or even an answer to a mystery.** Flashbacks can be in the form of a scene, a paragraph, a sentence, or even a single word. Flashbacks will come naturally out of character, setting, and plot development. It's tricky to write an effective flashback. Therefore, the purpose in using it must always be clear to the author and the reader.

Developing and Concluding Story Threads While Building Structure

At this point, we've established the external monologues along with the beginning internal monologue on the Story Plan Checklist. You should see the cohesive development of your story in this cycling sequence. Every part of your story should be so tangled up in cohesive elements that what you come out with *has* to be utterly solid. Every aspect of the book should fit together with and build on every other aspect. Your Story Plan Checklist builds the structure of your story by following story threads from beginning, to middle, to end. If any of your threads aren't strong enough, or "sag" anyplace, you'll see it in the checklist. It's a guarantee that, if the thread isn't properly developed within the Story Plan Checklist, it won't be properly developed within the context of your story. This same thing is true from outline to final draft. If your story threads aren't properly developed within your outline, they won't be properly developed in the final draft.

The best part of a cohesively built story is that your readers will invest themselves in it mentally, emotionally, and possibly even physically (if you can make them cry or bite their nails, you've got them hook, line, and sinker!). You've created a net the readers won't want to get out of until they know everything, and they'll feel like they're leaving a piece of themselves behind each time they reluctantly set the book down--especially that last time when they read "The End".

Story Plan Checklist Middle and End Sequences

At this point, we've established the beginning external and internal monologues for the first story spark. You should see the cohesive development of your story on the checklist in this sequence. You're nowhere near done though. To complete the Story Plan Checklist, you need to be brainstorming like crazy so you can come up with logical middle and end sparks. These sparks each need their own internal monologues, namely:

- Character conflicts (internal)
- Evolving goals and motivations
- Plot conflicts (external)

There's little chance of completing this checklist in the wrong way--trust your instincts and let your story guide you.

In *Death on the Nile*, the author had expended the use of the first spark by chapter eleven and really needed another to carry the character and plot conflicts through the middle section of the book.

The middle section of the book not only features a new story spark, it also incorporates an influx of suspects--many of whom are secondary characters (and therefore not necessarily detailed in the Story Plan Checklist the way the main characters were in the beginning). Some of these characters weren't involved in the story in the beginning, and so, to avoid confusion, it makes the most sense to introduce them in the middle portion of the Story Plan Checklist, where their motives and conflicts can be clearly defined. For this reason and for clarity, they're detailed on the checklist *after* the middle story spark is injected.

It's important to stress here that identifying secondary characters this late in the story is unusual and generally would only be done for a mystery or one with an extremely complex plot that features many important characters. Few other genres can rival the sheer number of characters introduced in a single mystery. Most stories will only have two or three important characters. That said, feel free to fill out your Story Plan Checklist in whatever way makes the most sense for you and your particular story. There is little chance of completing this checklist in the wrong way--trust your instincts and let your story guide you.

Note that, for efficiency, I've included character (outside and self POV) descriptions within the introductions. The middle story spark goes something like this:

Middle Story Spark:

Simon and Linnet believe they've escaped, but Jacqueline spent her last shilling to buy passage on the cruise, and now they're trapped with her. Before the journey can even begin, it's obvious that the group won't enjoy smooth sailing. Jacqueline is determined to have her revenge. Poirot has a vague, uneasy feeling that something bad will happen. When a boulder is apparently aimed at Linnet's head on the first day's visit ashore, Jacqueline is immediately suspected but proves to have been far from where the incident took place. The next morning, Linnet is found dead, with a "J" written in blood on the wall beside her stateroom bed, her string of pearls missing. That Jacqueline had a motive for killing Linnet is undeniable. Is her guilt, however, too obvious? Colonel Johnny Race, a Secret Service agent and an old friend of Poirot's, has also come on the cruise, revealing that he's seeking an enemy spy on board the *Karnak*. Also on board is Dr. Carl Bessner, a doctor. As Race and Poirot investigate, they find a boatload of others who also have motives for wanting the heiress out of the way.

Secondary Character Introductions:

- ***Louise Bourget:*** Linnet's vivacious Latin maid of the last couple months.
- ***Mr. Fleetwood:*** An engineer on the *Karnak*, Linnet's former

maid's ex-fiancé.

- ***Andrew Pennington:*** Linnet's American lawyer and trustee, best friend of her father. Linnet has known her "Uncle Andrew" since she was a little girl.
- ***Tim Allerton:*** A tall, thin young man threatened by consumption some years ago. He's content to spend his life with his doting mother, whom he gets along with comfortably. He tells his mother that "a little flutter" on the Stock Exchange has allowed them to take a trip to Egypt and to the Nile.
- ***Miss Marie Van Schuyler:*** A very wealthy, elderly American snob who refuses to speak to anyone who doesn't meet her most exacting standards. Inclined to be very careful with her health, she brings her nurse everywhere she goes, including on holiday, and orders her around like a slave.
- ***Symbolic Element:*** A velvet stole, last seen in the observation saloon. She calls attention to its loss just prior to Linnet's murder, and a search is done for it without success. (Characteristically worn by a wealthy woman who loves to flaunt her status, the stole, in this particular instance, also becomes an important plot device.)
- ***Miss Bowers:*** Of an incurious, unmoved personality by nature, Miss Bowers is Marie Van Schuyler's infinitely capable, efficient nurse.
- ***Cornelia Robson:*** Marie Van Schuyler's cousin, invited to join her for the holiday. A big, clumsy, unselfish woman not considered a social success, but of an amiable disposition and disposed to like all her fellow creatures.
- ***Rosalie Otterbourne:*** The daughter of Mrs. Salome Otterbourne, an author of risqué romantic books that don't sell anymore. Rosalie is often sulky, distracted, and rude, always unhappy. The two are on holiday after being kicked out of a hotel in Jerusalem.
- ***Symbolic Element:*** A small pearl-handled pistol--a dainty toy that looks to foolish to be real--is found in Rosalie's handbag. (When Poirot confronts her about it, Rosalie denies she owns a pistol at all, and even lets him go through her handbag to prove it. As Poirot expects, as it's highly against character for Rosalie to

own or carry around a gun, the pistol is nowhere to be found. Later, it's discovered that Jacqueline actually has two pistols and slipped one into Rosalie's purse, then later took it back.)

- ***James Fanthrop:*** A shy, youthful Englishman, the nephew of William Carmichael, the senior partner of Carmichael, Grant & Carmichael, Linnet's British lawyers. Intensely quiet, he rarely speaks, yet listens and watches attentively.
- ***Signor Guido Richetti:*** An energetic Italian archeologist studying temples and ruins.
- ***Mr. Ferguson:*** A bitter, belligerent, anti-capitalist Englishman with radical ideals, believing that, to build up, one must first break down and destroy. He claims he's "studying conditions" rather than on holiday.

Middle Sequence Character Internal Conflicts:

- ***Poirot:*** Afraid for Linnet and her husband, Poirot advises them not to return to the boat after their visit ashore. He senses something is about to happen--something he can't prevent, especially when (the night of the murder) he's excessively sleepy and sleeps so hard he hears nothing all night, uncharacteristic for a light sleeper.
- ***Jacqueline:*** After Linnet goes to bed (on the night she's killed), Jacqueline is so filled with rage for his betrayal, she shoots Simon in the leg with a pistol that's kicked away under a sofa (and which later is discovered to have disappeared completely). Full of repentance, Jacqueline is taken to be sedated and watched over by Miss Bowers. A "J" is drawn on the wall in Linnet's room, apparently in order to incriminate Jacqueline. With the nurse's presence by her bedside all night, Jacqueline is relieved to have an unshakeable alibi for the time of Linnet's death. But her tension as the chief suspect grows when her pistol is recovered from the Nile, wrapped in a velvet stole with a bloody handkerchief.
- ***Simon:*** Linnet and Simon were determined to stand and fight Jacqueline's craziness, and so he stays up long after Linnet goes to bed and puts up with Jacqueline's drunken abuse. After she shoots him in the leg, he becomes fearful that she'll kill her-

self. He insists she must be kept an eye on so she doesn't do anything rash to herself.

- ***Louise:*** Louise is cunning...and worried because Poirot overheard a heated discussion she'd been having with Fleetwood earlier in the voyage.
- ***Fleetwood:*** Linnet Ridgeway had discovered that Fleetwood, the man her former maid had been in love with, already had a wife and three children in Egypt. When Linnet told her (previous) maid this, the woman broke up with Fleetwood. Infuriated because her interference ruined his life, Fleetwood admitted to Louise that he wanted to kill the meddling Linnet, always dressed up in her pearls and lording it all over the place with never a thought that she'd destroyed a man's life.
- ***Pennington:*** Pennington met up with Linnet and her new husband in Cairo and came aboard with them. He's anxious about getting her to sign certain business documents he brought with him.
- ***Tim:*** Tim detests his bad luck--rotten health, never bad enough to be really interesting, yet not good enough for him to have led the life he would have chosen. With very little money and no congenial occupation, he considers his life a thoroughly lukewarm, tame existence. He's taken to "shaking it up" with what he believes to be a harmless venture...until he sees Hercule Poirot and almost gets cold feet.
- ***Miss Van Schuyler:*** Only one person knows that Miss Van Schuyler is a rabid kleptomaniac--her favored "clip" jewelry, especially pearls. Miss Van Schuyler is all about keeping up proper appearances, so this fact must not get out to the public.
- ***Miss Bowers:*** Miss Bowers always keeps a sharp lookout for Miss Van Schulyer's eccentric habit of stealing. Sensitive to her patient's aversion to scandal, Miss Bowers discreetly replaces anything Miss Van Schuyler takes.
- ***Cornelia:*** It's Cornelia's fate to either be bullied or instructed. Never a talker, she's perpetually a listener. It's Cornelia who Jacqueline decides to confide in, almost maniacally so, the night Linnet is killed.
- ***Rosalie:*** Rosalie is horribly jealous, finding it unfair that one

person should have so much money, success, good looks, and love as Linnet Ridgeway. Though Rosalie's mother is a self-professed teetotaler, she's exactly the opposite, to the great worry and embarrassment of her burdened daughter.

- ***James:*** Linnet has never met Jim and so therefore doesn't recognize him as a representative of her English solicitors, sent incognito on board the *Karnak*. James is anxious to thwart his rival Pennington's plans to steal Linnet's fortune right from under her nose.
- ***Richetti:*** Richetti is grim and unforgiving when Linnet Ridgeway opens and reads a telegraph intended for him--a ridiculous one about vegetables that seems to make no sense.
- ***Ferguson:*** Ferguson is disgusted by Linnet Ridgeway's policy of slaving hundreds and thousands of workers for a mere pittance to keep her in silk stockings and useless luxuries--she is one of the richest women in the world, but has never done day of hard work in her life. He believes she should be shot as an example.

Middle Sequence Evolving Goals and Motivations:

- ***Poirot:*** Poirot reasons that it's probable that the murderer was a witness of the scene between Jacqueline and Simon in the observation saloon, and that the killer noted where the pistol went under the settee. After the saloon was vacant, the murderer procured the pistol--his idea being that Jacqueline would be thought guilty of the crime. However, Poirot has two questions: Why was the pistol thrown overboard? The stole, wrapped around the gun, wouldn't have muffled the sound of a shot. The pistol would have only made a pop anyway when it was fired. The handkerchief was clearly used to get rid of fingerprints.
- ***Jacqueline:*** Jacqueline begs Simon to believe she didn't kill Linnet. She fears he'll never walk again after what she's done.
- ***Simon:*** Brushing aside Jacqueline's concerns about his injury and any idea that he believes she killed his wife, he worries continuously for her state of mind and forgives her.
- ***Louise:*** Linnet is last seen alive by Louise at approximately

11:30 P.M. Louise comes to Dr. Bessner's cabin for an interview with Poirot and Colonel Race the day after the murder. Simon is convalescing in the doctor's room and overhears Louise imply she could have seen the murderer.

- ***Fleetwood:*** With a motive like revenge, he might have overheard the scene and noted the position of the pistol, taken it to Linnet's stateroom; shot her, tracing the initial "J" in blood next to the victim to implicate Jacqueline; and thrown the pistol overboard. The cheap handkerchief wrapped around the pistol inside the velvet stole would more likely belong to a working man like Fleetwood than to the well-to-do passengers.
- ***Pennington:*** Wrongdoing in his dealings with Linnet's fortune, and her unexpected marriage, put him a financial quandary. He hopes to get her signature on documents that will help him conceal his fraud. The boulder that nearly hits Linnet was dislodged, possibly by accident but more likely on purpose, by Pennington. During the ten-minute interval between when Simon was left alone with an injured leg in the saloon and when James returned to search for the pistol, Pennington could have taken the gun and used it to kill Linnet.
- ***Tim:*** Like Pennington, Tim could have taken the pistol. However, his motive for murdering Linnet is weak. Yet he's very concerned about the missing pearls.
- ***Miss Van Schuyler:*** Miss Van Schuyler claims to have heard a splash, as if something was thrown overboard, the night of Linnet's murder. The velvet stole the pistol was wrapped in belonged to her. Her motive for murdering Linnet could have been the string of perfect pearls, which Miss Van Schuyler clipped and Miss Bowers returned the morning after Linnet is discovered murdered.
- ***Miss Bowers:*** Miss Bowers is cleared of suspicion, as she had no opportunity to take the pistol (she was tending to Jacqueline) before James Fanthorp returned to search for it under the settee.
- ***Cornelia:*** Cornelia is cleared of suspicion, as she had no opportunity to take the pistol before it was searched for and found missing.

- ***Rosalie:*** Rosalie denies hearing or seeing anything that night. Rosalie disliked Linnet and was envious of her, but any motive on her part is grossly inadequate. Nevertheless, she seems to know more than she's telling--such as the fact that her mother is a secret drunk, and she doesn't want anyone else to know. Rosalie dumps her mother's stash of spirits into the Nile. As for whether she saw anyone while she dumped the bottles...she refuses to tell.
- ***James:*** James could have pocketed the pistol while declaring himself unable to find it. His motive for doing so, or for killing Linnet, would be anybody's guess.
- ***Richetti:*** Like Pennington and Tim, Richetti could have taken the pistol. Linnet had opened a telegram meant for him, a telegram that seemingly made no sense to anyone...except to someone familiar with the South African rebellion and spy codes.
- ***Ferguson:*** Though Ferguson had the opportunity to get the pistol, he has no known motive for murdering Linnet outside of disgust and contempt for her someone as spoiled and selfish as she is.

Middle Sequence External Plot Conflicts:

Louise is discovered missing, then stabbed and killed in her cabin. The corner of a thousand-franc note is found in her hand. There can be no doubt that her attempt to blackmail the murderer ended fatally.

Cohesion between characters, settings, and plot in the middle section really fuses the story on a molecular level. The end section completes the story, providing both enlightenment and logical resolutions to all conflicts.

Incorporating Twists

We said earlier that most twists come at the end of a story. But this isn't to say you couldn't have twists at other points in the story as well as more than one twist, each coming at various intervals. Adding twists to your stories are exciting to read because the author leads the reader so effectively to believe one thing (a thing that *also* makes perfectly logical and cohesive sense) while completely turning the tables at the last minute.

Putting twists into each story spark is a sure-fire way to turn a suspenseful story into a nail-biting one. To get started, ask yourself, *In light of the rest of my story and the cohesiveness I need to provide, what's the most shocking thing I could have happen? What is the reader absolutely not expecting?*

A twist should be set up properly from the very beginning of the book to make it believable. It must fit logically and cohesively with what you've already set up in the beginning and middle of the book. Using an outline can help you prepare for that without requiring you to write an entire draft before you realize your resolutions are too predictable. Resolutions need to fit perfectly with every angle this twist presents.

Think about the book (and the movie, which is just as good) *Presumed Innocent,* by Scott Turow. If you haven't read or watched this before, I encourage you to do it at your earliest opportunity. The twist at the end utterly haunted me for years afterward. The truth was there before my eyes the whole time, yet I never saw it, and it punched me in the stomach brutally when it came.

A twist is so breathtaking because it comes out of nowhere (despite the fact that the reader will have to concede that all the evidence to point to it was there from the start) and it satisfies the reader worlds more than a predictable outcome ever can. In some cases, the twist may be the very thing the reader wanted to happen but didn't dare let himself hope for.

When I finished the outline for *Undercover Angel,* the seventh book in my Incognito Series, I found myself with a story that made complete sense, following the course that I'd set up from the beginning and throughout the middle to the end. Nevertheless, I was ultimately disappointed with the outcome and knew my readers would be, too. The resolutions were simply too predictable to truly satisfy me. So I sat down and thought to myself, *What is the most shocking thing I could possibly make happen in order to make the reader gasp when she gets to the end of the sto-*

ry? When I realized what it was, I went back into my outline and reshaped it from start to finish to fit this new twist as well (better, really) as the predictable resolutions did. When my critique partner read the outline, she said she'd fully expected the predictable resolution and never had the slightest clue about the twist until it hit her square in the stomach--and she loved it. This trick worked to fulfill the breathtaking longing in the reader for an unexpected shock.

Always look for the unexpected twist in your story because it makes it so memorable. There are always obvious scenarios that can be developed in response to the sparks introduced in your story but your goal is to generate the unexpected in your readers. Discombobulate them within the confines of logic, satisfactory resolutions, and cohesion.

Let's take a look at examples of end sequence external plot conflicts from *Death on the Nile* again. Incidentally, this book most definitely had a twist ending that made it utterly breathtaking and satisfying when I read it the first time.

Take note that only the main characters have end sequence internal monologues completed. The secondary characters in this mystery had their internal monologues fully detailed in the middle section of the book--but they are secondary characters who filled a specific role and performed specific, necessary tasks within the middle section of the book.

This is no way implies or assumes that these characters are irrelevant in the end. It's simply that the main characters introduced in the beginning of the novel are the ones who bring the resolutions for all other characters. One way to express this is to consider the secondary characters' internal monologues as short term, while the main characters' must be long term.

Also keep in mind that mystery books are by definition complex and filled with a seemingly endless supply of characters, so this Story Plan Checklist is much more complicated than, say, one of the examples included in Appendix D. In a novel like *Death on the Nile*, most of the secondary characters (and/or their subplots) are red herrings. The reader needs to have a solid idea of their internal conflicts, goals and motivations, and external plot conflicts to flesh the novel out. You'll also notice that all of the subplots and red herrings in *Death on the Nile* are cohesive and fit in with the major conflict wonderfully.

End Story Spark:

Just as Mrs. Otterbourne is about to reveal the name of Louise's killer, she's shot through an open cabin door.

End Sequence Internal Conflicts:

- ***Poirot:*** Poirot must weed out the suspects one by one. Miss Van Schuyler took Linnet's pearls, but Miss Bowers returned them at which time Poirot discovers the necklace is fake. Pennington's shoddy business dealings with Linnet's fortune are uncovered, and Jim's quest to save her is revealed. The spy Colonel Race came aboard to find turns out to be Mr. Richetti, whose coded letter was opened in error by Linnet earlier in the novel. The jewel thief is Tim Allerton, but Poirot allows him give the pearls up to avoid prosecution. Poirot is a romantic, and he sees that Rosalie and Tim are in love when Rosalie admits she saw Tim leave Linnet's stateroom the night she was killed. Mr. Ferguson is a member of the British aristocracy.
- ***Jacqueline:*** The evidence against Jacqueline is too convenient. Besides, her alibi is airtight. All she wants is to return to the man she loves.
- ***Simon:*** The pain in Simon's leg appears too much for him to dwell on his wife's recent decent. Fervently, he defends Jacqueline's innocence. He and Jacqueline can put the past behind them and come together again.

End Sequence Evolving Goals and Motivations:

- ***Poirot:*** Poirot reveals that Simon and Jacqueline have worked together to murder Linnet. Simon's shooting was staged, leaving a stray bullet lodged in the leg of a table (not in Simon's leg). After the gun went off, he pulled a nail-polish-saturated handkerchief out of his pocket, leading everyone in the room to believe he'd been shot. A Miss Bowers is called to care for Jacqueline in her room. Someone else is sent to summon Dr. Bessner in the care of Simon's injured leg...leaving Simon alone in the saloon. He grabbed the pistol and ran to Linnet's cabin. He shot her, using her blood to write the incriminating "J" on the cabin wall. Back in the saloon, he shot himself in the leg for real (using the velvet stole to muffle this second shot). Then he threw the pistol wrapped in the stole through the window to dispose of it.

In order to cover their tracks, Jacqueline committed a second and third murder. Louise dropped the hint to Poirot that she saw someone leave Linnet's stateroom the night of her murder in front of Simon so she could begin to blackmail him. Simon informed Jacqueline of the fact, and she stabbed Louise with one of Dr. Bessner's surgical knives. When Simon realized that Mrs. Otterbourne was about to reveal Jacqueline's role in Louise's murder, he cried out in his fevered state, effectively warning Jacqueline to make a desperate shot at Mrs. Otterbourne through the open door.

- ***Jacqueline:*** Jacqueline saw Simon was obsessed with the idea of marrying, killing, and gaining access to Linnet's fortune as soon as the two met. She knew he was too childishly simple to pull it off himself, especially considering his lack of subtlety and imagination. What other choice did she have? To protect him, she had to become involved in his plan. Seeing Linnet take Simon from her so ruthlessly, without a shred of caring for her old friend, produced hate and the inability to forgive in Jacqueline. Her love for Simon was beyond reason. A woman in love is a danger to everyone around her, especially herself.
- ***Simon:*** Simon married Linnet to get her money, plain and simple. Sure, he hated being married to a controlling woman--being owned by her. But he knew if he married her and she died, he'd be rightful heir to her fortune. Then he and Jacqueline could have their happily ever after.

<u>End Sequence External Plot Conflict Resolutions:</u>

Poirot allows the murderous couple to escape justice when Jacqueline shoots Simon, then herself with the second pistol Jacqueline slipped into Rosalie's handbag and later retrieved.

A couple of reminders:

- Blank or sparse sections are invitations to do more work.
- Mix up the sections of the checklist as you're inspired.
- You can use the checklist for a brand new project, books you've written one or more drafts of, and stories you've started but you're not sure where to go with them after a few chapters.
- Don't worry if your writing is your best on the check-list--it's for your own use.
- For an average novel, the checklist will usually end up being 5 to 10 pages long. What may add to the length are more than three story sparks as well as additional characters important enough to the story to have their own external and internal monologues.
- How you know whether a spark is still working is if your story isn't boring at any point. If it's starting to get dull, you need to inject a story spark to get things going again.

The Cohesion Test

Did you feel as though you'd read *Death on the Nile* after going over its Story Plan Checklist in this chapter? You should feel something very close to that. The same goes for the other Story Plan Checklist examples in Appendix D. Everything important to your book is included on the checklist; therefore it feels as complete and cohesive as a full story.

But how does a writer know for sure if his characters, settings, and plots are truly cohesive? Outside of the fact that your Story Plan Checklist should read like a mini version of the story, look for the obvious:

- Are there any sections on the checklist you didn't fill

out?

- Did you leave important characters off the list? If you put them on now and filled out their basic external and internal monologues, would the story be more cohesive?
- Are your story sparks intriguing enough, or can you punch them up more?
- Do your settings truly fit the characters and plot, or are they simply *there*?
- Do beginning, middle, and end internal monologues follow a progressive, logical course?
- Are resolutions logical? Predictable? Would a twist ending be more effective and exciting?

If you've covered all of the points above, and you want to be absolutely sure, ask yourself the magical seven questions of cohesion below. All must be answered with a resounding *Yes!* or your story needs more work.

- Are conflicts, goals, and motivations defined enough to pinpoint within the high-concept blurb?
- Do internal and external conflicts, goals, and motivations intersect, collide, and impact?
- Do characters have believable, identifiable, and compelling conflicts, goals, and motivations they care about deeply?
- Are the character's conflicts, goals, and motivations urgent and causal (can't have one without the other)?
- Do the characters have the skills to achieve the goal if sufficiently motivated?
- Are the main characters directly involved in resolutions of internal and external plot conflicts?
- If the story was set anywhere else, would the setting make the characters and plot less cohesive?

Anything but that definitive "Yes" to each question means you need to go back and work on your cohesion in the area that received a "No" or "Not sure". All elements must reach a molecular level of bonding.

You'll find a Story Plan Checklist (followed by a cohesion test) for your own use in Appendix C. If you'd like to view full Story Plan Checklists for more novels, see Appendix D. In Appendix E, we'll work together on exercises to help you flex your Story Plan Checklist muscles.

Tips For Wrapping Up Your Story:

1. Make connections between all of your plots and subplots. If internal and external conflicts (and goals and motivations) don't intersect, collide and experience impact, you're writing separate books *in the same manuscript.*
2. Don't worry if your internal and external conflicts lump together. It just shows how cohesive your story elements are--everything's working together toward the resolution.
3. Your Story Plan Checklist builds the structure of your story by following story threads from beginning, through middle, to end. If any of your threads aren't strong enough, or "sag" anywhere, you'll see it in the checklist. It's a guarantee that, if the thread isn't properly developed within the checklist, it won't be properly developed within your story.
4. Your checklist should read like a well-developed synopsis--which is why it can so easily be transformed into one. More about that later.

STAGE 2: EVALUATING THE BLUEPRINT

After you've set your blueprint outline and Story Plan Checklist aside for all the time you can spare, plan on spending a couple days or a week re-evaluating the strength of your story before you begin writing the book.

Though your blueprint will probably be very strong at this point, you may need to do a little revision of the outline and tightening of the checklist to achieve a solid story with strong connections and cohesion.

When you're satisfied with the evaluation, you're ready to begin writing the book!

LAYER II, PART B
Strengthening the Foundation

STAGE 3: WRITING THE FIRST DRAFT

By now, I'm sure you're wondering how a Story Plan Checklist fits in with an outline, and how either can help you write your first draft. As we've established, a Story Plan Checklist is just what it implies--a checklist that connects all the dots of your story (specifically, the internal and external conflicts, and the goals and motivations) and ensures that you close up any gaps in the logic while providing absolute cohesion between character, setting, and plot throughout your story. While the checklist absolutely *helps* a writer who's working with no other guide, the purpose of it isn't to take the place of an outline, where the crafting of scenes takes place, but to enhance and complete it. When you've finished your outline, developing the checklist (which should be simple at this point) will show you vividly whether your story is successful from start to finish.

Can you use the Story Plan Checklist without an outline to write your first draft? I've often said that there's no *wrong* way to write a book, but there are *ineffective* ways of writing. I stand by the truth of the fact that the clearer a writer's vision of a story before the actual writing begins (and a full outline and a completed Story Plan Checklist *will* guarantee that), the more fleshed out and solid that story will be once it makes it to paper. And, if you work out the kinks through outlining in some fashion, you'll absolutely reduce the number of revisions (and drafts) required. The checklist is intended to be used as a final check that the story is solid and ready to be turned into a fully realized manuscript.

If you've produced only a Story Plan Checklist to guide you but you aren't pairing it with an outline, you will end up using, in essence, an instinctive method of writing. In other words, when you're writing the book, you'll have to be in a constant state of brainstorming, searching out the correct paths to progress your story. The Story Plan Checklist on its own will certainly aid you in understanding your characters, settings, and plots better and will help you along this road of discovery. However, if you don't have a written outline beyond the checklist to help you when you sit down to write, what you come up with to flesh out each scene will need to stem directly from your brainstorming--not from written-down, crafted scenes, such as what an outline provides. (This is why it's so important to do the outline in Layer I.)

For that reason, I can't recommend strongly enough that you use an outline and the Story Plan Checklist together in writing your first draft. Use them together as a check and balance system. That's what we'll be doing in this section of Layer II.

So, that said, I'm going to start here under the assumption that you've completed a scene-by-scene outline and a Story Plan Checklist, and, as we discussed in the last section of Layer II: Part A, that you've set both aside for as long as you possibly can in order to give yourself distance to evaluate the strength of the story.

Once you take the project out to begin the true first draft of the story, you'll notice that you have everything you need to begin writing. The blueprint you created for yourself contains everything your book will contain, only on a much smaller scale, and will include a scene-by-scene breakdown of the entire story including all the major points (internal and external conflicts, and goals and motivations) from your Story Plan Checklist that ensure utterly cohesion. Your characters fit perfectly with both the plot and setting you've come up with. When you begin writing, you might actually see in your mind the "house" of your story going up with each scene--board by board, wall by wall, ceiling and window and door!

Because your outline blueprint contains a summary of what happens in every single scene of your book, when you sit down to write, you're simply following the breakdown of what you've already decided needs to happen in each one, and because your Story Plan Checklist did its magic, you won't leave out any major points that build in cohesion along the way. Additionally, you won't stare at the blank page, wondering how to fill it so the chance of suffering from writer's block is minimal. Your outline will tell you what to compose scene by scene. With each written scene, your story will progress--many times rapidly, especially if you're using a writing goals sheet (see chapter ten of *First Draft Outline* for more information on how to create one) and complete the number of scenes you set for yourself each day.

Though in the first edition of this book, I was instructed by staff at that publishing house to create a way to merge the outline and Story Plan Checklist into one document, doing so was never my intention in the initial creation of this book nor the method I've been describing in developing a Story Plan Checklist. In my mind, that would be suggesting to an author that she do much more work than she really needs to.

The reason I'm including that process in this revised second edition of the book in the next several pages is because doing so on paper is a more visual method of providing an example of how you use your outline and checklist as you write your first draft. That said, you're certainly not required to merge these two documents. When I'm writing the first draft, the Story Plan Checklist of that book is always in the back of my mind. I don't have to merge the two on paper to get the benefit of having developed it. Of course if it helps you to merge them as I will below, feel free. Don't make more work for yourself if it doesn't help you.

Over the course of the next pages, I've included step-by-step guidelines to show you how the outline and Story Plan Checklist work together when writing the book. The checklist covers the most important points of your story (usually condensed). Your outline may contain them in greater detail. In any case, in whatever form, these elements need to be brought out in the scenes of your story as you write them. The best way to show you this is by using the actual first scene of an outline (from one of my novella releases) interspersed with the necessary elements from a completed checklist. Following this, I'll show you how I used this solidly cohesive blueprint to write the first draft.

A quick reminder we learned from Layer II, Part A: The beginning story spark sets up the conflict. The middle story spark (or possibly more than one middle story spark) complicates the situation. Finally, the ending story spark resolves the conflict and the situation.

When writing outlined scenes, the first question to answer is who the point of view character is because it's that character's information you'll be concerned with in that particular scene. Remember we talked about the no-no of head-hopping in Layer II. Based on that and though, as a writer you'll have omniscient knowledge of other characters internal conflicts and goals and motivations, the POV character in each scene won't have inside knowledge about any other character but herself.

Your first scene is most certainly one of the most crucial--if not *the* most crucial in your story. This is the one what will either hook or lost editors, agents and readers. It's also the scene where you're setting up your story, and, therefore, it needs to convey a great deal very quickly (your outline will be fairly bursting with it all, as you'll see). That said, you can't overwhelm that first scene with too much of anything. It's a tricky balance best learned with the frequent practice outlining, writing and revising.

Remember that writing isn't an exact science, and what I'll give you here are guidelines that may not work for every book and are most certainly not set in stone. Use your own instincts with the information I'm including here. If it makes more sense for your story to do something else than what I recommend, then do that.

One other thing we'll talk more about in the revisions stage that applies here is that it's generally considered poor writing to use *self*-descriptions of point of view characters; that said, if you can do it without annoying the reader, go ahead. In most cases, have other characters describe the POV character. So, in your opening scene, you wouldn't include a description of the POV character. You should include descriptions of other important character(s) in the scene.

Now, take a look at how I've combined portions of a Layer I outline (taken from the free-form summary outline done in a scene-by-scene outline capsule) with a Layer II Story Plan Checklist (though I didn't specify which was which, since the two work together). Note that for clarity, I placed checklist items in the way that made the most sense in terms of which items I thought I might use first while writing the scene. Writing in general will help you figure out what should go where within the written scene.

Story Plan Checklist insert:

Title:
In Cahoots With Cupid, Book 2 of the Kaleidoscope Series

Genre:
Contemporary Romance Novella

POV Specification:
Angela Lewis and Kiowa "Ki" Mackenzie

Length of Book/Number of Sparks:
Approximately 12,500 words/2 story sparks

High-Concept Blurb:
Angela Lewis has devoted her life to seeing that everyone she cares for is happy. But when she returns home to Fever, Texas for a wedding, she remembers the one instance where she'd turned her back on something she wanted for herself. Kiowa Mackenzie is five years younger than her and had pursued Angela with the energy of a stallion when they were younger. Even now, he seems to have no inclination to stop, though she insists she's too old for him and she's not interested in falling in love again. Best man Ki has every intention of tackling the bridesmaids to make sure maid of honor Angela catches the bride's bouquet!

Summary Outline Capsule:

Day: February 12th
Chapter: Chapter 1
POV Character: Angela Lewis

Additional Characters: Ki Mackenzie
Location: Lubbock International Airport
Approximate Time: Late morning
Draft of Scene: Angela's flight gets into Lubbock, TX, Lubbock International Airport.

Character Introductions:

Angela: 39-year-old business owner, Maid of Honor at the upcoming wedding that takes place in the story, coming home to Fever, Texas after almost fifteen years away--with no small amount of trepidation.

Description (Outside POV):

Angela: Generous to a fault, she treats her employees and co-workers as family. After growing up on a ranch, she misses having a large, extended family, so her employees have become the family she lost when she fled Fever. Now that her friend and employee Keri is marrying her cousin, she knows she has to find a replacement at Kaleidoscope Office Services, but she hates the idea. Whoever she hires will become part of her family, just as Keri has been. It's been a month and two weeks since Keri gave her resignation preceding her Valentine's Day wedding.

Description (Self POV):

Angela: My high adventure life is a front for the truth: I'm afraid of life and love. Each time I realized I had a fear all these years, I confronted it. In the most dramatic way possible. I refuse to live with fear. I climbed Argentine Patagonia's because I'm afraid of heights; explored Guatemalan jungles because I'm afraid of bugs and the dark; explored Egyptian archeological digs because I found myself not wanting to leave home; and jumped out of a plane because I'm afraid of not having a safety net. So why did I return each time even more afraid of the thing I blindly feared before that? The one fear I refuse to confront is my fear of love. I know Ki has a crush on me, but I won't let myself believe it's true love.

Summary Outline Capsule

She's supposed to meet Keri (her close friend and co-worker) and Joshua (her cousin) in Baggage Claim. She's not feeling good. She didn't sleep last night, couldn't eat before her flight, tried to read on the plane to keep herself from thinking too much (all of which have increased her susceptibility to the airsickness she's now experiencing).

Airsickness, a form of motion, is brought on by air travel. Common signs and symptoms include: Nausea, vomiting, sweating, malaise, vertigo, dizziness, loss of appetite, cold sweating, skin pallor, difficulty concentrating, confusion, drowsiness, headache, and increased fatigue.

Angela is coming from La Crosse, WI, where she lives and works. The time zone is the same as in Lubbock, TX.

February 12th weather in Lubbock: Max temp: 57; Min temp: 28; Average: 43; Precip: .03; Record high temp: 86 in 1962.

Compared to the light snow falling in freezing WI when she left earlier that morning, it's difficult to imagine she's in the same country.

Setting Descriptions:

Fever, Texas (fictional) is a speck of a town a good ways from any city of consequence. Considered to be at the center of the South Plains, Fever is located between the Permian Basin to the south and the Texas Panhandle to the north. Seemingly endless, red-dirt roads stretch toward a brilliant orange/pink horizon. What little "town" there is to speak of amounts to a gas station with basic groceries, a hotel that rarely does brisk business, and a hearty-platter diner.

Angela and Ki grew up in a circle of cooperative ranches. The one they lived on is the Lewis Ranch. Ki's father had been a ranch hand there throughout his childhood. The ranch is jointly owned by Angela's father, his younger brother, and their sister. The neighboring ranches in the area include the Lewis Ranch, the Triple Aces Ranch, the May Ranch, and the Sanford Ranch.

Occupational Skills:

Angela: Angela owns Kaleidoscope Office Building, a strip mall that contains her two businesses: Kaleidoscope Office Services makes copies, types and prints, and does basic desktop publishing for small business and personal use. Her employees are Keri Woods (who's marrying Angela's cousin) and Aimee Cooper. Veronica "Roni" Spencer and Dex Everett handle the graphic design done at Lewis Graphics by Design. Angela's the aggressive salesperson for both businesses, sometimes effortlessly drumming up business for them. The other business in the building is Two Brothers Accounting, which she's invested in. Billy LaPointe and Rob Channing are accountants and tax preparers. Shayna Cavanay is their secretary/receptionist.

Summary Outline Capsule

Because she's the maid of honor, she's coming 2 days before the wedding to help Keri get ready. The bridesmaids (Aimee, Roni, and Shayna) will be coming in tomorrow. Angela is paying for their flights and giving them paid leave during these days. Dex is staying behind to handle any work that comes in for both shops. As much as possible, he'll divert deadlines to February 16th, when they'll all return. Shayna's ex-husband is taking her young son Ty during these days, but Shayna is worried sick about it. Billy and Rob are staying behind because they're up to their ears in work.

Ki is the one there to meet Angela at the airport.

Character Introductions:

Ki: 35-year-old engineer, Best Man at the wedding, who has his sights set on winning the woman he's loved most of his life while she's home--even if he has to enlist Cupid in his quest to succeed!

Summary Outline Capsule

Physical description of Ki: Tall, lean, and tan. Blondish-brown hair and baby blue eyes.

Occupational Skills:

Ki: He and his brother Wings, or "Mac" as everyone calls him, co-own Mackenzie Environment & Infrastructure, an engineering firm. Los Angeles marks the headquarters of their successful business. Both he and Mac have extensive experience and schooling in engineering and wastewater treatment. They travel all over the United States, spending a few months working on major upgrades of a wastewater treatment plant, more if there are problems.

Summary Outline Capsule

She never expected to see Ki waiting, especially since she just saw him at Christmas-time. He'd been on a project in Washington state and jogged over to Wisconsin to have dinner with her. In addition to his frequent visits, he calls her 4 or 5 times a week, and she loves these conversations.

Ki convinced Joshua and Keri to let him pick her up--what with wedding preparations, they agreed. They hug and kiss, and she can't help but think how good it feels to have his arms around her again. When she steps back, she says she's really glad to see him. He has a way of making her feel comforted, cherished and taken care of all at the same time. He says, "Wow, three out of four *what's* all at the same time. And at least one *how*." She's not sure what he means, but he goes to get the luggage instead of answering.

BEGINNING STORY SPARK:

Angela is dreading coming home, even as she's looking forward to the wedding of her cousin and close friend, whom she'd played matchmaker to get together. She'd just never expected the marriage to take place at the Lewis Ranch, since her cousin and his father had been estranged for years. Apparently the two have reconciled and the wedding at the ranch is part of that reconciliation. She hasn't been home for almost fifteen years--not since the funeral of Ki's parents and she didn't return to the Lewis Ranch that time.

As much as Angela has tried to block out the memories in the years she fled her husband in the dead of night, she can still recall too easily how much she loved Mason Broderbund. She understood her father's hero worship for the man because she shared it completely. Mason had been raised with her--not as a brother--and he'd always been older, *mysterious* compared to the other boys she knew her age. She'd been crazy about him for as long as she could remember. When she graduated from college with her business degree and came home, he swept her off her feet, making her forget her own dreams.

She never wanted to believe he was using her to get her share of the ranch, cheating on her with any available female in the vicinity, turning her against *herself* so easily. She'd accepted full blame for not being able to hold on to his love. For not being enough for him. The grip of the terror she'd held herself in with worrying he would dump her still held her motionless at times. He might not have hurt her more than the one time, but she let him do everything else. She let it go on for years. Sometimes she was grateful he beat her so badly that one time and one time only. Those ruthless punches woke her up to who she was, what she'd become, what she couldn't remain.

Character Internal Conflicts:

Angela: In the quiet whisperings of her mind, Angela continues to hear her old destructive voice telling her that without Mason she can't have love, can't have her family, can't have forgiveness for her obsessive love turned sin for a man who didn't deserve it.

The worst part had been that her father sided with her husband when Mason destroyed her faith, confidence and ability to trust anyone else to love her, but how can she blame her father when she never told him what Mason did to her?

She hasn't been able to return home for her father, nor for her own good. Home--where the jagged pieces of herself are scattered beyond retrieval. Mason continues to work on the Lewis Ranch, now as ranch foreman, to this day. He's her father's pride and joy. Angela believes her father chose Mason over her.

Because of all her fears, she can't allow herself to accept that Ki is serious about her. But the fact is that only he makes her happy. No one means more to her than he does--even if they can't be together the way she won't let herself believe he wants them to be. Only Ki fills the lonely ache inside her with his phone calls, his outrageous trips across the country just to have dinner with her, the way he's always there for her when she most needs him to be. She's conflicted about the fact that her friends love him and believe he's the perfect man for her. She can't even get herself to believe he's not because she knows she can never be the right woman for him after what happened to her, after what she did. She's too afraid to confront this fear.

Summary Outline Capsule

But, at the moment, she's too sick to dwell on anything too long. She's also embarrassed that she got sick at all. Not once during her "fear confrontation adventures" had she ever gotten sick. She suggests that Ki drop her off at a hotel if he wants to miss the "action"--she could hurl at any minute. He says he's taking care of her personally. Returning the favor for the way she took care of him last time she was home after his parents were killed. She insists that that was different. He says there's no difference. He needed someone and she was there for him. He's doing the same. She's touched.

This outlined first scene, which is a cross between an outline and your checklist, has everything necessary to begin writing. However, most writers will need time to brainstorm before writing a scene to come up with the best ways to start the story. I always advise authors not to get stuck on the first sentence. Yes, the first sentence is very important, but it's more important to finish writing the scene. You can always come back later and revise it into something that immediately hooks a reader's interest.

A tip about your story's first--and last--sentences: Begin looking for both as soon as you start outlining a story. The most effective beginning sentences are the ones that grab the reader's attention and brings her into the story without an instant of delay or confusion. (See Layer III for a tip on using dialogue as a beginning sentence.) In the same way, the most effective ending sentences are the ones that make the reader reluctant to leave the story and yet forces her to smile because it perfectly ties up the book she's just finished.

I can't help you write your opening sentence, but I can tell you to make it kick open the door to your story with instant impact that's readily absorbed--you don't want the reader's mind to go, "Huh? What does that mean?" You want her to think, "Great! I'm here. Let's go!" which really does convey the sense that she understands what's happening, wants to know more, and she's eagerly moving into the story with your POV character.

As for the ending sentence of a book, look for it early, too. Most effectively, it's a phrase, thought or situation that comes up often enough in the book that the reader will recognize it immediately. You want something familiar and comforting to readers. On its own, this ending sentence will give the reader the sense that all is ending well, exactly as it should, and happily ever after is on the horizon for these lovable characters.

For instance, in the story of the outlined scene you just read, *In Cahoots With Cupid*, the hero, Ki, wants to enlist the aid of Cupid to win Angela's love. Oh, but where to find Cupid? In fact, this "Cupid" is both a character- and plot-defining Symbolic Element in the story. Cupid comes along in the form of the baby boy Angela's old friend, Maggie May, has. Maggie May calls her baby "her little cupid", and Ki agrees that the tyke looks like Cupid himself in his droopy cloth diaper. All of this (and the title, of course) helped me to come up with the most obvious and satisfying ending sentence. Ki thanks "Cupid" for helping him get his girl, and Maggie May exclaims, "I just knew you two were in cahoots!"

You'll also need to brainstorm before writing a scene to come up with the best way to incorporate descriptions (of the setting and character variety), backstory, and conflicts without overwhelming the reader. Remember, you want to kick open the door of your story, but, once the reader is inside, you want her walking beside your POV character, eagerly discovering (and able to absorb) as the story folds. All of this must be natural and organic. Resist any urge to do a giant information dump right up front. You only want to *introduce* your character, setting and plot in this first scene--and to mix them all together so (1) they make sense; (2) they convey bits of information about character, setting and plot that are intriguing and lead the reader to want to know more about all three; and (3) they lead naturally into the next scene, which will progress character, setting and plot to another level of the story, almost like taking stairs one at a time toward the top of a building.

Your outline shows the progression you need to take on the journey of writing this book. Whenever you introduce a new POV character, you follow the same process. In other words, when I introduced Ki as the second POV character in chapter two of *In Cahoots With Cupid*, I pulled out the same list of Story Plan Checklist elements I did for Angela, except I used Ki's information in this chapter.

It was at the end of this second scene that I finally introduced the external plot conflicts. That might surprise you, because you may be thinking that the plot has to be introduced immediately. You're right. But remember that your first story spark is what infuses the beginning of the story. That spark will include the portion of the plot you need introduced immediately. Ideally, you should only introduce external plot conflicts or goals and motivations (don't forgot, internal conflicts and goals and motivations come one at a time) after main character internal conflicts (which are based on the first story spark) have been established.

Now, keep in mind that the story we're using as an example here was a novella and had a grand total of eight scenes, which I alternated between my two POV characters. A novel will probably take several more scenes to fully introduce main character internal conflicts or goals and motivations, followed by the external plot conflicts--most likely the full beginning of your book. Remember, we said in Section A of Layer II that if you have a 75,000-word novel with three story sparks, the first comes right in the beginning within the first few chapters, the second will come around the halfway mark of the book (around 40,000 to

55,000 words in) with the last just near the end at maybe 75,000 to 80,000 words in.

In chapter three of *In Cahoots With Cupid* (Angela's POV), I introduced Angela's goals and motivations. Chapter four was in Ki's POV, and his goals and motivations came into play. Up until this point, I was *setting up* (note those words carefully because what we've done thus far is introduce) all of these things, just as you will be for many, many more scenes in your own story. Chapters five and six of my story fully fleshed out internal conflicts, goals and motivations, and plot conflicts. Up to this point, these things were set up, introduced and hinted at, but not brought out fully. Now was the time to make a true impact with them.

Chapter seven introduced the ending story spark, which begins the cycle of progressing internal conflicts, goals and motivations, and plot conflicts all over again. In a book, you'd repeat what you've already done previously with this new set of evolving points: You set up (introduce and hint at) one at a time with the different POV characters, and this will take many scenes to accomplish. This is followed by fully fleshing out all of these things until you're ready to inject another story spark. If you have more than three, naturally, you'd repeat this cycle after each one.

Normally, books have three internal monologue cycles. The final cycle will inject the ending story spark. Remember, what happens now will happen fairly quickly, in the last 10,000 words or so (depending on the size of your book, of course). While this invigorates your story *incidentally*, what it's most doing is illuminating and resolving so you can begin tying up your conflicts and bringing about logical resolutions to them.

In my story, I only had two story sparks (because novellas rarely have more than two). We mentioned earlier that additional sparks almost always increase length since you're building a more complicated story. So chapter seven injected the second one, and the cycling went even more quickly this time. Final internal conflicts and goals and motivations were illuminated, then tied up with the external plot conflict that led to the resolutions.

This whole process takes a significant amount of practice to learn and especially for it to become instinctive in the course of writing a book. Chances are, you won't get it exactly right the first time even when you've got a few or a dozen books under your belt. Revision will help you smooth out any rough edges in your first draft. Information dumps or illogical passages that stall you (or critique partners) during a revision will be alerting you to a section that needs to be reworked--either by putting the information elsewhere in the book, breaking it up and scattering it throughout several scenes, or cutting, condensing, and polishing it so it flows better and makes more sense.

In my first draft of *In Cahoots With Cupid,* I realized (with a little help from my critique friends) that the prologue I started in Ki's POV was nothing more than a huge information dump. During revision, I condensed the material down to half its original size and placed it later in the story, as my new chapter four. Then I smoothed out all the chapters that came before and after it, so they flowed into and fit this one.

Another area that I later revised was Angela's occupation. What you see in the outlined scene is what I started out with. Again, this was far too much information in a place that wasn't ready to accept it. I hadn't introduced her employees, so it didn't make sense to include a detailed explanation of what Angela did for a living and who she employed there. That information got condensed, smoothed and incorporated into chapter three, where it made perfect sense, considering the fact that she did finally meet up with her former employee, Keri, in that scene.

Revision is a necessary, natural part of writing. Every first draft needs it. However, a writer who starts a project with all the necessary groundwork will probably have few, if any, *major* problems with her first draft when it's finished. Her revision will amount to minor editing and rearranging, cutting, condensing or polishing. We'll go over that in Layer III.

While I won't claim it happens with every book for every author, I do believe that the best books--the ones that have creators and muses who love them--are written with a magical element infusing the process. What you read of the combined Story Plan Checklist and outline for *In Cahoots With Cupid* probably sounded as flat to you as it did to me when I took out the outline in preparation to write the story. Everything I needed was there. I just needed to brainstorm to figure out how I was going to arrange these things and then begin writing to bring about that magical infusion.

When I was writing the first draft, though, I took that detailed summary I provided myself in the outline, and I used it to bring my characters, settings, and plots to life. All three of these felt amazingly real and vivid to me from the very first sentence I wrote. I wanted to know more about all three. My senses were completely stimulated by what was coming out during this writing process. Because of that, I could bring the reader into this world I'd created, introduce her to my characters, and make her care about the conflicts they were facing.

Below, you'll find what I ended up with after writing, revising, and editing and polishing the first draft:

In Cahoots With Cupid
{Kaleidoscope Series, Book 2}

Karen Wiesner

Chapter 1

February 12th

Her stomach felt like she'd swallowed a big box of the very worst flavors in Bertie Bott's Every Flavor Beans. Angela Lewis closed her eyes and halted on the disembarkment ramp, causing several passengers to mutter rudely as they shoved past her. ***[Author's note: I chose my first two sentences based on the fact that I wanted the heroine to be experiencing airsickness, and this brings the reader directly into the story with empathy and a touch of humor. Within the first two sentences, POV character should always be introduced with the full name in the most creative way you can come up with. The reason for her sickness is because I had this idea in the outlining stages of the story that the hero is thinking a lot about traditional wedding***

vows since his best friend Joshua told him he was getting married and wants the hero to be his Best Man. Part of the vows are "in sickness and in health". So the hero will be taking care of the heroine to prove he can be the man she needs. Later, she loses her purse, and "for richer and for poorer" comes in to flesh this angle out.] The roiling in her middle worsened. Little if any sleep last night, nothing to eat today, reading on the plane to keep herself from thinking too much about what in the world she was doing coming home...

Airsickness. Ugh. At least Keri and Joshua would be waiting for her at Baggage Claim instead of her family or anyone from the Lewis Ranch. ***[Author's note: Here you see a hint of her internal conflict. After all, why would she want anyone other than family or those who lived at her family's ranch {the reader will deduce this because the heroine's last name is the same} to pick her up from the airport? This will make the reader wonder what happened to make her not want them to greet her as soon as she gets off the plane.]***

Keri...what am I going to do about her resignation?

Angela shook off her thought. She'd have to face it, but not today. Not until after she returned to La Crosse, Wisconsin. Besides, she was thrilled Keri and Joshua were engaged. She, along with Dandy, the crotchety, loveable old foreman on her family's ranch, had gone to the trouble of matchmaking for just this reason--to see Keri and Joshua happy at long last. ***[Author's note: This story was the second in a series. That's always complicated because, with a series, you want to include a very basic summary of what happened in the previous story, but, since it's not the focus of this one, it has to tell everything necessary in just a few short sentences. I dropped in this bit of background here, where it enhances the reader's knowledge without overwhelming, then revisited the issue in the chapter three, where a fuller--but still very concise--explanation was needed. I should add that in my first draft of this story, I included the full explanation of how Angela's employee (and friend) Keri had fallen madly in love with Angela's cousin over Christmas, due to Angela and Dandy's matchmaking. Keri resigned in or-***

der to concentrate on planning her wedding, and Angela is bothered greatly at the thought of "replacing" her at Kaleidoscope Office Services. Two of my critique partners tripped over this great hunk of information that really wasn't needed fully at this point. I cropped it down here to all that's really needed. The rest, I sprinkled throughout chapter three, where it actually did fit.]

Angela took a few slow, deep breaths, trying to fight her nausea. ***[Author's note: Remember that long list of airsickness symptoms in the outline? Instead of including the list, I put the symptoms into action. The reader feels empathy because actual feelings are evoked from the symptoms the heroine experiences. This is a way to turn passive information into active prose. Again, notice it's sprinkled throughout the scene instead of included in one clump.]*** Then she forced herself forward. The Lubbock International Airport was crowded. The weather through the plane windows had looked gorgeous with the sun shining brightly, the day unseasonably warm, according to the pilot, at seventy-three degrees. Because of her sickness, the warmth only made her feel feverish now. Back in La Crosse that morning, light snow had been falling. It was hard to believe she'd been in the same country just hours ago.

Jostled about by those who apparently didn't have time to be polite, Angela was thrust into Baggage Claim, already filled to capacity with passengers and loved ones. She huddled into the nearest space against the wall and spent another long minute trying to talk her stomach into calming down. When she couldn't, she accepted her best bet was to find Keri and Joshua and get out of the dizzy airport.

The last person she expected to be coming toward her was Kiowa Mackenzie. Dressed in comfortably worn jeans, a denim work shirt under a light jacket, and his old Resistol suede felt cowboy hat and boots, he took her breath away.

The many faces of Ki. Today the tall, muscular cowboy I remember he was growing into by the time I left home; last time I saw him, the sharp, sexy businessman. ***[Author's note: This description--coming on the heels of the last paragraph, where***

the reader is given a nice picture of what the hero is wearing--is much more natural than a block that contains hair color, eye color, height, weight...yet it conveys a very clear image in the mind. Notice that the hero's physical description is interspersed all through this scene, giving the reader time for form her own mental picture.]

His skin was as tan as it would be if he'd spent the last few months in Miami instead of overcast Renton, Washington, a small city south of Seattle, where she knew he'd been at Christmas. He'd been working on a major upgrade of a wastewater treatment plant. He and his brother Wings, or "Mac" as everyone called him, co-owned Mackenzie Environment & Infrastructure, an engineering firm. Los Angeles marked the headquarters of their successful business. Both he and Mac had extensive experience and schooling in engineering and wastewater treatment. They traveled all over the United States, spending a few months on each project, more if there were problems. Angela knew that part of what Ki loved about his career came down to the fact that he wasn't always doing the same thing. While his permanent location was situated in the dinky little ranch town of Fever, Texas she and the two brothers had grown up in, he returned only a few times a year. ***[Author's note: The reader learns a lot in this paragraph--and not simply the fact that the hero is an engineer and co-owns a successful business with his brother. That portion of what the reader learns is highlighted. That amounted to three, concise sentences. The rest of the paragraph gives the reader more personal information. The heroine knows where this man is at all times--they're in almost constant contact despite the fact that they're in different states. That speaks of an intimacy that impacts their relationship on multiple levels. It'll also make the reader wonder why the heroine is hemming and hawing in accepting him as the perfect man for her.]***

And I haven't been home since-- ***[Author's note: Here again, just a very effective hint of the first story spark and the heroine's internal conflict. This will nag the reader's mind each time she's given another piece of this intriguing puzzle.]***

Deep grooves surrounded his smiling mouth, scattering her thoughts and drawing her own lips up against her will. She recalled their greeting last time he flew into La Crosse to see her.

"What are you doing here?"

"It's Christmas. I was hoping to take you to dinner."

"To... You came here from Washington for dinner?"

He chuckled. "You act like that's out-of-the-ordinary."

No, that wasn't strange for Ki. No matter where his projects ended up, he came to see her in Wisconsin often. When he couldn't visit, he called her four or five times a week.

I don't know what I'd do if he didn't. I live for those phone calls. Those visits. He goes straight to my head every single time with all his flirting. And those hello and goodbye kisses... ***[Author's note: Take a look at the highlighted section above. It really adds to the paragraph where we learn that the hero and heroine are in constant contact with each other. The reader now learns that he flew to see her on Christmas a few months ago--from his project in Renton, Washington to her home in La Crosse, Wisconsin. And he came just to take her to dinner. This is something he does often. When he can't, he calls frequently. The way this information is conveyed isn't a summary, like you saw in the outline. This is where that magical element comes in as a writer strives to take what was flat, basic information in an outline in order to turn it into more than mere words. The reader uses all her senses with the characters. The liveliness of active, interesting prose can make readers forget they're reading as they're transported with your characters fully into the world you've created.]***

Even as she opened her arms for his expected hug, she asked, "What are you doing here, Ki? Keri and Joshua were supposed to meet me."

"I convinced them to let me do it. Do you mind?"

She drew back slightly. "Of course not. Never."

He enveloped her again, and she closed her eyes, breathing in the familiar, intoxicating scent of his cologne. Why did his arms always feel so right? During those three-hour-long phone conversations with him, she imagined herself in his arms, growing warm and drowsy against his chest.

Just like all those times, the memory of his kiss shattered the comforting aspects of being swallowed up in his strong embrace. He never kissed her the way he should, the way she told himself he ought to. She often teased him about how he lost that ingrained gentleman quality of his when he said hello or goodbye. When he eased away now, she stopped breathing altogether--forgot how--with his gaze hungry on her lips. Heat raced through her veins, straight to her nerve endings, in anticipation.

Unfortunately, her churning stomach couldn't be denied even with the intense desire she knew she shouldn't feel for this childhood friend who meant more to her than any other.

"You don't look so good, angel," he murmured, cradling his cool hand against her burning cheek. "I'd say you look white as a ghost if you weren't green."

She grinned uneasily. "Airsickness. I've never had it, but I've been around others who have. I need to get out of here."

"I've got Dramamine back at my apartment."

"Let's go."

He leaned forward and dropped a kiss on her mouth, reminding her of the deep, forget-my-own-name kiss he would have given her if she wasn't sick. "Stay here out of traffic. I'll get your luggage."

Angela leaned back against the wall, her eyes glued to the man who'd infused her childhood with confidence. His crush on her had been outrageous, sweet...a complete whirlwind of happiness. Tempering his incurable flirtations, his charm seduced her even now. She could come up with a million reasons why she wasn't the right woman for him, why he deserved so much better than a shell of the person she was as a teenager, the whole woman she was meant to be now...and wasn't. The fact that he'd just turned thirty-five and she'd been thirty-nine for a long time was one good excuse--one as good as any. ***[Author's note: You'll notice that in setting up her internal conflicts, the reader doesn't get it all in one big information dump. It comes in hints that layer on top of each other, allowing the reader to absorb them...and allowing her intrigue to grow of the situation. Also note from***

the outlined scene with checklist items interspersed that all ***of the heroine's internal conflicts aren't included in this chapter. Obviously, that would be too much information for a single scene. Earlier in chapter two, we talked about how you introduce characters a little at a time--the way you meet people in real life. In a novella, that process necessarily has to be speeded up. In a novel, this would take the whole of the beginning of the book to fully bring out.]***

She admired his patience as he watched for her suitcase to come around the carousel, the way he tipped his old cowboy hat back. She loved those blondish-brown curls at his neck, the baby blue eyes that checked on her frequently as he waited. Why did her chest feel so heavy if it was her stomach that was in chaos? She worried she'd cry when he came back to her with her heavy suitcase. With his free hand, he drew her tenderly against his side, obviously to shelter her against the bustling traffic all around them as they made their way out of the airport. ***[Author's note: This is a romantic story. Sexual tension is something that has to start from the beginning and hum throughout the story. It's subtle in this story, but still very active. In a romance, the author has the challenge of making the readers not only care about her hero and heroine individually but to want to see them come together for their own happily ever after. So sexual tension needs romantic intimacy to satisfy the reader.]***

They boarded the shuttle bus to the parking lot.

"How you feeling?" he asked when they found a seat together.

"Is it possible to want to sleep and throw up at the same time?" she murmured.

His arm already around her, he pressed her head to his shoulder, stroking her hair. "I'll get you somewhere you can do both."

Instinctive laughter burst out of her, and she groaned at the commotion the act caused her insides. "I'm really glad you're here, Ki. You make me feel comforted, cherished and taken care of all at the same time."

"Wow, three out of four *what's* all at the same time. And at least one *how*."

Confused, she looked up at him. "What?"

His grin was just a little crooked--something she loved every time it set her heart to racing. "Nothing. You've never been airsick before?"

"You're talking about someone who's climbed Argentine Patagonia's mile-high sheer faces and granite spires that stretch thirteen thousand feel into the sky; navigated treacherous Guatemalan jungles; explored Egyptian archeological digs with a field school and nearly got buried in a cave-in; and jumped out of a plane flying 13,500 feet above the earth, falling at a rate of a hundred and twenty-five miles per hour... Ugh, why did I have to remember that, of all things?" Angela prided herself on a healthy lifestyle filled with adventure that covered her deepest, unshakable fears. ***[Author's note: Notice the subtle injection of the fact that these adventures she goes on cover fears. This will become very important later in the story. For now, it'll nag the reader who wants another piece of the puzzle that makes up the heroine.]*** "Save yourself, Ki. Drop me off at a hotel and you can miss the 'action'." The motion of the bus was making her feel like she would hurl at any moment.

"You remember last time you came home?"

His parents' funeral.

Angela and Ki had grown up in a circle of cooperative ranches. The one they lived on was the Lewis Ranch. Ki's father had been a ranch hand there throughout his childhood. The ranch was jointly owned by Angela's father, his younger brother--Joshua's father--and their sister Crystal, who'd married the cowboy who got her pregnant. The entanglement lasted all of a month. When Crystal's son Shawn was a teenager, she left him with her brothers and moved to La Crosse, Wisconsin. Crystal had long since taken up travel as a career, and she rarely came home now--not even for weddings and funerals.

And I inadvertently followed in Aunt Crystal's footsteps. But how could I have not come home for Ki when his parents were killed in that plane crash, even if I could never come home for myself? ***[Author's note: Here's another personal touch. In the paragraph just before this one, the reader is given some set-up information concerning setting and relationships. I could have***

easily included the internal dialogue in this paragraph with that--as more informational prose. But I wanted to make this information personal. The heroine is conveying her internal conflicts in a very intimate way that the reader will respond to in the same intimate way--making her care about these characters.]

Angela squeezed her arms around Ki's waist, and he nodded, looking down at her. "Just returning the favor for the way you took care of me, angel."

"That was different," she murmured, her gaze locked with his soft one in the shadow of the brim of his hat.

"I needed you. I couldn't have survived without you there for me. There's nothing I wouldn't do for you, Angela Butterfly Lewis. Just ask me, and I'm yours."

The fierceness in his voice reminded her of the only other man who called her by her embarrassing middle name.

Daddy who always called me his beautiful butterfly. Daddy who sided with my husband when Mason destroyed my faith, confidence and ability to trust anyone else to love me. But how can I blame Daddy when I never told him what Mason did?

Still, she hadn't been able to return home for her father, nor for her own good. Home--where the jagged pieces of herself were scattered beyond retrieval. She'd been grateful when Dandy asked her not to come home for his funeral. He'd wanted her to remember him as he was. Dandy had realized she wasn't ready to face her past then.

But for Ki she had returned.

And, whether or not I'm ready now, I'm home.

Against her better judgment, she'd be Keri's Maid of Honor on the Valentine's Day wedding, which would take place on the Lewis family ranch. *I'll never get through it. Not without...*

"You'll be busy as the Best Man. How can I ask you to be there for me, Ki?"

The back of his free hand brushed her cheek, his thumb lingering on her bottom lip. "You don't have to ask me, angel. I'm still yours. Always yours."

His words evoked the memory of his words when he was only

thirteen. *"I'm gonna marry you, Angela Butterfly Lewis. You mark my words good, honey. Someday I'm gonna marry you, right here on your daddy's ranch. Don't matter if you're ninety-four and I'm just comin' into my golden years. Someday you're gonna love me the way I love you. For always."* ***[Author's note: I love flashbacks, especially these short ones that achieve the same purpose as if I'd written out an entire scene that took place in the past. I get a vivid picture of ranch with a slightly gawky kid in cowboy hat and boots holding out a bouquet of wild daisies he picked to the heroine (who's also much younger). Short flashbacks are a great way to break up standard prose with something personal and intriguing. How the reader envisions them in her own mind is part of the magic of storytelling. If the reader is coming up with her own images, she's very much involved in the story. Allow that! Encourage it! It's what makes your book one that goes on the keeper shelf.]***

Shaky as she felt, Angela couldn't prevent herself from smiling. Kiowa Mackenzie hadn't changed one iota in almost thirty years. He was still chasing her like a jackrabbit with a one-track mind, and she still couldn't decide whether to set him loose for some other nice girl...or to let him catch her. ***[Author's note: Now that you're finished reading this scene, go back and skim it once more, taking particular notice of the mix of narration, dialogue, internal dialogue, flashback, introspection, description. These are all varied enough that the reader barely notices the writing--she's completely in the scene. If you had long blocks of any one of these, it would take the reader*** out ***of the scene because the writing will have called attention to itself. Also, take note of the last sentence. Does it effectively set the reader up for what's going to happen next? The reader has been introduced to a lot, but in small doses that have whetted her appetite to learn more about Angela and Ki, more about Fever, Texas, and more about what conflicts are associated with Angela coming home and Ki winning her heart at long last {characters, setting and plot working in wonderful cohesion, right from the very start!}. Not only should the last sentence of a scene give the reader some idea where the story is***

going, but it most definitely needs to make her want to huddle deeper into her chair so nothing can prevent her from reading on.]

Using an outline followed by the connect-the-dots Story Plan Checklist to produce a solid blueprint you can use to write the true first draft of your book should eventually become easy, because you got all the hard work out of the way first by laying a solid story foundation, ensuring that your major points are providing the framework of the book, and you built a cohesively layer through these things.

In the fifteen years I've been steadily selling books to publishers, writing the book has become the *easy* part of the whole production process. For the most part, my first drafts have been *final* drafts, requiring minimal revision. Usually a final edit and polish complete the job. Most of my editorial revisions are basic, commonsense suggestions to refine word usage and smooth out the flow of sentences. I've been very fortunate to enjoy both good reviews and a warm reception from readers. Additionally, I'm able to complete more books each year because I use the most effective methods for completing projects. One other benefit I've discovered is that this wonderful Story Plan Checklist has another use I've alluded to previously in this book. With it, I can produce a synopsis of the project to submit to publishers and agents with little guesswork involved--a synopsis that's amazingly concise yet contains everything a synopsis needs to hook editors and agents. In Layer IV, I'll show you how to do just that.

STAGE 4: CREATING A PUNCH LIST

In Stages 1 through 3, we learned to evaluate our blueprint (outline), build a cohesive story with a Story Plan Checklist, and combine the two to help with the writing of the first draft. This brings us to Stage 4.

Before you hand a home-builder that last payment, you're advised by experts to do a final walk-through with him. On the day of the walkthrough, the builder will carry a clipboard and room-by-room checklist to record notes and check off items found to be satisfactory. He'll look above, below, and behind everywhere he and his flashlight can reach. By the end of the walk-through, your builder will have compiled a "punch list" of items that must be attended to before the job is considered complete. This punch list organizes and states those details that remain incomplete--items that are broken, lacking parts, or requiring your review. Basically, these are items in need of final attention. Unless there are major problems to be corrected that would prevent you from doing so, you're ready to accept the keys and move into your new home.

In writing, a punch list encompasses the same ideas. You've completed a story blueprint, a Story Plan Checklist, and you've used these to write the first draft of your story. If all went well, what you've ended up with is extremely solid (though probably not ready for anyone else to see yet). Now you'll create a punch list of all items that need to be attended to in the revision and editing and polishing of this finished book, before you submit the work to critique partners followed by agents or publishers.

Here's an example of what this might look like:

Problem	How to Fix	Chapter/Page #(s)
Need to make Justine more suspicious of Lucy	Has Justine found out previously that Lucy has been caught by their superiors filtering money from terrorist accounts to overseas banks for her own use? Justine saved her the first time it happened by vouching for her potential value to the Network. So Justine recognizes the account Reggie discovered as one of the	Chapter 2

	ones Lucy was supposed to have closed years ago. Is Lucy somewhere she shouldn't be? Do her fingerprints show up in Alex's kitchen? Justine discovers Lucy hacked into the files to discover Dez and Justine's history and she found out about Dennis Omrinski. Lucy realized Carianne was involved and approached her about making money again. Justine is able to trace Lucy's communications with the buyer.	Chapter 20 Chapter 31

A very basic worksheet you can use as your punch list is included in Appendix C.

Setting the First Draft of Your Book Aside

In *Plotting & Editing*, Sherry-Anne Jacobs says, "In the first flush of enthusiasm about your success in completing a manuscript, you'll be wearing rose-colored spectacles. And probably a big grin." This is definitely not the time to start sending the book out to publishers who might wipe that silly grin off your face in a mortifying hurry. Once again, you need to set your project aside to give yourself time to gain objectivity and a rest. Yes, again!

In the course of an average year, I alternate my time between outlining, writing, revising, editing and polishing 5-10 novels or novellas. For instance, in 2012, I:

- outlined 5 novels
- wrote 4 novels
- revised and polished 2 novels, 10 reissued novels and 11 reissued short stories
- completed editor revisions for 3 novels and 4 short stories, 8 novels and 5 short stories that were to be reissued, and 1 writing reference
- prepared 8 novel proposals along with 11 novel and 11 short stories reissue proposals
- and had 3 novels and 5 short stories published, and 8 novels and 5 short story reissues published

If you look at the Works-In-Progress page on my website: https://karenwiesner.weebly.com/works-in-progress.html, you'll see how I juggled my work for multiple years in a row, month by month.

All of my projects are done in the stages I mentioned before. I *love* that I'm never doing the same thing in terms of outlining, writing, revising, or editing and polishing a project. I move from outlining one book, to revising a different one, to writing something else altogether, layering and building and developing the book into something wonderful. I'm always fresh, always enthusiastic, always eager to complete a project a little more, knowing my work will be solid and ready to send to editors when the stages are at last done.

The reason I'm telling you this isn't to show off but because the only way this is possible is because I write in stages, which allows me to be productive without being overwhelmed in the least. Additionally, if I didn't set each project aside after each stage of development, I wouldn't be able to accomplish this much, and my enthusiasm for each project would be severely limited, since I would have to perform all the steps of development in immediate succession. Additionally, I'd be sending less-than-perfect manuscripts to publishers, and that's *never* a good thing. In chapter ten of *First Draft Outline*, I give specifics on how to allow all this shelf-time in your schedule--without losing *any* momentum in your career--through the use of realistic, careful scheduling, and goals sheets. It's not only possible to be one or more books ahead of your releases (or submissions), it's the *only* way to continue your career writing several quality books a year.

Most people think that I must work 24 hours a day based on my productivity. That's the really amazing part of this whole method. I don't have to. I set aside eight o'clock to noon or two p.m. on weekdays for projects and I can take off every weekend and a lot of time in the summer for a break, yet I'm constantly moving forward. At the time of this writing in November 2014, I've completed all of my 2015 contracts and started several of my 2016 ones, which means I'm working more than a year ahead of releases.

There are only three things writers need to do to be productive:

1) Work in stages. (Anyone can learn this, given a little time, and it's simply logical to work this way. There's nothing magical or even "hard-wired" about it!)
2) Use annual goals and project goals sheets. (Not difficult to learn at all. *First Draft Outline* and the *First Draft Outline Bonus Companion Booklet* have templates for both of these worksheets.)
3) Sit down and do the work. (No magic formula for this one either, but I play head-games with myself all the time to get my work done. For instance, I tell myself that if finish the work I'm supposed to this morning, I can play a computer or X-Box game all afternoon. Believe me, that's a huge motivation for me. Find something that motivates you. Motivation lights a fire inside you the way simply lecturing yourself can't.)

You can really see using this system that, even if you have only one or two hours per day to work, you'll always be progressing and building very solid, high-quality stories. Conceivably, you could double your output in a year's time while doing some of the best writing you've ever done in your life.

But, yes, after you've set the groundwork with working in stages and goal-setting, it really does come down to an issue of exactly what Ray Bradbury advised that student: You have to sit down and write what you planned to write during the time you planned to write it.

A good rule of thumb for unpublished writers is to stay one to two projects ahead of your *submissions*. For a published author, you should stay one to two projects ahead of your *releases*. Three to six months before a new year, you need to either be thinking--or preferably *working*--on next year's projects.

Now that we've completed another step in this project, put everything pertaining to the project back in the story folder and set it aside for as long as you're able.

***

The second layer of a story involves building a proper frame-work--cohesive characters, settings, and plots--on the foundation you laid with your outline blueprint and Story Plan Checklist, and writing the first draft based on these. With these elements, you create an extremely strong layer--something that will take the finishing touches beautifully. In the next chapter, we'll go in-depth into the final layers of your story, which involves revising, and editing and polishing the first draft of your book.

LAYER III
Decorating

Once a builder has completed the house, interior painting, staining, and caulking are done, with carpeting as the last step. At that point, interior design becomes the priority. Room arrangements, color schemes, and window treatments, based on knowledge of what's available in the owner's price range and what's appropriate for each use, become the finishing touches. Everything that's done is a layer in develop the house into a home. It's in the final decorations that a solid house truly becomes a thing of beauty and a source of pride. Most new homeowners are dying to throw a party and show it off.

In writing, we have a similar layering. We've created layers through story folder creation, brainstorming, researching, sketching, outlining, developing a Story Plan Checklist, writing the first draft. (Imagine if you skip more than one of those steps! Your book is missing all those layers, and you'll definitely notice that it lacks texture, quality, and strength as a result.)

Now we'll talk about the layers of strength and beauty that are added to a story through revising, editing and polishing the first draft of the book. During this time, we rearrange, punch up the word colors of the book, clarify and beautify with the finishing touches that make it shine. Once you've finished this step, you'll be dying to send it out to those brave readers willing to take on the assessment of an unpublished work--those who will hopefully love it as much as you do. Even if they don't, they may help you see the strengths and weaknesses more clearly, and you can make the necessary changes before you begin submitting to publishers and agents.

The stages involved with this layer include:

1. Revising
2. Involving critique partners

3. Setting the final draft aside
4. Final editing and polishing

Earlier, we discussed the fact that writing and revision are two completely separate processes that require different mindsets, and therefore shouldn't be done at the same time. While writing a book, a simple need to polish words, sentences, or paragraphs can become a complete rewrite. This isn't a productive way to work when you're attempting to *finish* the first draft of the book. An unfortunate side effect of revising, editing, and polishing your story while you're still writing it is that you don't get the necessary distance from it in order to be able to revise effectively. You need to enter the revision phase with fresh, objective eyes once the first draft of the book is finished. Only then can you see the story as it really is. I love what Stephen King says about this process: "I'm rediscovering my own book, and usually liking it. That changes. By the time a book is actually in print, I've been over it a dozen times or more, can quote whole passages, and only wish the damned old smelly thing would go away. That's later, though; the first read-through is usually pretty fine."

We also discussed earlier how, if you're building a house, you wouldn't start painting before all the walls were up. You wouldn't put in carpet before the plumbing and wiring were done because you'd end up having to tear out the carpeting in order to get the necessary plumbing and wiring in where they should be. Paint and carpet are the polish of a completed room; they're final steps in dressing it up. In the same way, writers should concentrate on finishing a full draft of the book before endeavoring to do any revision, editing or polishing.

By this point, you've completed a story blueprint, discovered the benefits of using a Story Plan Checklist to create a cohesive outline, and you've written the first draft of the book. Between these steps, you've let your story rest quietly on a shelf, ideally for a month or more each time. Stephen King calls this a "recuperation time", and it really is, considering the blood, sweat, and tears you've expended. When you take the manuscript down again to begin revisions, followed by editing and polishing, "you'll find reading your book over after a six-week layoff to be a strange, often exhilarating experience. It's yours, you'll recognize it as yours...and yet it will also be like reading the work of someone else...This is the way it should be, the reason you waited. ..."

STAGE 1: REVISING

Marguerite Smith said, "Motivation is when your dreams put on work clothes." *Revision* can also be aptly described as when your dreams put on work clothes. The process is equivalent to getting on your hands and knees to scrub a filthy floor until it shines. It's the grunge work of being a writer, but it's well worth the effort you put into it. And revision and editing and polishing add a very definite extra layer to your story. Without it, your story probably won't read smoothly, nor will it shine.

What's the best way to revise? Below, we'll discuss ways to go about revision effectively.

Minimizing the Work

Let's first talk about the difference between the revision process and the editing and polishing process, because these, too, are separate jobs that can--but ideally *shouldn't*--take place at the same time.

These writing processes are similar to what builders face. It's not unusual to make design changes during construction, but builders want to minimize them. Moving a wall, for instance, can be expensive, especially if it's already been framed in and drywalled. During construction, periodic visits are made to the building site in order to monitor the home's progress. This allows the owner and builder to detect problems earlier and therefore take corrective action.

In the same way, in the process of writing a book, you want to minimize major changes to your book, like rewriting an entire story thread, or adding, deleting, or revising multiple chapters--they'll cost you a lot of time and effort (hence the need for a blueprint and Story Plan Checklist, where these kinds of revisions take only a fraction of that time and effort). If you've gone back to your blueprint often while writing the first draft to make sure your story is progressing the way it needs to and your story has passed the Cohesion Test, you'll detect problems early and be able take corrective action. This prevents major revisions at the end of a project, when you've already committed hundreds of pages to a solid structure. Terry Brooks said about this: "I believe, especially with long fiction, that an outline keeps you organized and focused over the course of the writing. I am not wedded to an outline once it is in place and will change it to suit the progress of the story and to accommodate new and better ideas, but I like having a blueprint to go back to. Also, having an outline forces you to think your story through and work out the kinks and bad spots. I do a lot less editing and rewriting when I take time to do the outline first."

What most writers call revising is actually just editing and polishing. Revision is the larger of the two jobs. We'll talk more about editing and polishing, which should be minor buffing up, later. Revision may or may not be major, especially if you've started with a story blueprint and a Story Plan Checklist. But it does involve tweaking characters, settings, and plots; and possibly rewriting, adding to, or deleting one or more scenes; and incorporating major research. When you revise, you evaluate (and fix) any of the following:

- Structure
- Character, setting, and plot credibility and the cohesion of these elements
- Depth of conflicts, goals, and motivations
- Scene worthiness
- Pacing
- Effectiveness of hints, tension and suspense, and resolutions
- Transitions
- Emotion and color
- Hooks and cliffhangers
- Character voice
- Consistency

- Adequacy of research
- Properly unfurled, developed, and concluded story threads
- Deepening of character enhancements/contrasts and the symbols of these

Revision is redoing or reshaping in an effort to make what's already there better, stronger, and, of course, utterly cohesive.

Maximizing the Benefits

After you've completed a first draft and allowed the book to sit for a long time, the next step is revision. While I used to do this step off the computer on a hard copy of the book, the work involved after the revision done by my own messy (practically unreadable) hand, having to make all those corrections within the story file on my computer, became too immense. Literally, there was never a single page that didn't have countless changes, additions, or deletions. I now find this job a world easier to do on the computer.

I strongly believe that revision should be done as quickly as possible, with as little interruption from the material as possible. This won't compromise the quality of your revision, I promise--just the opposite, in fact! Ideally, if you can set aside a block of time of about a week (three days is generally the maximum time it takes me, but I always allow for a week) to work exclusively on the revision, you'll find that your story will be more consistent, and you'll remember details much better. In my case, I remember things photographically--I could argue that I memorize the entire book during this time, and any error will jump out at me as I work. During revision days, I may even be woken from sound sleep because a glaring error in some portion of the book will emerge from my subconscious. The whole book is quite literally laid out in my mind, ready to be accessed at a moment's notice during this short revision period. If revision on a project is broken up over a period of days or weeks, especially if you're working on other projects during this time, the book will most certainly suffer from consistency issues, and possibly even structural and cohesion problems. If you can set aside that crucial, uninterrupted block of time to focus on revision, your story will benefit from it immeasurably.

To get started, read through your punch list, which you've used to organize and state the items in need of final attention. Fix firmly in your mind the details you need to attend to while reading your book from start to finish. Check off what you've finished at the end of each work day so you'll know what you need to deal with when you come back to the revision.

Yes, during this time you'll be working on fixing more serious problems, but you probably will be doing some editing and polishing during this stage as well. You're there; it wouldn't make any sense to not clean up something small but not quite right that clearly needs a little elbow grease. However, what you're really looking for during the revision is anything in your story that doesn't work or doesn't make sense.

One way I keep my project consistent is to have a notebook next to me while I'm reading to revise. I jot down the timeline and various other details, including the page number the detail is mentioned on. If I later have a question while revising about, say, when a certain event took place, I can always look in the notebook to make sure I've kept those facts consistent. Whenever and as often as this detail is mentioned in the story, I'll write down the page number for it in the notebook. I might decide to change the fact later, and this way I have a list of all the places affected by the change.

You may have very little left to do once when you complete this process.

STAGE 2: INVOLVING CRITIQUE PARTNERS

Everyone knows writers can get too close to their own work. It's an occupational hazard. While you may feel that you've got a story beyond compare, it may need a little more work and you simply can't see it. That's why it's so important *now* to turn your beloved opus over to a trusted spouse, friend, or, preferably, a critique partner (or three) for a critical read. The opinion of others is very important. You're not ready to send that book out to a publisher/editor or agent until you've had enough reader reactions to judge the strength of your accomplishment.

STAGE 3: SETTING THE FINAL DRAFT ASIDE

Allow yourself to set your final draft aside for several weeks after you get a critique for it. Right now, you might be sick of your book and stinging from some of the glaring holes others saw that you somehow managed to miss.

I highly recommend that you give yourself this time to digest the comments a critique partner made about your beloved baby, too. At this stage, your desire may be to haul off and lay her out flat. Don't do it! After you've initially read her comments, send her this note without any embellishments: "Thanks for all the work you put into critiquing my story. I'll get back to you in a few weeks if I have any questions or comments about your evaluation." Then folder-up that project again with her comments. Put it away in your story cupboard and do something else. I guarantee that her comments, if left on a low backburner in your mind, will do their work. When you return for the final editing and polishing, hopefully for the last time before you begin submitting to publishers/editors or agents, you might even agree with your friend on several points. You'll also feel better about everything, and you'll be able to evaluate, unbiased, what needs to be done to shine up that book.

You might be wondering how many times you can set your book aside before it goes to an editor. I've suggested you set it aside for a few months after the outline is complete, before you begin writing the book. I've suggested you set it aside after the first draft is done, before you begin revising. And now, set it aside again, after the critical reads and before you complete final editing and polishing, before sending it off to a publisher/editor or agent. As with a good wine or cheese, the more shelf-time you give each book, the stronger it'll be. And the better for you to see your story clearly.

STAGE 4: FINAL EDITING AND POLISHING

While only you can choose whether this is absolutely your last chance to catch flaws before the book goes out to the important people who can publish it, in general, editing and polishing should be almost as simple as reading through the manuscript and making minor adjustments that allow the words to flow like music to the ear. A solid blueprint and Story Plan Checklist virtually ensure that. But send your manuscript out only when you feel it's ready to go.

I've never tried to do this stage on my computer because I miss too much that way. For some reason, human eyes aren't equipped to see subtle problems and certainly not typos on a computer screen. Pages need to be printed; then revision can be done with a pen or pencil away from the computer. When you finish that, make corrections from your marked-up pages on the computer file of the book. The good news is that, if you did all the work involved in outlining your story before writing it, this step in the process will be easy. In this stage, I may only mark or fix something every few pages, making final computer corrections to the story file much simpler this time around. This is another reason I strongly suggest editing and polishing corrections be made by hand on a hard copy then transferred to your computer file of the story page by page--the transfer actually helps you edit and polish as you're working, making the story another layer stronger.

I usually complete this step within a day or two, just as for revising, and for the same reasons stated in that section.

Uncovering the Diamond in the Rough

Everyone knows that "a diamond in the rough" is a metaphor referring to the original unpolished state of diamond gemstones, especially those that have the potential to become high-quality jewels. Most stories are rough diamonds at this stage. Someone who works in a diamond mine or designs jewelry will get as excited at the sight of a rough, potentially perfect diamond as someone who loves to wear expensive jewelry will over a fine cut diamond. In their mind's eye, these experts can already see the finished, faceted jewel that will emerge when the gemstone is put through the steps of cutting and polishing.

Writers also get excited about their stories at the beginning of nearly every stage, since they've had a good amount of time away from the project and they may have a picture in their mind's eye of what will emerge during this step in the process.

Editing and polishing are a lot like the process of turning a rough gemstone into a finished one. You're cutting the bad, replacing it with the good, and polishing up what remains until it shines. This is a final step in publication of a book, called copyediting in publishing circles, and defined as the correction and enhancement of grammar, vocabulary, and punctuation details.

The process of editing and polishing involves any or all of the following:

- Rearranging sentences or paragraphs
- Showing, not telling, where most needed
- Tightening sentences and individual words (such as changing passive to active and dull to impacting; cleaning up repetitiveness)
- Smoothing out roughness and making purple prose more natural
- Punching up tension and suspense
- Ensuring variation in sentence construction and length
- Varying and enriching words

Editing and Polishing Tricks

Bernard Malamud said that he wrote each book at least three times: "Once to understand it, a second time to improve the prose, and a third time to compel it to say what it still must say." While I won't argue the order stated with a Pulitzer Prize–winning author, writers unquestionably do need to remove clutter to make a story understandable, to prevent tripping hazards caused by clumsy prose, and to infuse a story with vivid, interesting narration that says succinctly what it is the author wants it to say, concurrently bringing the whole story to life.

Putting on work clothes for the final step closer to your dream--where a story really comes into its own--you'll no doubt feel a sense of gratification, realizing your baby is almost ready to leave the relatively safe nest you've provided, hopefully to make you proud. Some basic tricks to help you with this process are included next.

Tip Sheet: Description

• **Don't write character descriptions in a single block (i.e., for more than three sentences) at *any* point in the book.** As Renni Browne and Dave King say in *Self-Editing for Fiction Writers*, "Your readers will find your story more engaging if they can meet your characters the way they meet people in real life: a little at a time. ..." Or, to put it another way, here's a gem from Tina Jens's "Such Horrible People" in *On Writing Horror*: "...don't drop chunks of your character sketch into the story like a brick into a fishbowl." Intersperse character description throughout a scene.

• **Unless the main character is the only one who has point of view in the story, avoid putting a POV character in the embarrassing position of having to describe *herself*.** Preferably, character descriptions should never be written from the same character's point of view (i.e., her own POV). More effectively, write them from other characters' POVs. Describing herself from her own POV, she'll either sound like she's going on and on about herself with every little detail of her looks, or she'll sound outright conceited. Of course if your story only has a single character POV without an omniscient narrator, you will have to write descriptions from her POV, but, again, these need to be interspersed carefully and used with the purpose of revealing the character's unique personality and emotions.

• **Don't inundate the reader with the same descriptions over and over, such as of eye color, hair color, etc.** Mention descriptions only once or twice each throughout an entire story. You might want to use these in moments of intense intimacy or within dialogue. In general, though, trust your reader to already have the fact stored away and used in the vision whenever a particular character is in a scene. As Dwight V. Swain says in *Creating Characters*: "*Show* how the character looks and acts, and then let your readers extract whatever feelings they wish from it."

This example of effective description from *Sense and Sensibility*, by Jane Austen, equally conveys personality:

Mrs. Jennings, Lady Middleton's mother, was a good-humoured, merry, fat, elderly woman, who walked a great deal, seemed very happy and rather vulgar. She was full of jokes and laughter, and before dinner was over had said many witty things on the subject of lovers and husbands, hoped they had not left their hearts behind them in Sussex, and pretended to see them blush whether they did or not.

- **Descriptions are more than adjectives!** Descriptions should never simply be adjectives tacked onto a person, place, or thing, such as in the following example of overdone description:

With a heavy sigh, he set down the black ceramic coffee mug, his green gaze settling heavily on the gilded clock ticking loudly against the familiar noises outside his solid oak office door.

When you reveal every last detail of your character and/or surroundings, as above, the reader--sure--can picture the scene, can even feel like she's right there...but she might not want to be now that you've hit her over the head with it. In the above paragraph, the reader does get a picture of the setting, the character, and the things around her. But it's the type of writing that calls attention to itself and thereby pulls the reader out of the story. Every writer's cardinal rule (and goal) should be to keep a reader reading.

Description can be turned into something vital to your story during your editing and polishing. We'll try some editing and polishing exercises in Appendix F.

Tip Sheet: Dialogue

• **Effective dialogue can transform a story into something unforgettable.** External dialogue is everything characters say out loud, to themselves occasionally, most often to other characters in the story. Dialogue is important in a story. Few writers would tell you otherwise, but few realize just how essential it is. You'll most notice how effective dialogue can be in fleshing out a story when you take it out of your writing. For instance, take a look at this passage written entirely without dialogue:

She told us there was five hundred dollars in the envelope. That what she was about to ask us was very unusual and we might not want to do it. If we did decide not to accept, the five hundred dollars was for us to forget all about her.

I told her I'd pretend she was my algebra lessons in high school.

Roger glared at me as if my sparkling wit might scare her off, and asked what she wanted us to do.

She leaned forward confidentially. She wanted us to dig up her husband's grave.

Roger and I simultaneously leaned forward. I begged her pardon.

Her husband was buried last night, she explained, and she wanted us to dig up the coffin.

It was clear from Roger's expression that he considered this task quite a bit less appealing than wild kinky sex. He asked her if she was kidding.

She shook her head, saying she was completely serious.

Was this the kind of thing she usually asked people in coffee shops? Maybe she walked in here by mistake thinking it was Maude and Vinny's Discount Graverobbing Emporium.

Now read the same passage as it's actually published--with effective and varied dialogue--in Jeff Strand's *Graverobbers Wanted (No Experience Necessary)*:

"Inside this envelope is five hundred dollars. What I'm going to ask is very unusual, and you may not want to do it. If you decide not to accept, the five hundred dollars is for you to forget all about me. Deal?"

"Sounds great," I said. "I'll just pretend you were my algebra lessons in high school."

Roger glares at me as if my sparkling wit might scare her off. "What do you want us to do?"

She leaned forward confidentially. "I want you to dig up my husband's grave."

Roger and I simultaneously leaned forward. "I beg your pardon?" I asked.

"My husband was buried last night, and I want you to dig up the coffin."

It was clear from Roger's expression that he considered this task quite a bit less appealing than wild kinky sex. "You're kidding, right?"

She shook her head. "I'm completely serious."

"Is this the kind of thing you usually ask people in coffee shops?" I inquired. "Are you sure you didn't walk in here by mistake thinking it was Maude and Vinny's Discount Graverobbing Emporium?"

Undeniably, dialogue truly adds spice and impact to any story, so use it effectively.

• **Passages or an entire chapter made up of nothing but dialogue can cause readers to lose focus on everything outside the dialogue.** You might laugh about that because it's so obvious, but, in my many years of critiquing unpublished contest entries, this is one of the most commonly made mistakes I've seen.

We discussed the importance of using dialogue effectively, but let's turn it around this time. Instead of taking the dialogue completely out of a passage to see how necessary it is, let's make the passage all dialogue. Look at the next example:

"Will it come back today?" Ramo asked.

"It may," I answered him. "More likely it will come after many suns, for the country where it has gone is far off."

"I do not care if the ship never comes," he said.

"Why do you say this?" I asked him.

"Why?" I asked again.

"Because I like it here with you," he said. "It is more fun than when the others were here. Tomorrow I am going to where the canoes are hidden and bring one back to Coral Cove. We will use it to fish in and to go looking around the island."

"They are too heavy for you to put into the water."

"You will see."

"You forget that I am the son of Chowig," he said.

"I do not forget," I answered. "But you are a small son. Someday you will be tall and strong and then you will be able to handle a big canoe."

The passage is pure dialogue, and it reads like bullets firing from a gun. (I call writing like this "dialogue bullets".) When dialogue is used exclusively, you don't find out who's talking, and you lose focus on the characters, their goals and motivations, and their emotions in the scene.

Now read an effectively written version of the same passage as it was published in Scott O'Dell's classic, *Island of the Blue Dolphins*:

The air was clear and we could look far out to sea in the direction the ship had gone.

"Will it come back today?" Ramo asked.

"It may," I answered him, though I did not think so. "More likely it will come after many suns, for the country where it has gone is far off."

Ramo looked up at me. His black eyes shone.

"I do not care if the ship never comes," he said.

"Why do you say this?" I asked him.

Ramo thought, making a hole in the earth with the point of his spear.

"Why?" I asked again.

"Because I like it here with you," he said. "It is more fun than when the others were here. Tomorrow I am going to where the canoes are hidden and bring one back to Coral Cove. We will use it to fish in and to go looking around the island."

"They are too heavy for you to put into the water."

"You will see."

Ramo threw out his chest. Around his neck was a string of sea-elephant teeth which someone had left behind. It was much too large for him and the teeth were broken, but they rattled as he thrust the spear down between us.

"You forget that I am the son of Chowig," he said.

"I do not forget," I answered. "But you are a small son. Someday you will be tall and strong and then you will be able to handle a big canoe."

The scene now has focus and the text takes you right inside the scene and the characters. You not only feel with them, you see what's around them in the scene and get a glimpse of what they're doing physically. The dialogue provides a catalyst to all this, advancing plot and characterization.

As a general rule, only use "dialogue bullets" when you need to create extreme tension. Here's an example, from Larry McMurtry's *Lonesome Dove*, of how this can be done proficiently without losing any of the texture:

"How's Maude Rainey?" he asked.

"She's in good health," Call said. "She fed me twice."

"Good thing it was just twice," Augustus said. "If you'd stayed a week you'd have had to rent an ox to get home on."

"She's anxious to sell you some more pigs," Call said, taking the jug and rinsing his mouth with whiskey.

"If Joe was to get kilt I might court her again," Augustus speculated.

"I hope you will," Call said. "Them twelve young ones ought to have a good father. What are the horses doing back here so soon?"

"Why, grazing, most likely," Augustus said.
"Didn't Pedro make a try?"
"No, he didn't, and for a very good reason," Augustus said.
"What reason would that be?"
"Because he died," Augustus said.

The dialogue in this passage effectively manages to convey characters, emotions, goals and motivations, plot, even setting, all sprinkled liberally with a good deal of humor.

• **Effective internal dialogue can flesh out your characters.** Internal monologue is everything the characters don't say out loud; these are essentially their thoughts. Not everyone can write this type of dialogue effectively, so play around with it for a while. There are two types of internal monologue, and you can use whichever one is most effective for a particular scene. The following example, from my novel *Falling Star*, is fine as is:

He was smooth all right. Nate chided himself as Rori disappeared into her father's house. With a little more practice, he could apply to snake charming school.

Add internal monologue and it really turns the paragraph into something personal and intriguing:

That was smooth, Nate chided himself as Rori disappeared into her father's house. *Very smooth. You could apply to snake charming school with a little more practice.*

The second example brings the reader directly into the character's thoughts and has much more impact.

• **Dialogue--what a character says and how he says it--reveals the inner person, and more.** The manner in which a character speaks and the particular words she chooses say something about her. Dialogue will and should reflect who the character is, even what she does for a living.

On the other hand, the occasional character who doesn't fit

her stereotyped mold is always intriguing to a reader. Make a bad boy or a cowboy philosophize about the poetic insight of Shakespeare. Make a wallflower put on a vixen red dress and stiletto heels and temporarily act out of character.

Take a look at this example of dialogue reflecting character from Marilyn Pappano's *A Dangerous Man*:

A faint tinge of color accompanied her next shrug. "The body. The muscles. The grace. You're obviously in very good shape, and you move very gracefully but with a great deal of control."

That control relaxed almost enough to allow him to smile--almost. "I wasn't aware you'd noticed."

"You're the only observant one." She went around to sit behind her desk and moved several items he'd placed there an inch or so to one side.

He adjusted the blinds, stepping back to avoid a shower of dust from the slats as they tilted, then warned, "Leave these just like this."

"Yes, sir." She offered him a mock salute. "You give orders very well. Did you get to do much of that in the Army?"

The dialogue reveals what the hero has done for a living as a retired Army master sergeant, and cleverly incorporates a bit of description. Hero and heroine are star-crossed lovers who parted badly once upon a time and have now been reunited by danger, which is hinted at here, in the dialogue that also touches on their situation, emotions, and conflicts very effectively.

• **Start your story with dialogue.** An old, very effective (and infrequently used) trick of the writer's trade is to snag a reader with a fascinating morsel of dialogue at the very beginning of a story. You can't lose. You begin with immediate action and conflict, and the reader is brought into the scene from that very first sentence. Look at these examples and judge for yourself. I'd be shocked if you didn't want to read more of each:

"Why are you writing a stupid parking ticket when there are

killers running around loose?"
--*Badge of Honor*, by Justine Davis

***

He looks like a walking corpse, Xizor thought.
--*Shadows of the Empire*, by Steve Perry

***

"Death," the proprietor said clearly, showing the stone.
--*On a Pale Horse*, by Piers Anthony

***

"I had the dream again last night."
--*The Seventh Night*, by Amanda Stevens

***

"I want to meet my dad."
--*Daniel's Gift*, by Barbara Freethy

***

"Ray Bans, a five o'clock shadow, and a black leather jacket."
--*Private Dancer*, by Suzanne Forster

• **Vary each character's dialogue.** How do you make your characters sound different? By making a conscious effort to do so. Make a list of your important characters. If you know their personalities, you'll have a good idea about certain things they would and wouldn't say, and ways they would and wouldn't say them. Are they prone to the vernacular--in other words, do they use street language? I know most writers have some kind of aversion to writing slang of any kind, but they're not doing justice to their characters if they don't take into account that many people do use slang--often, and as a habit and a choice.

Or do characters "sound" more like English professors? And, again, this shouldn't be the writer's choice. Some writers use dialogue that makes *all* their characters sound like English professors, and the dialogue becomes monotonous because it's not varied from character to character. That's not good or even effective writing.

Do characters use dialogue somewhere between slang and uptight English professor? Do characters use a lot of internal dialogue? If you don't know the answers to these questions, spend more time on this in the editing and polishing stage.

In chapter three of *First Draft Outline*, there's a section called Additional Outline Aids that discusses the creation of dialogue worksheets which you can easily create for all your main characters to keep track of their unique dialogue idiosyncrasies. Sometimes dialogue comes easily and you won't need to map out or think about how a certain character would talk. Other times, you'll have to sit down and map out specific words or phrases certain characters would use. Create tags or mannerisms for some of them. Once you've figured out who says what and how she'll say it, go through your book from start to finish and mold her dialogue to the specifics you've mapped out for her.

Dialogue can be turned into a catalyst for a dynamic story during your editing and polishing.

Tip Sheet: Introspection

• **Get inside your character's head!** The dictionary definition of *introspection* is "observation or examination of one's own mental and emotional state". By showing a character's introspection, you give the reader the ability to get to know the character from the inside out. A character's behavior in any given situation will both characterize her and create emotion. Hence, behavior and reactions work hand in hand (but they needn't be linear as a rule). Behavior, in essence, is the action, which is almost always followed by a reaction. Working within a specific point of view, follow action with that character's reaction to the behavior. Look at this simplified example from Linda Howard's *Cover of Night*, with just the behavior-reaction-introspection sequence pulled out:

Cal reached back under the blanket and put his hand on her hip, silently pulling her even closer to him. **(behavior)**

Tears stung her eyes as she nestled close, as close as she could get. **(reaction)**

This--this was what she'd missed most, the quiet companionship in the night, the knowledge that she wasn't alone. She wanted him to hold her, wanted to feel his arms around her. **(introspection)**

When he'd held her and Neenah after the frightening episode with Mellor, **(behavior)** for the first time in a long while Cate had felt...safe. **(reaction)**

Not just because Cal had protected them, though she was bemused to realize that was indeed part of her response; some primitive reactions evidently don't go away. The biggest part of it, though, was that suddenly she hadn't felt so alone. **(introspection)**

Behavior and reaction almost inevitably lead to introspection. Without introspection, readers will feel as though they're watching your characters through a pane of glass they can't get past. They can see and hear your characters, but rarely will they experience what the characters are going through without effective introspection. Let's take a look at the above example without introspection:

Cal reached back under the blanket and put his hand on her hip, silently pulling her even closer to him.

Tears stung her eyes as she nestled close, as close as she could get.

"Go back to sleep," he whispered softly. "You'll need all the rest you can get."

Below is the published version from *Cover of Night*. You'll see what a difference it makes to get inside the POV character's head:

Cal reached back under the blanket and put his hand on her hip, silently pulling her even closer to him.

Tears stung her eyes as she nestled close, as close as she could get.

This--this was what she'd missed most, the quiet companionship in the night, the knowledge that she wasn't alone. They hadn't so much as kissed, yet somehow, on some level, they were already linked. She felt it as surely as she knew when the twins were all right, or when they were getting into trouble. She didn't have to see them; she didn't have to hear them; she just knew.

"Go back to sleep," he whispered softly. "You'll need all the rest you can get."

She wanted him to hold her, wanted to feel his arms around her. When he'd held her and Neenah after the frightening episode with Mellor, for the first time in a long while Cate had felt...safe. Not just because Cal had protected them, though she was bemused to realize that was indeed part of her response; some primitive reactions evidently don't go away. The biggest part of it, though, was that suddenly she hadn't felt so alone.

Your story comes to life through introspection in a way that can't be overstressed. It fleshes out characters, settings, and plots.

• **Write effectively enough that the reader has the same reaction as the POV character.** When editing and polishing sentences, make a much more focused effort to bring the reader directly into the story so she can participate actively. In scenes of intense emotion, if the reader doesn't feel the same reaction as the POV character, you haven't written the scene effectively. Take these examples from Angela Hunt's *A Time To Mend* (the second being the published version):

Jacquelyn felt a scream rise in her throat, begging for release, but she clamped her lips shut to imprison it.

***

A scream clawed in Jacquelyn's throat, begging for release, but her clamped lips imprisoned it.

While both work well, in the first version, the word *felt* separates the reader from the character. We're looking at her. In the second version, we're right there with her, feeling the scream clawing its way up her (our) throat while her (our) lips refuse to allow it escape.

Introspection can turn a good story into a compelling, moving, touching...you get the picture. Use your editing and polishing to make sure you've done the very best job you possibly can to make your story a compelling one.

Tip Sheet: Effective Revision Choices

• **Sentence structures and lengths need to be varied.** Like good music needs to have long and short notes, high and low, varying beginnings and endings, a good writer should never allow every sentence to start or flow in exactly the same way. Take the example below:

She needed to make a loaf of bread. She went to the store to make her purchases. She bought bread ingredients. She took her purchases home.

Sounds terrible, doesn't it? I wish I could tell you I don't see this very often, but the horrifying truth is that I see this careless sort of writing from both new and experienced writers. Vary sentence structures and lengths so the lines flow into the ear like music, as in this revised version:

She slammed the cupboard with a grimace.
I'm Old Mother Hubbard. No flour, no yeast. How do you make homemade bread with an empty cupboard?
Sighing, she grabbed her keys. At least the store was just around the corner. And she could get her dog some biscuits while she was at it.

A world better, isn't it? Pay special attention to the way every sentence begins here. There are a million different ways to start a sentence without a pronoun of some kind. Look at the variations in each sentence above, the variety of sentence *lengths.* When you're editing and polishing, these are exactly the kinds of things you want to fix.

• **Does passive voice = boring; active voice = exciting?** Most writers will tell you, yes, those equations are absolutely correct. But what exactly are these passive and active voices everyone involved in writing talks about endlessly? In *Conflict, Action & Suspense,* author William Noble says that "active voice with its direct and straightforward verb use rivets our attention....The passive voice works best to change the pace, to stretch and extend narrative, or to diminish emphasis on action and suspense." Therefore, both passive and active voices are viable, depending on what kind of scene you're writing. An action scene requires an active voice, while a dramatic, emotional scene may call for a passive voice.

What has most authors, publishers, and agents in an uproar concerns the actual words used--are the words active or passive? The most instant form of action is what propels a sentence. Learning to write in an active voice is important to the overall appeal and impact of your story. For instance, here's a paragraph from my romantic comedy novella, "Silver Bells, Wedding Bell," written in the most passive manner possible:

She was racing across the distance between her and the open phone kiosk. Luggage was being knocked over, small children were hurtled in her rush. The men and women who glared at her were side-stepped.

This was revised before publication so it had a much more active voice:

She raced across the distance between her and the open phone kiosk, knocking over luggage, hurtling small children, side-stepping glaring men and women.

How many times did you stumble over the passive use of the words *was* and *were* in the first version? Like music, words very much have sounds as a reader reads. The words can flow easily, or they can cause a sort of clumsiness as they're read. That first example above "sounds" very plodding, almost thoughtful, and the reader is really watching the action from a distance--none of conveyed what I hope. The second example reads fast, smooth, but with a punch, and the reader feels the rush and tumble along with the character.

Your editing and polishing needs to weed out these passively, plodding sentences, to be replaced with tight active sentences.

We'll talk about cleaning up the overuse of words like "was" and "were" soon.

• ***Never* tell, always show?** Another point that's harped on in writing circles is the necessity of showing, not telling. Showing is very much about creating an immediate scene. The characters are there, and the reader moves along with them. Telling is merely a secondhand report of what happened to the characters in play. While there are certain uses for telling versus showing (i.e., you don't want to write an entire scene to convey a single, small point), you really do have to consider that a story told is very much like a newspaper article--it contains all the facts, none of the emotions. It's dry and often monotonous. Therefore, a story told is one that has nowhere near the compelling, immediate action of a story shown. While I'm not sure if it affected the impact *The Friday Night Knitting Club* made on readers around the world, since the book turned into an instant bestseller, take a look at the writing style. A lot of the book is told rather than shown, it's almost like short newspaper articles fill most of the scenes. This is a literary fiction leeway that few other genres are allowed.

Unlike books, movies can't tell anything at all--they *have* to show. Books should be presented in much the same way because each reader forms a "movie" of the story in her head as she's reading. Your choice of active showing is what puts the movie in her head. It's unlikely that a told story will achieve the same effect. Here's an example of telling:

I went upstairs and laid him down on our pallet. I lay down beside him. For a time, his pulse beat fast, his heart pounding. But toward midnight, both faded away. I fell asleep with my baby in my arms for the last time.

While this is a perfectly acceptable means of conveying information if it's necessary to avoid writing a whole scene, the poignant way this scene was *shown* in Geraldine Brooks's *Year of Wonders* brought out every bit of heartache and anguish felt by this young, grieving mother who loses her child to the plague:

I crooned to him as I climbed the stairs and laid him down upon our pallet. He lay just as I placed him, his arms splayed limply. I lay down beside him and drew him close. I pretended to myself that he would wake in the wee hours with his usual lusty cry for milk. For a time his little pulse beat fast, his tiny heart pounding. But toward midnight the rhythms became broken and weak and finally fluttered and faded away. I told him I loved him and would never forget him, and then I folded my body around my dead baby and wept until finally, for the last time, I fell asleep with him in my arms.

The first time I read this in context with the rest of the book, I cried. I doubt many would have the same reaction to the told version preceding it.

While editing and polishing, you'll have your final opportunity to change these instances of telling instead of showing. Pump your story full of everything and anything that will get the movie rolling in your reader's mind as he reads.

• **Watch adverb usage.** Go over your story with a highlighter, picking out all the adverbs that end with *-ly*. You can't and won't--and contrary to what most experts will tell you--you *shouldn't* get rid of all of them. Adverbs have their place, just as adjectives do, so don't go crazy on this point and turn out an adverb-free story as if you'll win an award just for managing this feat. That said, it is very true that adverb-overwhelmed narrative tends to bog a story down. There's usually a better (less *boring*) way of writing these words that so easily pepper a first draft, such as in this example:

Guilt ran thickly through Jacquelyn's blood.

***

Jacquelyn's blood ran thick with guilt.
--*A Time to Mend*, by Angela Hunt

A lot is conveyed in the second version that wasn't in the first, so the change involved more than simply cleaning up an adverb. In the second version (the published one), the delivery of the sentence itself is action-packed and to the point. You can almost feel shame, a violent and dirty emotion, polluting the character's veins. You want images like this to come through as you're editing and polishing, so watch for opportunities to refine them.

- **Avoid overused words.** *Was/wasn't, were/weren't, did/didn't, have/haven't, is/isn't, are/aren't, to be/been* are some the most common culprits. Using a different color highlighter or your computer search function, highlight these words to see how often you're using them, then try to find viable substitutes for them. When I critique someone else's work or judge a contest entry, I usually find *hundreds* of these within just a few pages. While you can't and shouldn't get rid of all of them, make sure you're using as much active voice as possible.

To give you an example of what a difference it makes to clean up these words, below you'll see basically the same sentence, but written without overused words in the second example:

He'd have known it anyway. Fury was something he felt like pure energy coming from it in waves. It was hot and powerful, rolling toward him like heat from a house fire.

***

He'd have known it anyway--he could feel fury as pure energy coming from it in waves, like heat from a house fire.

--*Constantine,* by John Shirley

Both of these examples say about the same thing. The difference is that the first is written in an unimaginative, overwhelming, passive voice, the second in an active, impacting one that's extremely effective. It's just tighter and clearer to read.

Remove the clutter of unnecessary words as much as possible in your editing and polishing. Do the same for a whole host of careless choices in sentence structure. One culprit that crops up inevitably is the little phrase *was going to*. In a sentence like "She was going to be strong and independent," the *was going to* can easily be replaced with *would*. Or better yet, *She'd*. The outcome, "She'd be strong and independent," is right to the point without unnecessary words to clutter it up.

• **Overused "idea stringers".** Replace words like *when, as, realized, wondered, occurred, felt, seem, appear, look*. These are some of the most overused words in existence because they string ideas together so easily. But if you see them more than once per page, they start to call attention to themselves. As with adverbs, you can't get rid of them all, but you can reword or vary them. One way to handle this situation is to replace these words with more effective words or phrases:

She was greeted by the scent of gingerbread when she stepped into her apartment.

***

The scent of gingerbread greeted her the instant she stepped into her apartment.

We also get rid of that dreaded *was* in this revision. *When* can also be replaced with *while, once, before/after, as*, etc. Another good way to deal with these worn words is to take them out completely, dividing the sentence into two or more sentences instead:

She realized she could have called out to him only after he walked away and turned the corner.

***

He walked away. She watched him in mute shock. Only after he turned the corner did the word "*Wait!*" fill her throat with violent need.

While the first example is succinct, it reads very slowly and is a bit unfocused. The second version has a lot more impact, putting the reader both in the scene and in the character's viewpoint, as well as eliminating overused words.

• **Start with a bang.** Avoid sentences that begin with *There was/were, It was, They were, He was.* They tend to slow things down, and risk putting your reader to sleep. An example of passive construction, and suggested revision follow:

There was no evidence that he had heard her.

***

If he heard her, he gave no indication.

This one is another example of the reader looking through a glass pane *at* your character versus being *with* the character. You truly do want your reader with your characters.

• **Wilt thou use contractions, or continue to live in the past?** I honestly don't know why contractions are an issue, but I've lost count of how many contemporary contest entries and books I've read in which the *writer* refuses to use contractions (and, yes, that emphasis is important to note because a writer who refuses to use contractions is one who refuses to allow her characters to decide how they will or won't speak). We live in the twenty-first century. Everyone uses contractions in verbal speech, and our written words should reflect that.

Remember that the words you use have an impact on the reader's perceptions of the characters. A character who never uses contractions will come off as stuffy, uptight, and snooty. Besides, using contractions will give your sentences more immediate impact. So please do use contractive forms of *had, have, will,* etc. as much as you can if you're writing a contemporary story.

Check out these examples, with the better ones coming from *The Ocean Between Us*, by Susan Wiggs:

She had said all those things many times before.

***

She'd said all those things many times before.

She still could not believe she had gone through with it.

***

She still couldn't believe she'd gone through with it.

While editing and polishing, you can easily use a highlighter or the search function of your word-processing program to make sure you don't inadvertently leave a *cannot* or *have not* in there.

• **As a general rule, avoid long sentences.** While it's true that a dramatic scene should have longer sentences than an action scene, be careful not to have too many. Overuse of long sentences makes the style of writing clunkier than it needs to (and should) be. Take this example, for instance:

It was too terrible to close his eyes, and they burned with an internal pressure while his mouth was locked open in a scream that never came--at least he still recognized the shapes around him as hallucinations.

Now the panting confusion of this sentence might seem extreme, but I see sentences like this all the time as a contest judge and critic. Sentences can't be readily comprehended, let alone absorbed, in this form. Most readers can digest a single action or idea, perhaps two, in a single sentence. Any more than that, and they start to get confused and can't follow the action.

Think about each portion of a sentence as one action/idea

that needs to be comprehended by the reader. For instance, one action/idea could be that the hero can't close his eyes. Next, he's realizing that he can at least still recognize the shapes as hallucinations. Then his mouth is locking open in a scream. You get the picture. Now let's look at this example as it was published in its more digestible, pleasing format in *Thunderhead*, by Douglas Preston and Lincoln Child:

It was too terrible. He could not close his eyes, and they burned with an internal pressure. His mouth was locked open in a scream that never came. At least he still recognized the shapes around him as hallucinations.

Imagine if every single sentence in your book was made up of three or four actions/ideas. It would read like you were plodding one mucky step after the other through a swamp.

Breaking up long sentences into two or more, as seen in the examples below, makes them much more immediate, and allows the reader to absorb what she's reading more easily.

Collet wheeled, his anger brimming as he thought, *They lured us upstairs with the intercom!* Searching the other side of the bar, he found a long line of horse stalls but no horses. Apparently the owner preferred a different kind of horsepower; the stalls had been converted into an impressive automotive parking facility, and the collection was astounding, including a black Ferrari, a pristine Rolls-Royce, an antique Astin Martin sports coupe, a vintage Porsche 356.

***

Collet wheeled, anger brimming. *They lured us upstairs with the intercom!* Searching the other side of the bar, he found a long line of horse stalls. No horses. Apparently the owner preferred a different kind of horsepower; the stalls had been converted into an impressive automotive parking facility. The collection was astounding--a black Ferrari, a pristine Rolls-Royce, an antique

Astin Martin sports coupe, a vintage Porsche 356.
--*The Da Vinci Code*, by Dan Brown

In the revised version, we get rid of *as*, *realized*, and *that*, and the result has a smoother rhythm and more impact. You'll also notice that the revised version just reads smoother, more like the music flow we're striving for as composing writers. Break your sentences up so readers can readily digest them.

The editing and polishing stage is the perfect time to be on the lookout for those overly long sentences. If you have to take a highlighter to each one so you're focused on fixing this problem, know that the end result will be well worth your effort.

- **Unassuming *it*.** I'm guilty of assuming that everyone will understand what I mean when I use the word *it*. Most writers do have some guilt in this regard. This happens most often in a first draft, but during editing and polishing, pay special attention to this little word to make sure you're not assuming your reader will know what you mean with its use. The word *it*, especially when used near the beginning of a sentence, loses focus and therefore impact on the reader. Don't let *it* sit there, assuming a role that hasn't been defined, explained, or adequately described. Try to make *it* more specific in your sentences, for instance:

It had taken a heavy toll on him, but he didn't appreciate seeing proof in the mirror.

This sentence begs a myriad of questions. *What* took a heavy toll? A death, an accusation, a sledge hammer? Any one of these and a million more could work. Luckily, this author didn't allow an *it* to assume itself to the reader.

The past year had taken a heavy toll on him, but he didn't appreciate seeing proof in the mirror.
--*The Da Vinci Code*, by Dan Brown

- **Don't make me repeat myself--avoid careless repetition.**

Watch for repeated words. If you have a noun or verb in the first paragraph of a page, then that same word again at the end of the same page, it literally jumps out at the reader. The same can be true if you repeat a word for no other reason except that you couldn't think of a better, similar, more effective one. Look carefully at the first paragraph in the example below, rife with repetition that jumps out with its overuse, then notice the differences in the published version:

It was daylight. Mortal time of day, not his, and I felt the need to see what the men had done to his once beautiful home, to see if I could indeed walk the exorcized grounds or sleep in the wooden boxes defiled by holy hosts and holy water.

I searched the wall until I found a low wooden door hanging partway open, open enough that I could squeeze my body through.

On the opposite side, the once beautiful gardens were overgrown with weeds and scrubby bushes. The abbey church that had undoubtedly once been beautiful was overgrown with scrubby bushes and weeds that surrounded the vaulted stone frames empty of their holy glass.

What had happened to the holy order that had once lived here? Did their ghosts still walk these quiet grounds, broken, desolate souls among broken dreams?

Did the vampire's soul walk with their broken, desolate souls?

***

It was daylight. Mortal time, not his, and I felt the need to see what the men had done to his home, to see if I could indeed walk the exorcized grounds or sleep in the boxes defiled by hosts and holy water.

I searched the wall until I found a low wooden door hanging partway open, enough that I could squeeze my body through.

On the opposite side, the once beautiful gardens were overgrown with weeds and scrubby bushes. The abbey church that had undoubtedly once been beautiful was covered with dead ivy that surrounded the vaulted stone frames empty of their holy glass.

What had happened to the order that had once lived here? Did their ghosts still walk these quiet grounds, desolate souls among broken dreams?

Did the vampire's soul walk with theirs?

--*Mina*, by Marie Kiraly

Fixing this kind of problem is an editing and polishing job that really requires a lot of uninterrupted focus.

• **Then again, all repetition isn't bad.** Save repetition for places where it drives the impact deeper in, rather than annoying the reader or calling attention to your words:

Nothing was enough. Sitting still wasn't enough. Getting his hands on her wasn't enough. He wanted to devour her whole.

--*Falling Star*, by Karen Wiesner

• **A thesaurus is not always a writer's best friend.** Another thing I feel I must mention is that newer writers tend to overuse their thesaurus. While variety is good, you don't want to sound like you've been using a thesaurus. For instance, in this sentence, I've clearly used my thesaurus way too often:

The redolent perfume of gingerbread accosted her the moment she strode into her ignoble tenement.

However, this type of "thesaurus talk" is perfectly acceptable if you use it as a character tag in dialogue. I remember a character in the TV series *thirtysomething* who spoke like a human thesaurus. He was one of the most intriguing people on the show. I can hear Miles Drentell quite distinctly saying:

"Ah! The redolent perfume of gingerbread accosted me the moment I strode into your ignoble tenement."

As with all guidelines, none of these suggestions are hard and fast rules. You'll know it's written the way it's meant to be when it won't be cut, replaced, or reworked in any other way. Only then will your editing and polishing be complete. In Appendix F, I'll present some examples for you to edit and polish.

***

The third layer of a story involves the finishing touches to make your story shine. With these elements, you'll create an extremely strong layer--something that will allow you to send your novel out with confidence to the people who can publish it. In the next chapter, we'll go through the steps required to prepare a proposal--including reworking your Story Plan Checklist into an effective synopsis!

LAYER IV
Preparing a Proposal

Now that you've completed a solid, polished story, you'll need to create an equally polished fiction proposal to present to an agent or editor. This extremely in-depth chapter will help you through every step in that process, as well as offer examples of each component of a solid proposal.

Let me preface everything I say later with this notice: If you already have a professional layout for your proposal packages that's been well received by editors and agents, then continue with your own style. Nevertheless, you might learn a few new things to help you make your proposals even more professional. What I'm about to give you is industry standard--most editors and agents approve of it, and I've received numerous comments on the professional quality of my submissions when I've used it. That said, if a publisher or agent has a list of formatting guidelines, then always follow it to a T.

A proposal that is equally efficient for an editor or agent consists of:

- Query letter
- Synopsis
- The first three chapters or first fifty pages (commonly called a partial) of the book

This chapter will take you through the steps to complete a query letter, a synopsis, and your partial, as well as provide information on how to package and submit your proposal. It will also include many tips for preparing a proposal so tantalizing, you're sure to get a request for the full manuscript. Finally, we'll go over some of the most common mistakes made when preparing a proposal.

THE QUERY LETTER

Most publishers accept unsolicited query letters that include a very brief summary of the story within the body of the letter. If they'll accept an unsolicited submission, or if you've already made contact at a conference or in response to a previous query, then there are several necessities for putting together a killer proposal:

- **24-pound white paper (92 bright).** The 20-pound variety is grayish, almost dirty looking, compared to 24-pound paper, and it's essentially see-through. If you lay one sheet on top of another, you can see the print on the bottom page. For an editor who spends all day looking at manuscripts, submissions prepared on 24-pound paper are much easier to read.
- **The right font.** Times New Roman is the most commonly requested font, even over the once-popular Courier. And use the same font consistently. Authors frequently make the mistake of not printing their query letter, synopsis, and partial in the same font. If your query letter is in Times New Roman, then make sure both the synopsis and partial are also in TNR.
- **One-inch margins all around, no page number on the first page, size 12 pitch.** Typewriters introduced selectable "pitch" so the machine could be switched between pica (10 characters per inch) and elite (12 per inch). The elite 12 pitch (pitch is called font size on a computer) has become standard. Make sure your query letter, synopsis, and partial match in all of these regards. Ensure consistency throughout each part of your proposal package.
- **Black ink only.** Editors aren't impressed by fancy submissions. They're impressed by professionalism. While a different color ink could be used in the heading of professional, personalized letterhead, it's not recommended for any other part of your submission.
- **Block style setup for the query and synopsis.** In

> other words, single-spaced, no indents, and each paragraph is followed by a blank line. Your partial, of course, will be in standard manuscript format of double-spaced, indented paragraphs.

Let's discuss the format of your query letter, starting from the top of the page. The first thing you need is your contact information, consisting of your name, address, e-mail address, fax number, and website URL(s) or blog. If you don't have personalized letterhead, you can create your own in your word-processing program, but keep it as simple as possible. Double space after your contact information.

Left-align your query. Except for your contact information, don't center or right-align any parts of the query, not even the date and your signature.

Include the name of an editor who's accepting submissions in the genre of the book you're querying. If you need to, check the publisher's website or call to inquire about this. Never submit blindly--you're guaranteed either to be tossed in the slush pile or to have your manuscript returned unread. Even if you're certain of who you want to submit to, it wouldn't hurt to call and check to make sure that editor is still working for this publisher. Many times, I've been moments from sending a query, made the call just to double-check, only to find out the editor had left the house permanently. It pays to be sure.

Check and double-check (during your call, or look for it on the website) that you've spelled the editor's name correctly. Follow the name of the editor with his title in the company (again, you may have to call and inquire about his official title, but this is crucial information--it proves you did some homework about him before you submitted), and then the publisher's address. Writers' organizations will have the most current information if you can't find a phone number or website.

Skip a line and insert the date. Skip another line following this to include your greeting. "Dear Ms./Mr. [Last Name]:" is always safe. (Use a colon; only personal letters end a greeting with a comma.) Never use a first name unless: (1) You know the editor very well--as in, you've met him at a conference and/or have had lengthy discussions with him in the past; (2) the editor has a unisex name and you don't know whether to call him (or her) Mr. or Ms. In the case of a name such as Terry Meadows, you would put "Dear Terry Meadows:" instead of "Dear Ms./Mr. Meadows:" Better yet, when you call to inquire, ask the receptionist who answers whether the editor is male or female.

The greeting is followed by another blank line. If you've met this editor before, or if he requested the material you're sending, refresh his memory in a succinct sentence or two in the first line of your query. Something like "I enjoyed discussing *The Story of My Heart* with you at the Pikes Peak Writer's Conference in April. Per your request, a proposal of this book is enclosed."

The next portion of your query letter is crucial. Many people lead their queries with something like "Please consider reviewing my book for publication." Any editor would assume that getting him to review your material is the point of your submission, so stating the fact is redundant, and the editor will already be bored.

A much better way to begin a query letter is by using the high-concept blurb you created in your Story Plan Checklist, though you might want to break it into two sentences instead of one, since some high-concept blurbs can get too long and wordy. You want to hook the editor into your story immediately. Remember, the basic structure of a high-concept blurb is: A character **(who)** wants **(what)** a goal because he's motivated **(why)**, but he faces conflict **(why not)**.

Fill in the blanks for your story:

________________________ **(name of character)** wants
________________________**(goal to be achieved)** because
____________ **(motivation for acting)** but he or she faces
______________________ **(conflict standing in the way)**.

If you find it more appropriate, you can also use your beginning story spark to start your letter.

Once you have the editor hooked with the very first sentence of your query, it's time to give a little more information about your story. In one to two paragraphs (no more than that, even if you're including a synopsis), sum up the most compelling elements of your story, including what makes your characters so interesting and what their conflicts, goals, and motivations are.

The paragraph that follows will include the most basic information about your story, including:

- Length (approximate length in number of words is preferred; i.e., 65,000 words, not 64,231 words)
- Genre of your story--be specific, even if your story straddles more than one category
- Whether the book is complete, or when you plan to complete it (it's best to say something like "end of November 2008" or "beginning of December 2008")
- Whether this book has won or finaled in any contests
- A very brief overview about the other stories in the series, if the book is part of a series
- Anything else that's important for the editor to know about the story

Following this paragraph, include your biography. Please note that the biographical section for a published author will probably differ from that of an unpublished or newer author. An unpublished author would include anything that makes him intriguing to an editor, such as:

- Any publishing credits (article or short story credits count, even if you're not published in book-length fiction)
- Organizations of which you're a member (and that are relevant to the submission and to writing in general)
- Any information that makes you an expert on the subject the book deals with, or any special research, etc., done in the area the book deals with
- Your day job, but only if it's intriguing or in some way parallels the submission (someone who teaches writing should always include that fact, but someone who works as a dishwasher at a restaurant wouldn't need

to divulge that unless the story prominently features a restaurant and/or dishwasher, but even then...)

Unless it in some way parallels your story, personal information isn't appropriate in a professional proposal--save the names and ages of your children, grandchildren, and pets for your author biography once you're published.

If you're a published author, you have several options for presenting your biography. You can include the important details in one or two paragraphs, or you can include your full-length biography separately immediately following the query letter. Naturally, you would only include information that is pertinent to your submission, or that in some way puts you or your body of work in a promising, impressive light. Include any of the following:

- Any advance reviews for this submission from other published authors
- Publishing credits (always include the publisher, release date, and formats the book is available in, along with any awards or nominations, and--in the most impressive cases--snippets of reviews you've received for your books, especially if they're in the same genre as the project you're submitting)
- Any awards you've received as an author, separate from your writing
- Writing organizations you belong to
- Information about your successful promotional endeavors as a published author
- Your website URL(s) and blog
- Anything else that's impressive and pertinent to your submission and/or your writing career

In the final paragraph of your query letter, tell the editor what you're enclosing in this package--usually your synopsis, the first three chapters of the book, and a SASE with sufficient postage for return of your proposal.

Whether to include a SASE or ask the editor or agent to recycle the partial is still up for debate in writing circles. There are several editors and agents who feel that asking them to recycle it is basically equivalent to saying "My work is garbage." For that reason, I always advise including a SASE with sufficient postage for the partial's return to you. Even if you ultimately throw the proposal away (it's usually *not* reusable), you won't inadvertently give the wrong impression.

Most authors also end the query with words similar to: "I'd be happy to send you the entire manuscript at your request. I look forward to hearing from you." These facts are obvious, but their expression is brief, and they do an acceptable job of closing your letter.

Finish off your query letter with something simple, not gushy, such as "Sincerely," or "Respectfully," followed by three to four blank lines. Type your name below where your signature will go, and *make sure that it matches the name you have at the top of the query with your contact information*! Believe it or not, I've actually seen some authors use two different names here--pen name for one and real for the other. How does the recipient know which is which? Unless you're a published author well known under this pen name, always use your real name everywhere in your proposal until you are published. This is something you discuss with an editor only after you're accepted with the publisher.

Once you're certain your query letter is ready to go, sign your name in ink in the blank space above your typed name.

Finally, include a simple list of what's enclosed in the package after this point. Generally, once the editor has finished reading the query letter, he'll use the enclosures listing to make sure you've included everything he needs.

If your query letter is longer than one page, staple the pages together.

In Appendix G, you'll find an example of an effective query letter for my book *Dead Drop*.

THE SYNOPSIS

Now we're going to talk about how to make your synopsis so outstanding, you'll have editors drooling to read more. You've already done all the hard work with your Story Plan Checklist, and we'll talk more about this soon.

The biggest problem I see with synopses is that authors don't know how to write them, or they assume an outline and a synopsis are the same thing. They're not--not at all. A synopsis, plain and simple, is a summary of your book set down in linear paragraph form. An outline is much more detailed. It covers all the major points of your story (character and plot conflicts), chapter by chapter. Nonfiction publishers typically ask for this; fiction publishers only occasionally want an outline.

When beginning your synopsis, start with the header at the top of the page. Your header should include the title of your book, followed immediately by the word *Synopsis* on the left; then, aligned on the right, your name followed by the page number. No header should appear on the first page. Following eight blank lines, center your title (all capitals, bold, and larger fonts are fine). Space down one and type the word *Synopsis*. After another space or two, include your name.

The recommended guideline for a synopsis is one single-spaced page for every 10,000 words (e.g., a 60,000-word novel results in a six-page synopsis), though complex stories might end up with more. However, industry standards have certainly dictated in the last few years that the shorter and more concise the synopsis, the better. Almost no editor will accept a synopsis longer than five to ten pages--which is about the length of a standard, uncomplicated Story Plan Checklist. Editors want to see the bare bones of a story, not extraneous information or flowery prose. They're looking for good writing as much as your ability to put the entire story into an easily understood, succinct block. However, worry later about the length of the synopsis. If it's much too long, you can cut it once you've got the basic structure down.

Remember that a synopsis is written in the present tense--unlike most stories. If you're referring to something that happened in your character's past in your synopsis, you would use past tense, but otherwise everything should be in present tense.

In general, write the synopsis when you're finished with your book or when you have a solid Story Plan Checklist. Always tie up your conflicts in the last few paragraphs of your synopsis. Never withhold the resolution in an attempt to leave the editors dying to find out how the book ends. Describe how the story is resolved in a way that will make editors want to see the flesh and blood on these bare bones.

Turning a Story Plan Checklist Into an Effective Synopsis

If you managed to fill out each item on your Story Plan Checklist, turning it into a synopsis should be pretty simple. All you really have to do is convert it to present tense (if it's not in that tense already) and arrange it in a logical, (mostly) chronological order. This might mean some cutting and pasting, so it works best to do this on your computer, with a copy of your original Story Plan Checklist saved elsewhere. Be sure to save the new copy under another name.

Read through your checklist a couple times, and you'll probably start seeing a sensible way to arrange the items. As you work, go ahead and remove the item specifications (in other words, you don't need to include "Beginning Story Spark", nor the character specification of the items).

Unless you think they are crucial to your story, some of the items from your checklist probably won't be needed in your synopsis:

- Working Title
- Working Genre(s)
- Working POV Specification
- Estimated Length of Book/Number of Sparks
- Description (Outside POV)
- Description (Self POV)
- Enhancement/Contrast
- Symbolic Element
- Setting Descriptions

Once you've read over your Story Plan Checklist a few times and you've gotten a good feel for how to assemble it into a synopsis that makes perfect sense, go over the items I've listed above and ask yourself if they fit in your synopsis, or if they can be cut. Absolutely essential to your synopsis will be these items:

- Identifying the Main Character(s)
- Character Introductions (though these might be significantly trimmed)
- Occupational Skills (again, you might trim some of what you've written in your checklist--a single line is usually all that's required)
- Beginning, middle, and end sparks, and the following sequence for each:
    a. Internal Character Conflicts
    b. Evolving Goals and Motivations
    c. External Plot Conflicts

Now, since your Story Plan Checklist is already arranged in beginning, middle, and end sections, you should see a clear progression as your checklist-turned-synopsis moves from character introductions to internal character and plot conflicts. Suspense will be built in because of your story sparks--which should be tantalizing on their own. If you see any areas that aren't in keeping with the progression, or sections that simply don't fit in your synopsis, feel free to cut. If you decide later you need it, you still have your Story Plan Checklist to refer back to.

Your Story Plan Checklist is written in such a way that it's unlikely you'll include too much information in your synopsis, but your page count will help you determine if your synopsis is too long. If your synopsis is longer than ten pages, you need to crop it to include only the *major* internal character and plot conflicts, and goals and motivations. If even these go very long, you can sum up a two-paragraph conflict into only a few sentences. And, yes, it may take you several passes to find a manner of doing this well. It helps to set the synopsis aside for a week or two after your first pass, then to come back and see if you can do more cropping. I've often found that once I've had a few weeks away from a ten-page synopsis, I can come back and immediately see what doesn't belong. In a few hours, the synopsis becomes a rubber-band-tight five pages.

Continue whittling until you no longer see any area that doesn't fit perfectly. You might want to send the synopsis to a critique partner and ask her for a reaction to it. The synopsis you've created here should make the reader feels as though he's read the book (and now he'll definitely *want* to read it!), and the resolution you offered in your concluding paragraph(s) should satisfy him.

We said our Story Plan Checklist didn't need to be our best writing. True. But a synopsis does need to include your best writing. So you may have to rework it slightly to really make the writing pop during this process.

How do you know when it's done? When absolutely nothing else could be taken out without compromising the story summary.

Once you've polished this synopsis until it shines, paperclip the pages to keep the synopsis separate from your partial.

In Appendix G, you'll find an example of the synopsis I created for *Dead Drop*, based on the Story Plan Checklist example in Appendix D. If you compare the Story Plan Checklist and the synopsis of this story side by side, you'll be able to see how simple it was to convert the Story Plan Checklist to synopsis format with careful whittling.

THE PARTIAL

Let's talk about how to make your partial so fascinating, editors absolutely won't be able to wait to see the full manuscript. We'll also cover how to put the proposal together once the query, synopsis, and partial are done.

Always include a cover page on top of your partial. The cover page text should be centered, beginning with the working title (which can be bold and in a larger font), then word count, followed by your contact information, including name, address, phone number, and e-mail address. No header should appear on the cover page.

Each page of the rest of your partial should have a header including the title of your book, left-aligned. Your name and the page number should be aligned on the right in the header on every page of the partial. On the first page of your partial following the cover page, space down eight lines and center your title (again, all capitals, bold, and a larger font are fine). After another space or two, include your name. Double space and begin to the left. It's acceptable to put the first two or three words in all capitals. Your next paragraph should be indented five spaces.

When you begin a new chapter after this point, make a hard page break, then start just as you did before, with the chapter number bolded and centered eight spaces down from the top of the page. Scene breaks can be indicated by a blank line, with the first one or two words following the blank line left-aligned. You can also use symbols to indicate a new scene is beginning--three asterisks with a blank line above and below them are the most common device for this. In order to be consistent with what you've done previously, if you've used all capitals for the first few words of the chapter, start at the left in all capitals for a new scene.

A partial is either the first three chapters (including a prologue), or the first fifty to sixty pages of the manuscript. Don't choose fifty pages from the middle of your book--that would be cheating, and it's frowned on by nearly all editors. Send the first fifty pages unless the editor specifically requests otherwise.

The partial doesn't have to be exactly fifty pages long. Remember that you want your partial to end on an exciting note. If the end of your scene on page fifty or thereabouts is tantalizing, great. If it's not, find a more suspenseful place to end your partial. Whatever you do, make the editor drool to read more.

Many of the things we discussed in creating a winning synopsis apply here. If editors don't see cohesive characters, settings, and plots, they won't request to see more of your manuscript. Also remember that these elements need to be developed almost as well (though much more succinctly) in the synopsis as in your book.

Your partial will be fairly long--use either a binder's clip or a rubber band to hold it all.

In Appendix F, you'll find an example of a cover page and a

short excerpt of *Dead Drop* (which I'm using here to represent just the initial pages of a partial). Double space yours.

PUTTING THE PROPOSAL TOGETHER

Once your proposal pages have been tapped together until all the edges are perfectly smooth, put everything together in the order you want it, usually:

- Bottom: synopsis
- Middle: partial
- Top: query letter

There's been a lot of debate over whether to put your synopsis before or after your partial. Ultimately, it's up to you. My thinking is, if I put my partial before my synopsis, and the editor reads my partial, is intrigued by it and wants to know more, then he has the synopsis left to read. The synopsis should whet his appetite for the full manuscript.

However, most editors have their own preferences as to which they read first, so no matter what you do, they'll end up doing what they want. It probably doesn't matter anyway. Just make sure your enclosure list at the end of your query letter matches the order of the documents in your package.

Paperclip a business card and your self-addressed, stamped envelope (SASE) to your query letter. Now, with everything together, put a sturdy, cardboard backing under the pile. Use extra-large rubber bands to secure the pile both vertically and horizontally. This will keep it looking neat. You're now ready to slip the bundle into an envelope that holds it easily without being so big that the bundle will slide around inside the envelope. The post office and other mailing services won't take much (or any) care in delivering your package--pack it well and send it First Class or Priority Mail to lessen the chances that the editor will end up with mere scraps of what you intended to submit.

The Six Deadly Proposal Sins

Let's go over the most common problems in fiction proposals and how to avoid them.

1. **Lack of sufficient characterization.** What's the most important part of a book? Hands down, characters. You can have the greatest plot on the face of the earth, but if you don't have even more exciting characters, you'll never pull it off. Creating amazing characters that reach out of your query, synopsis, and partial and grab an editor by the heart should be your paramount task when you're putting together a proposal. Nothing else you do will be even remotely as important. In fact, I'd go so far as to say that if you completely flub your proposal format, but your story characterization is outstanding, no editor will care about your faux pas. Great characters can right a thousand wrongs.

2. **Stories that lack cohesion.** A story must be made up of cohesive elements. Characters, settings, and plot must fit together organically. All story threads--from the main ones to the minor ones--must have a unity that leads to steady development and satisfactory resolution. Give editors and agent something to look forward to with pacing that heightens the intrigue. When an editor or agent sees a lack of cohesion in your proposal, it's a clear indication that you haven't spent enough time thinking your story through and beginning with a solid foundation.

3. **Not starting with a bang.** Synopses and manuscript introductions should begin with something intriguing. Within the first ten pages, you need to have the editor or agent hooked. What happens in your story will carry over to your synopsis, so if the book doesn't start with anything important or interesting actually happening, your synopsis will also start in a boring way. Start and end every single chapter or scene in your synopsis and

story with a bang.

4. **Passive writing.** I'm sure most of you have heard more about this than you care to, but if you submit a proposal rife with passive writing, not only will the editor not want to see more of your manuscript, he won't be interested in future submissions from you either. Learn how to write in an active voice, show don't tell, and give your prose impact and a natural, intriguing flow.

5. **Not knowing the difference between a synopsis and an outline.** Editors almost always ask for a synopsis--not an outline--with a partial. Once you sell to a publisher and you have an editor you're comfortable with, he may want to see your outline before you write a book--and you can sell future books to him based on only this, or on an in-depth synopsis. However, before you sell your first novel, and possibly for a few projects afterward, you'll need to submit a tight synopsis. There's no better way to learn how to write one of these than by starting with a Story Plan Checklist.

6. **Head-hopping.** Head-hopping is annoying. A huge percentage of editors and agents won't accept it because trying to figure out who's in viewpoint from one minute to the next grows frustrating. *Only one POV character per scene*--make that a rule from this point forward and don't step over that line, because following this rule really will make your stories radically better.

Tip Sheet: Proposal Tricks of the Trade

Some of the strange no-no's below might amuse you, but the fact is that I wouldn't have to mention them if an author somewhere, sometime had not done exactly these things. Be a professional.

- If you're a published author, never include promotional items from previous releases.

- Unless you're a professional illustrator and you're submitting a children's story, the editor you haven't yet sold your manuscript to isn't interested in what you've come up with for cover art, no matter how outstanding. Don't put the cart before the horse by including anything by way of cover art for your book.

- Never try to thank or bribe an editor with a gift enclosed along with your proposal.

- Don't be presumptive by using a pen name or including a dedication in your proposal--those things are discussed only *after* a book has gone to contract. Horse before the cart, remember?

- Including a copyright symbol on any part of the proposal is unnecessary and has a tendency to make editors think you're an amateur, paranoid, or both.

- Always include sufficient postage on your SASE, with your address and the name of the editor or publisher already printed on the envelope. What would you do if a stranger sent you something that required more postage to return than was included? You'd probably throw it away. So would an editor, justifiably.

- Always get delivery confirmation at the post office. (The under-a-dollar cost will save you a headache or two, and a phone call to the publisher to find out if the package was received; you can find out yourself within a few days that it arrived.) While it's acceptable to send a postcard so the editor can let you know your package was received, you want him to concentrate on your proposal, not little tasks that will take him away from his regular editing.

• Never send your package via Media Mail--if it's undeliverable, the post office may throw it out without contacting you. While this doesn't always happen, it does occur frequently. You can contact your local USPS to see what regulations they follow, but it's not really worth taking the risk.

• Within your proposal, include only contact information that you actually use. If you don't want an editor calling you at home or work, don't include those phone numbers. If you almost never check your e-mail, then don't include an e-mail address. If your website is infrequently or even never updated, you might not want to include your website URL, since the site will reflect poorly on you if the editor or agent decides to visit.

• Word count is generally figured by multiplying the number of pages in the completed manuscript by 250 (which is the average number of words per page, in a double-spaced manuscript with 12-point type). Always round your word count to the nearest thousand. So, if your completed book has 203 pages, multiply that number by 250 to get 50,750 words. You'd round this to 51,000 and say your book has approximately 51,000 words.

• Even when you're published, you have to be a professional. Give your current publisher and any other publisher you submit to (whether by e-mail or snail mail) the benefit of a submission that meets his requirements, that's submitted according to his guidelines, and that treats him like a professional. Don't send a personal letter that includes a submission to any publisher unless you have a very good working relationship with him, he's encouraged you to send informal book pitches, and this format is acceptable to him. When unsure, always opt for a full proposal including a professional query letter, synopsis, and partial. Don't slack in being a professional because you feel you're above it. There will never be a time in your career when you can act in an unprofessional manner and not have it come back to bite you in the butt.

•Learn how to write a professional query letter, biography, and synopsis, and keep your skills sharp throughout your career. You'll always need to know these things, considering the rate at which publishers come and go and at which authors either slip into obscurity or have to start all over again. Trust me, these are skills you can't really afford to lose.

•Before you send your proposal out, make sure you let someone else (or better yet--two or three others) who has good writing skills and an eye for typos critique it. Don't rely on your own editing skills or your word-processor's spell-checker. Make sure your submission is error-free and that everything looks clean and professional. This also means no coffee stains or perfume--cigarette smoke and pet hair are also highly offensive to sensitive people. Take those things into account when preparing your submission. You might want to either keep your office free of cigarettes or pets, or to prepare your submission elsewhere, where smoke and pet hair aren't problems.

•If this proposal is being submitted in response to an editor's request, it's a good idea to include a photocopy of his original request behind the query letter (noting that you've included it after your query). Editors ask a lot of authors to submit, so this is a nice reminder of how the two of you originally met or of what was originally requested of you.

•Send out your very best material. This may mean preparing your submission and letting it sit on a shelf for a week or two, or possibly longer, before going back to view it with fresh eyes. Only then can you be confident in sending it to an editor or agent. Most editors and agents remember their first impression of an author for years to come. Make sure their first impression of you is that you're a professional who's spent a considerable about of time preparing a perfect proposal with this specific editor/agent in mind.

- Finally, don't feel like everything I've said here is written in stone. As long as everything in your proposal is consistent, I doubt too many editors would be offended by a slightly different setup. Just make sure you provide every editor you submit to the most professional, consistent, and intriguing proposal possible.

***

Creating a killer fiction proposal is no more an easy task than planning a book, writing it, and revising it. The contents of your query letter, synopsis, and partial--not to mention how you package them--will play a part in how the editor or agent you submit to responds to your story. Armed with a clean, professional setup and a story that you've made utterly irresistible in each portion of your proposal, you can have editors and agents not only requesting the full manuscript but begging for it immediately if not sooner.

EPILOGUE
The Cohesive Story

We've established, from comparing the process of building a house to the process of building a story, that there are three distinct layering steps:

- Stage 1: Planning for and laying a foundation
- Stage 2: Writing
- Stage 3: Revising

Layers mean *strength* in story building just as they do in house-building. Without layering, a story is one-dimensional, unbelievable, and boring. Layering also has the effect of producing cohesion of all elements. Characters must blend naturally into your setting, just as plot must develop as an organic part of your character and setting. If a story doesn't work, it could very well be because your character, setting, and/or plot elements aren't cohesive. Each element hinges on the other two, and they must fuse irrevocably.

My main hope is that going through the Story Plan Checklist process has vividly shown you the need for cohesive story elements in each story you write, and that you can now use these steps in crafting your own wonderfully fused story.

In Appendix E, I'll take you through the process of building cohesion step by step. If you want a little more experience in using the Story Plan Checklist, read through those I've created from published books in Appendix D. At that point, you can inject the blank Story Plan Checklist included in Appendix C with your own sparks to set off a beauty of a story.

The editing and polishing exercises in Appendix F should help you with the finishing touches to make your story shine like a gem.

"DO I HAVE TO DO THIS FOREVER?"

After *First Draft Outline* came out, I was frequently asked whether all the pre-writing steps, checklists, and worksheets had to be completed with each writing project. As I said then, I'll say now for both *First Draft Outline* and *Cohesive Story Building* readers:

I promise you, you won't always have to fill out so many worksheets and checklists--unless you want to continue with them. The longer you write, the more books you finish, the easier it should become. Writers grow more adept in our writing the longer we do it.

If you've never written a book before, you'll need the direction both of my books (and plenty of others) can give you. If you simply can't get some portion of your book to work, then all the checklists and exercises should help you figure out where your story is stuck or going wrong.

A writer usually spends a lifetime honing his or her process of writing. But the first step is locking down what works for you and what doesn't. Once you've used a method like those I advocate in my books often enough, you'll find that a lot of the writing process has become instinctive for you. You'll understand the importance of solid characterization now, whereas you may not have before. You'll comprehend how well-placed descriptions can enhance all the other parts of a book. Because so much of this has become instinctive for you, you may not have to formally complete setting sketches or plot sketches, etc., anymore. You'll do those things within the framework of your research and then within the outlining.

Whatever stage in your writing, I don't ever believe you should do more work than you need to. If you find yourself getting bogged down (either by the amount of time allotted--too much or too little--to each step, by an ability to progress with a step, or for any other reason), move on to the next step. If you don't need to follow a particular step in the process because you've already done it or it would just be unnecessary for you, you shouldn't do it. All of this stuff is designed to get writers thinking about areas that they've always seen as part of a whole, but that they've never before *separated* from the whole. In the beginning, you may need to perform all of those steps, filling out endless worksheets, etc., as you learn how to sufficiently develop each aspect of a book. But only do what you feel *benefits* you and your story.

All this said, I believe an outline is a crucial layer in developing every story. I don't really think you can "instinctively" grow out of needing one of those because it's really the ideal place the hard work of writing a book should be done.

***

Story building is truly an art. Writers have, or can learn, the tools to build an incredible story.

How amazing that words can create people readers want to meet personally, and build worlds that readers want to visit. Words make people laugh, cry, chew their nails to the quick, get mad enough to have a physical reaction, fall in love. Words possibly even change lives.

A layering process of writing sets up the stages necessary to complete a cohesive, irresistible dream book that is hauntingly unforgettable to everyone who reads it.

Remember, the worksheets, examples checklists, and other aids used in this book are also available separately in an electronic, useable file for your own writing. It's called "*Cohesive Story Building Bonus Companion Booklet* ", available from the publisher of this book. A print edition can be purchased as well.

APPENDIX A
Glossary

Action: the advancement of plot and subplot threads from scene to scene.

Aftereffects of resolution: an emotional reaction or an event which carries the story goal or a subplot thread beyond its resolution.

Black moment: the bleakest moment in the book, where the reader is lead to believe that the main character's future may never be happy because the obstacles appear monumental and the story goal seems unachievable. The black moment comes at the end of the middle section of the book.

Brainstorming: creative "brewing" of an idea, during which stories come to life in spurts.

Capsule: formatted outline capsules contain single-scene summaries. Each capsule contains the day; the chapter and scene numbers; the point-of-view character; additional characters; the location and time; any facts, notes, or questions necessary to the development of the scene; and, finally, the draft of what happens in the scene.

Character internal conflicts: emotional problems (brought about by external conflicts) that make a character reluctant to achieve a goal, keeping him from learning a life lesson and making the choice to act. In fiction, internal character conflicts are why external plot conflicts can't be resolved. The character can't have his goal until he faces the conflict. The audience must be able to identify with the internal and external conflicts the character faces in order to feel involved and to care about the outcome. Character growth throughout the story is key to a satisfactory resolution.

Character sketches: details about a character, including physical descriptions and mannerisms, personality traits, background, internal and external conflicts, occupation, and miscellaneous facts.

Cohesion/cohesive: in writing, matching characters, settings, and plot to one another in such a way that each part of a story is drawn together and fused until they become inseparable.

Conflict: the opposition to the happy resolution of the story goal; the clash between good and evil that motivates the main characters to act. May be internal or external.

Consistency: the steady flow of each plot and subplot thread from the beginning of the book, through the middle, to the resolution.

Contrast: a method for building action and suspense by providing baffling, opposing characteristics in character, setting, or plot. A contrast can be a subtle, balanced, or extreme element in opposition to what the writer has already established for a character, plot, or setting.

Description: in-depth details about characters and settings that allow the reader to use the full range of his senses. Self-pov descriptions are a character describing herself. Outside pov description is any other character describing another character.

Detailed construction outline: in writing, a scene-by-scene summary containing all the information necessary for the writer to begin working on a daily basis, from the start of the project to the finish.

Dialogue: words spoken (external) or thought (internal monologue) by a character.

Downtime: a point following the black moment, in which the main character takes release from the action to reflect on what happily-ever-after could have been. During downtime, the character believes that the story goal is unachievable, and he will seemingly give up the fight. More extreme form of release; relief from agony. Downtime must be followed by suspense.

Draft: either the initial full writing of a manuscript, or a start-to-finish overhaul of a manuscript.

Editing and polishing: the process of turning a rough story into a finished one by cutting the bad, replacing it with the good, and polishing up what remains until it shines. Involves making minor changes in an outline or manuscript in order to smooth the arrangement of sentences, tighten words and sentences, and so on.

End scene notes: in the preliminary sketches, end scenes are ideas about the story that you know go into the finals section of the book at some point.

Enhancement: an enhancement is a subtle, balanced, or extreme element that complements what the writer has already established as a character's traits.

Evolving goals and motivations: goals are what the character wants and needs. Motivation gives him drive and purpose to achieve the goal. Goals must be urgent enough to motivate the character to go through hardship and self-sacrifice. Multiple goals collide and impact the characters, forcing tough choices in the pursuit of reaching their purpose. Focused on the goal, the character is pushed toward it by believable, emotional, and compelling motives that won't let him quit. Because he cares deeply about the outcome, his anxiety is doubled. The intensity of the character's anxiety pressures him to make choices and changes, thereby creating worry and awe in the reader. Goals and motivations are constantly evolving to fit character and plot conflicts.

External monologues: free-form summaries that refer to a single facet of the exterior conflicts of a story. These must be cohesive with internal monologues, as they work together to form a complete story.

Flashbacks: a memory or description of a pivotal event that occurred previous to the current story timeline; used to build suspense, slow down the action, provide missing details, illuminate hidden motivation, or reveal an answer to a mystery.

Foreshadowing: a method for building action and suspense by hinting at what is to come.

Formatted outline: the final version of your outline; ideally the first draft of your book written scene by scene in formatted outline capsules.

Foundation: in writing, an outline in some form and/or a Story Plan Checklist.

Framework: in writing, the first draft of a story, necessary to define structure.

Genre: bookstore classification of the category or type of book (e.g., mystery, romance, fantasy).

Internal monologues: free-form summaries that refer to a single facet of the interior conflicts of a story; building a story from the inside out. These must be cohesive with external monologues, as they work together to form a complete story.

Introspection: a character's observation of his own mental or emotional state; or, thoughts of the situation he faces.

Layering: strengthening an existing plot line by deepening characters, adding new subplot threads, and further enhancing cohesion in the story.

Linear writing: working in a chronological and progressive manner from beginning to end.

Long-term threads or goals: the story goal (and, in a romance, the romance thread). Long-term threads in your story are the goals that all your main characters are fighting for.

Miscellaneous scene notes: ideas you have about a story that don't fit chronologically into the outline where your summary outline ends, or ideas that you might want to explore later but aren't sure really belong in the story.

Mood: the feeling or atmosphere of a scene, carefully constructed through description, dialogue, introspection, and action. Mood often elevates suspense.

Nonlinear writing: working out of order or skipping around during the process of building your story structure. The opposite of working in chronological order.

Outline: in publishing terms, a summary of all the major points of your story (character and plot conflicts), chapter by chapter or scene by scene.

Pacing: the rate at which each plot and subplot thread progresses from the beginning of the book, through the middle course of the book, to its satisfactory resolution.

Partial: the first three chapters (or fifty pages) of a book.

Plot: internal and external story threads; must be cohesive with character and setting.

Plot external conflicts: the central tangible or outer problem standing squarely in the character's way that must be faced and solved by that character. The character wants to restore the stability that was taken from him by the external conflict, and this produces his desire to act--although the character's internal conflicts will create an agonizing tug of war with the plot conflicts. He has to make tough choices that come down to whether or not to face and solve the problem. Plot external conflicts must be urgent and require immediate attention. The audience must be able to identify with the internal and external conflicts the character faces in order to feel involved and to care about the outcome.

Plot sketch: a document outlining the story goal and subplot threads, including tension, releases, downtimes and the black moments, resolutions, and aftereffects of resolution.

Preliminary sketches: the foundation of your story, including character, setting and plot sketches, and scene summary notes.

Project folder: a large folder containing all the materials relevant to a specific story idea.

Proposal: submission to an agent or publisher that includes a query letter, synopsis, and partial.

Punch list: organizes and states items that remain incomplete or broken, that are lacking parts, or that require your review; items in need of final attention. A goal sheet prepared after the completion of the first draft of the book that includes a running list of changes that must be made to the draft.

Query letter: an introductory letter that includes book and author information; can be submitted independently or as the cover letter of a full proposal package.

Release: any temporary easement of either romantic/sexual tension or plot tension. Milder form of downtime; relief from anxiety. Release must be immediately followed by tension to keep the reader interested.

Research list: a list of areas to be researched for a particular story.

Resolution: the satisfying, logical conclusion of story threads.

Revision: reworking material in an effort to make what's already there better and stronger. In a less ideal situation, making significant changes to an outline or draft, such as adding or deleting plot threads, or completely rewriting certain sections. In a milder form, tweaking characters, settings, and plots, and incorporating research.

Romance thread: a dominant romantic and/or sexual relationship between main characters.

Romantic/sexual tension: any type of suspense or exaggerated awareness that brings the romance thread to the fever pitch of anticipation.

Sag: a lull (usually in the middle of a story) caused by weak plotting or pacing, and requiring a new story spark to infuse the plot with action.

Scene summary notes: in the preliminary sketches, the scene summary notes are the first attempt to set down the basics of what happens in the book starting from the beginning and moving from scene to scene chronologically.

Sensory description: using the senses of sight, touch, smell, hearing, taste, and feeling to set the mood or tone of a scene; brings the reader directly into the story and involves him.

Setting: details and descriptions of various locations and time periods in a story; must be cohesive with character and plot.

Setting sketches: details and descriptions of various locations and time periods in a story.

Shelf-time: a period of time during which the writer stops working on a story and allows it to sit on a shelf. Shelf-time gives the writer a fresh perspective when he next picks up the book.

Simple falsework sketch: in writing, a very simple story sketch, which is basically a jumping-off point that gets a writer immersed in his story. The writer may create more sketches--general and detailed--to get the story moving forward again if it stalls.

Story blueprint: similar to an outline, the foundation of a story, including character, setting, and plot sketches; a guideline used to create and assemble a story.

Story folder: a large folder containing all the materials relevant to a specific book idea.

Story goal: the major, long-term plot thread that continues from the beginning of the book until the very end. Every subplot thread and all characters are involved in achieving the story goal.

Story Plan Checklist: an in-depth guideline that targets the key elements necessary in building a cohesive story; includes basic, external, and internal monologues.

Story spark: something intriguing that ignites a story scenario and carries it along toward fruition; each story requires at least two to sustain it; novels generally have three. A story spark must infuse and reinfuse the story, and a new one must be injected at certain points in order to support the length and complexity of a story. The beginning story spark sets up the conflict. The middle story spark (or sparks) complicates the situation. Finally, the end story spark resolves the conflict.

Subplot threads: the secondary plots that make up a story, usually translating into short-term quests toward the resolution of the story goal.

Suspense: the sensation of agony coupled with uncertainty in the reader; more intense form of tension that produces dread in the characters and readers.

Symbolic element: something that defines a character, defines the situation he's in, or does both. May or may not be a tangible object that enhances and/or contrasts and thereby develops the character and plot in deeper ways.

Synopsis: a summary of your book set down in linear paragraph form.

Tension: the sensation of anxiety coupled with anticipation in the reader; less intense form of suspense that produces hope in the characters and readers. Tension alternates with release to keep the reader on edge.

Theme: the dominate idea driving the story; story goal and theme can be used interchangeably.

Threads: internal and external conflicts (also frequently referred to as plots and subplots).

APPENDIX B
Worksheets from *First Draft Outline*

Worksheet 1: Character Sketch
Worksheet 2A: General Setting Sketch
Worksheet 2B: Character Setting Sketch
Worksheet 3: Plot Sketch
Worksheet 4: Formatted Outline Capsule

Worksheet 1: Character Sketch

Title:

Character Name:

Nickname:

Birth Date/Place:

Character Role: (hero, heroine, secondary character, villain)

Physical Descriptions:

Age:

Race:

Eye Color:

Hair Color/Style:

Build (Height/Weight):

Skin Tone:

Style of Dress:

Characteristics or mannerisms:

Personality Traits:

Background:

Internal Conflicts:

External Conflicts:

Occupation/Education:

Miscellaneous Notes:

Worksheet 2A: General Setting Sketch

Title:

Name of Setting:

Characters Living in This Time Period and Region:

Year or Time Period:

Season:

State:

City or Town:

Miscellaneous Notes:

Worksheet 2B: Character Setting Sketch

Title:

Character Name:

General Settings for This Character (See Corresponding Worksheet 2A for Details):

Character's Home:

City or Town (See Corresponding Worksheet 2A):

Neighborhood Character Lives In:

Street Character Lives On:

Character's Neighbors:

Character's Home (Apartment, House, Mansion, Trailer, Ranch, etc.):

Home Interior:

Character's Workplace:

City or Town (See Corresponding Worksheet 2A for De tails):

Business Name:

Type of Business:

Neighborhood:

Street:

Individual Workspace:

Co-workers:

Miscellaneous Notes:

Worksheet 3: Plot Sketch

Title:

Story Goal:

Romance Thread (Optional):

Subplot Threads:

#2

#3

#4

#5

#6

#7

#8

Additional

Plot Tension:

Romantic/Sexual Tension (Optional):

Release:

Downtime:

Black Moment:

Resolution:

Aftereffects of Resolution (Optional):

Worksheet 4: Formatted Outline Capsule

Title:

Day:

Chapter and Scene #:

POV character:

Additional Characters:

Location:

Approximate Time:

Facts Necessary:

Notes:

Questions:

Draft of scene:

APPENDIX C
Story Checklists

Checklist 1: Story Plan Checklist
Checklist 2: Cohesion Checklist
Checklist 3: Punch Checklist
Checklist 4: Revision Checklist
Checklist 5: Editing and Polishing Checklist

Story Plan Checklist

Title:

Genre(s):

POV Specification:

High-Concept Blurb:

Estimated Length of Book/Number of Sparks:

BEGINNING STORY SPARK:

Identifying the Main Character(s):

Character Introductions:
- *First Character:*

- *Second Character:*

Description (Outside POV):
- *First Character:*

- *Second Character:*

Description (Self POV):

- *First Character:*

- *Second Character:*

Occupational Skills:

- *First Character:*

- *Second Character:*

Enhancement/Contrast:

- *First Character:*

- *Second Character:*

Symbolic Element:

- *First Character:*

- *Second Character:*

Setting Descriptions:

- *First Character:*

- *Second Character:*

Character Conflicts (Internal):

- *First Character:*

- *Second Character:*

Evolving Goals and Motivations:

- *First Character:*

- *Second Character:*

Plot Conflicts (External):

MIDDLE STORY SPARK:

Character Conflicts (Internal):

- *First Character:*

- *Second Character:*

Evolving Goals and Motivations:

- *First Character:*

- *Second Character:*

Plot Conflicts (External):

END STORY SPARK:

Character Conflicts (Internal):

- *First Character:*

- *Second Character:*

Evolving Goals and Motivations:

- *First Character:*

- *Second Character:*

Plot Conflict (External) Resolutions:

Cohesion Checklist

How do you know if your characters, settings, and plots are truly cohesive? Once you finish your Story Plan Checklist, check the obvious first:

- Does your Story Plan Checklist read like a mini version of the story?
- Are there any sections on the checklist you didn't fill out?
- Did you leave important characters off the list? If you put them on now and filled out their basics, and external and internal monologues, would the story be more cohesive?
- Are your story sparks intriguing enough, or can you punch them up more?
- Do your settings truly fit the characters and plot, or are they simply *there*?
- Do beginning, middle, and end internal monologues follow a progressive, logical course?
- Are resolutions logical? Predictable? Would a twist ending be more effective and exciting?

If you're satisfied that your story is cohesive, try one final test to be absolutely sure. Below, circle the answer that best fits your reaction to the question. Remember, anything but a resounding "Yes!" to each question means you need to go back to that element of your story and work in more cohesion.

Question	Answer	Areas to Rework
Are conflicts, goals, and motivations defined enough to pinpoint within the high-concept blurb?	Yes! No Not Sure	• Conflicts • Goals and Motivations • High-Concept Blurb
Do internal and external conflicts, goals, and mo-	Yes!	• Internal and Exter-

tivations intersect, collide, and impact?	No Not Sure	nal Conflicts • Goals and Motivations
Do characters have believable, identifiable, and compelling conflicts, goals, and motivations they care about deeply?	Yes! No Not Sure	• Characters • Conflicts • Goals and Motivations
Are each character's conflicts, goals, and motivations urgent and causal (can't have one without the other)?	Yes! No Not Sure	• Characters • Conflicts • Goals and Motivations • Plot
Do the characters have the skills to achieve the goal if sufficiently motivated?	Yes! No Not Sure	• Characters • Occupations • Goals and Motivations • Plot
Are the main characters directly involved in resolutions of internal and external plot conflicts?	Yes! No Not Sure	• Characters • Conflicts • Goals and Motivations • Plot
If the story was set anywhere else, would the setting make the characters and plot less cohesive?	Yes! No Not Sure	• Settings • Characters • Conflicts • Goals and Motivations Plot

Punch Checklist

Items that need to be attended to in the revision and/or in the editing and polishing.

Title:

Problem	How to Fix	Chapter/Page #(s)

Revision Checklist

You should pay special attention to a number of items as you're evaluating and revising:

- Structure
- Character, setting, and plot credibility and the cohesion of these elements
- Depth of conflicts, goals, and motivations
- Scene worthiness
- Pacing
- Effectiveness of hints, tension and suspense, and resolutions
- Transitions
- Emotion and color
- Hooks and cliffhangers
- Character voice
- Consistency
- Adequacy of research
- Properly unfurled, developed, and concluded story threads
- Deepening of character enhancements/contrasts and the symbols of these

The table below will help you build consistency. In the first column, include the timeline or other detail. In the second column, include every page number on which the detail is mentioned. For instance:

Timeline or Detail	Page in Ms.
First murder occurred at 7:32 P.M.	*3, 12, 91–93*
Andrea moved to New York in 1995.	*7*

Timeline or Detail	Page in Ms.

Editing and Polishing Checklist

The process of editing and polishing involves any or all of the following:

- Rearranging sentences or paragraphs
- Showing, not telling, where most needed
- Tightening sentences and individual words (such as changing passive to active, and dull to impacting; cleaning up repetitiveness)
- Smoothing out roughness and making purple prose more natural
- Punching up tension and suspense
- Ensuring variation in sentence construction and length
- Word enrichment

Additionally, evaluate these areas as you edit and polish:

Description

__Have I interspersed character descriptions throughout scenes instead of in a single block?

__Have I described characters from another character's POV? (i.e., characters are *not* describing themselves)

__Have I mentioned descriptive details (hair and eye color, etc.) only once or twice within the story?

__Have I kept adjectives in descriptions to a minimum?

Dialogue

__Have I used external and internal dialogue effectively?

__Have I avoided dialogue bullets except to create extreme tension?

__Have I used dialogue to reveal my characters' personalities, goals and motivations, etc.?

__Does each character's dialogue fit that character?

__Would my story or the individual scenes be more effective if started with intriguing dialogue?

__Do all of my characters "speak" differently?

Introspection
__Have I effectively used introspection to allow readers to get inside my characters' heads?
__Have I written with such emotional impact, readers will experience the same emotions as my characters?

Miscellaneous
__Have I varied my sentence length and structure?
__Have I written each sentence in an active voice that ensures the most impact?
__Are my scenes compellingly shown, with telling reserved only for those instances in which a scene doesn't need to be built around a minor point?
__Have I cleaned up as many adverbs as I can?
__Have I revised sentences to avoid as many of these overused words as I can? *Was/wasn't, were/weren't, did/didn't, have/haven't, is/isn't, are/aren't, to be/been*
__Have I removed unnecessary clutter, particularly in changing *was going to* to *would*?
__Have I fixed as many overused idea stringers, like *when, as, realized, wondered, occurred, felt, seem, appear,* and *look* as possible?
__Have I revised passive sentences that begin with *There was/were, It was, They were, He was*?
__If I'm writing a contemporary story, have I used contractions?
__Do I have any long, hard-to-absorb sentences? Can they be revised as two or more sentences for more immediacy?
__Have I defined exactly what "it" is, especially at the beginning of sentences?
__Have I avoided careless repetition unless the repetition drives the impact deeper?
__Does anything I've written make it sound like I used the thesaurus too freely?

APPENDIX D
Story Plan Checklist Examples

Example 1: *Dead Drop*, by Karen Wiesner
Example 2: *I Am Legend*, by Richard Matheson
Example 3: *Harry Potter and the Chamber of Secrets*, by J.K. Rowling
Example 4: *The Friday Night Knitting Club*, by Kate Jacobs

Story Plan Checklist Example

Title:
Dead Drop, Book 4 of the Incognito Series, by Karen Wiesner

Genre:
Romance, action/adventure, suspense

POV Specification:
Scenes are either from Roan's POV, or Perry's

Estimated Length of Book/Number of Sparks: 60,000 words/3 sparks

HIGH-CONCEPT BLURB/BEGINNING STORY SPARK

After being approached by a recruiter, a man is unwillingly inducted into a covert government organization. Daniel Sands was inducted at the age of 20 against his will. Parris "Perry" L'Engle, the only woman Roan ever loved, was never convinced that the car accident that took his life was legitimate, regardless of the evidence to the fact. She's never stopped searching for him. Alone, Perry gave birth to a child Daniel never knew she was carrying. Twenty-five years later, when their son is approached by the same covert agency that tried to recruit Daniel before his disappearance, Perry knows the man she loves isn't dead. As an FBI agent, Perry is determined to find Daniel--the only man who can save their son from the same fate that destroyed both of their lives.

Main Character Overviews:

- ***Daniel Sands*** (always referred to as Daniel to prevent confusion with his son), 20 years old when inducted. Daniel had flirted constantly with every woman around him, whether the woman was attractive or not. He loved to make women feel good. Grandmothers, little girls, beautiful women--everyone loved him. Effortlessly, he made himself irresistible to all females in his path. He was fun-loving. While he'd been restless almost constantly, he'd also been happy. He possessed a seemingly endless supply of energy and the tenacity to draw others into his perpetual excitement about life. Daniel Sands believed in world peace, love making the world going around, being a neighbor to everyone he met and doing good to everyone, including the wicked.

- ***Roan Emory*** (the former Daniel Sands). 45 years old when the story opens and a Network operative, has been trained to be an emotionless, calculating machine, silky-smooth and sensual in his manner. Restless, reckless, he nevertheless never fails to do what he needs to.
- ***Parris "Perry" L'Engle*** (45 years old when the story opens) is a highly respected woman, mother, daughter and FBI agent. Perry has an inextinguishable fire, an ambitious drive to keep plugging on until the answers eluding everyone else come to her through sheer force of will or seduction. Those around her see her as very capable and driven, skilled at her profession. However, as both of her parents are also FBI agents, they believe that if they haven't found an explanation for Daniel's disappearance 25 years ago, then it truly must have been an unfortunate accident. Perhaps, they and her own partner believe, Perry is projecting unrealistic wishes into the situation.

  Perry defines herself by the roles she plays as mother, FBI agent, daughter, lover. When she had Daniel in her life, she was completely satisfied and felt whole. Since his death, she sees herself as only half a person, even with her son, and, as such, there's nothing she wouldn't do to get back the missing piece of herself. Her life has become her son, her work, and searching for the man she lost. She's unwilling to accept that she might never get her life and love back. To Perry, admitting to the car accident is admitting that Daniel really is dead. She's nowhere near ready to do that.

Occupational Skills:

- **Daniel:** Taught microbiology at the university, but his real love was his research into strengthening the human immune system to resist multiple diseases. He'd accumulated a massive body of work and was much touted in the academic field. He was blessed with genius level IQ that had justifiably caught the attention of some of the largest intelligence networks in the world, including NASA and the American government.
- **Roan:** Network operative. He can disappear into thin air, kill with the stealth and precision of an otherworldly being. If he doesn't want to be found, he won't be. He's the most dangerous man in the world. And he wants out or wants it to end.
- **Perry:** Her parents' positive influence led her to follow in their footsteps by becoming an FBI agent. Her mother is the Special Agent in Charge (SAC) of the Minneapolis field office, where her father also is an agent.

Symbolic Element:

- **Roan:** The ability to play elaborate classical pieces on the piano. This balanced his scientific side with a touch of the artistic and lends a romanticism when he realizes. Also, he's a man hard as granite, and he needed softness. As Roan, he owns a grand piano yet never plays it because to do so would resurrect memories of a life stolen from him. The first time he plays it after Perry enters his life again is the signal that the defenses and guards he's constructed for himself are beginning to crumble.
- **Perry:** A love of growing roses, particularly lush, blackish-red blossoms in a hybrid tea rose called Ink Spots. It's in her rose garden that Roan makes his "dead drops" to keep in touch with her after they come together again, and it's this same rose that reunites them in the end.

Secondary Character Overview:

Danny Sands, Perry and Daniel's son (always referred to as Danny to prevent confusion with his father). Engaged to Aimee. Like his father, his research makes him a fanatically workaholic. He's strong, independent, capable, not afraid to face anything in life. He won't hide behind his mother if the recruiter steps beyond request. Danny teaches microbiology at the university, but his real love was his research into strengthening the human immune system to resist multiple diseases. Danny had become interested in the massive body of work his father left behind early on, and he's taken over his father's much touted work in the academic field. Danny is also blessed with genius level IQs that has justifiably caught the attention of some of the largest intelligence networks in the world, including NASA and the American government.

Setting Descriptions:

- **Perry:** Perry lives in a picturesque neighborhood just outside the city. Instead of traffic and sirens at midnight, she hears crickets and the wind's breath. She owns a 1923-era, craftsman style home, surrounded by fragrant woods and the explosively lush, colorful garden she loved babying throughout the year. The interior boasts knotty pine walls stained a warm honey; beamed, twenty-foot ceilings; and expansive rooms filled with plump, oversized chairs, generous tables, and a profusion of pillows and throws that help create the informal coziness she prizes. In the living room is a polished Bosendorfer piano.
- **Roan:** The Network was the most covert organization in the world with branches all over the globe. It was funded by a major technology corporation that designed innovative equipment both for public use--computers, cell and satellite phones, software and the like--and devices to which only the Network had access. The corporation, Expanding Technology Industries--ETI--functioned exactly as a real business did

and was the perfect cover for the Network. Below the ETI skyscraper in Chicago, in an underground bunker deep in the earth was the Network headquarters, inaccessible to anyone without clearance.

The American government sanctioned the organization, but only the highest officials knew about it, including the President and a select committee in the White House, called Oversight. In the half-century the Network had been in existence--formed by the then-President of the United States along with Captain Tom McKee, a career officer and a decorated war hero--it'd had surprisingly few bumps. Tom McKee had been the first Network head. When McKee had been killed unexpectedly, his daughter--who'd also had a lifetime of military training--stepped in. Shannon McKee fills the role of 1st-in-command--head of the Oversight Committee, which acted as liaison in Washington, D.C. between the government and the Network.

Having the unchallenged authority and skill to disable and destroy criminals the way few other law enforcement agencies can, the Network takes over where regular law enforcement leaves off. The organization represents an absolute justice in a world overrun with evil. The price for that justice is high, requiring the life of every man and woman who serves it. For them, there is no life and no love, only duty.

Roan's Conflicts (Internal):

The only way to keep himself sane in this insane place was to shut down his emotions and put everything into his work. Nothing has challenged those safeguards in the twenty-five years since he was inducted. But, after so many years on the edge, he wants out or wants it to end. An operative on the edge, death is the only way to end the pressure, the oppression, the lack of freedom the Network offers him. He'll never be completely free of the Network, especially not to return to the life he had with Perry. They'll never let him go. Having his freedom out in the world would be dangerous for them. Even if they willingly let him go and cut all ties with him, wiped away his memories of them and his years in service, enemies of the Network will see him as collateral. His presence outside could cripple them in a short time. Only legitimate death will free him.

Plot Conflicts (External):

A week before Daniel disappeared, Perry had overheard a voice just outside his office door. Later, Daniel told her that the man refused to give his name or the government organization he worked for, had told Daniel to tell no one anything about the meeting where Daniel had been propositioned to join a covert government organization. Daniel had been promised the moon. The price? His life. He would have to give up everything he knew, even his family. Those he loved. Stopping short of laughing in the man's face, Daniel had turned him down flat. Though Perry had only just completed her FBI training at that time and had accepted a job at the Minneapolis field office, she'd spent a lifetime with two FBI agents. At the time she'd assumed the fact that she came up with absolutely nothing on this supposed government agent was because she didn't have the skills or the clearance to find him. Now, 25 years later, she's discovered that the man is an enigma. She has no idea who he was, and she's never been able to locate him.

On the heels of the strange, hush-hush attempt to recruit Daniel, Perry had come up with endless scenarios about what could have taken place that day. Almost all of those she'd come up with pointed to the fact that Daniel Sands wasn't dead. Yet she's been unable to locate him and solid evidence--however slight--that the only man she's ever loved is still alive. Nevertheless, there are too many strange things about Daniel's death for Perry to let it go. He was on a rural road in the middle of nowhere--there wasn't a house for over a mile. He was over 25 miles from home, in an area where he didn't know anyone. His teaching assistant had confirmed that a call had come in at about 5:30 that day, and Daniel had left immediately after it, looking extremely upset. Perry herself had had a last-minute doctor's appointment. That appointment had confirmed her suspicions for the past few weeks--she was pregnant. The cause of Daniel's accident had never been discovered, but the front end of his car had been badly damaged before it'd blown up. His body hadn't been recovered, but his blood had been found in the smoking hull of his car.

Perry's Conflicts (Internal):

There's a good possibility Perry had never really known Daniel Sands at all and an even better possibility Daniel willingly gave up his life to join this secret government organization. He'd gone along with the faked car accident, surrendered his very blood to make it look authentic. He'd willingly given her up, their love and life together. He'd conceded loss on all of it for the chance to discover more than he could 'ever have believed possible'. As hard as she rebelled against it, there are plenty of reasons Daniel would give up everything. His research had been so important to him. His thirst for knowledge was unbearable even for him. He'd spent his life meeting problems head-on--problems that had been insurmountable for nearly everyone who came before him--and solving them. If the recruiter had given Daniel an utterly compelling, impossible problem to solve and the resources to solve it, Perry can imagine that Daniel would have given up his life as he knew it to discover what had been hidden from him in that life. His confident, almost cocky mind no doubt convinced him he'd return to his original life when he finished. For the first time, he may have met his match and discovered there was no going back.

Roan's Evolving Motivations and Goals:

He believes in nothing, nothing except the missions he's called to do.

Perry's Evolving Motivations and Goals:

Outside Danny's office, she hears voices. One of them is her son's, the other makes her go stock still and cold. She recognizes it as belonging to the recruiter who'd propositioned Daniel 25 years ago. She listens to him give the same recruiting pitch to Danny. Horrified, she vows to protect her son at all cost. But how?

Perry realizes she might be able to find Daniel after all these years, by following this recruiter.

MIDDLE STORY SPARK

Upon following the recruiter, Perry meets the man called Roan Emory...quite possibly Daniel Sands.

Perry's Conflicts (Internal):

She's horrified by the ramifications. This unemotional man who'd held her throat in his powerful hand and promised he'd kill her if she didn't do what he told her to could be the man she'd loved, a man who'd once held her heart completely in his sway. She would have followed him to the ends of the earth just to have him look in her direction. To have him give her that melting smile that made her feel all the love she'd ever need in the world. The grief Perry has never fully allowed herself to feel--because she couldn't accept Daniel was truly dead--comes over her, and she's immobilized and overwhelmed by it. Even if that man is Daniel, she now knows he's truly dead to her.

Perry's Evolving Motivations and Goals:

Perry has to find out the truth and possibly face that Daniel had given up the life he knew voluntarily. He might be aware the organization he works for is trying to recruit his son. He could very well be willing to do anything to see to it personally that his son follows in his footsteps. She has to protect her son, possibly from his own father. She realizes she has to make plans, but she's at a complete loss as to how. Her mother has done her a favor by putting Danny and Aimee in protective custody, but it's a temporary solution. Her son won't live his life, running, living in fear, anyway. Perry now knows that there is no fairness with this organization. If they want Danny, they'll have him, one way or another.

Plot Conflicts (External):

For the past few years, the Network's Alpha Mission had been to bring down the most dangerous terrorist group in the world--

R.E.D. R.E.D. is an invisible, highly militant terrorist group out of Mexico. They're both elusive and vast, spread out all over the world in small groups called remote command centers. R.E.D. is led by a man called 'the Black Pope', a ruthless killer who seems to have God--or the devil--on his side. Roan was to infiltrate and then destroy R.E.D. from the inside out. That's what he's been doing for the past year, but his contact, whom he passes information to, never leads him to the next level within the group. He hasn't gotten anywhere near the Black Pope because the Remote Command Centres (R.C.C.'s) are self-contained. Only the highest figures within the organization have access to him. All the information Roan has passed to his contact has panned out. Roan has also been able to get valuable information from them without his contact knowing. Nevertheless, his contact had gotten suspicious of him not long ago for no accountable reason and pulled out of their deal. Befitting his role as a traitor, Roan has retaliated and the Network has descended on R.E.D., destroying R.C.C.'s one after another with a vengeance. Roan has vowed to take them apart a piece at a time. Roan and his team have just retrieved a briefcase nuclear weapon R.E.D. has developed.

Roan's Conflicts (Internal):

Knowing that Perry married Lincoln Sands, the late Daniel Sands' older brother, less than six months after his death, Roan believes Danny is Linc's son. He'd never had any real choice about joining the Network. Once they'd decided they wanted him, everything had been arranged without his approval, including Parris being out of contact that day so he couldn't verify the car accident he'd been told she'd been in wasn't real. By the time he'd figured that out, it was too late to do anything about it, outside of fighting them and making his training hard on them, making them regret bringing him in against his will. They'd told him Perry betrayed him by being secretly in love with his brother and getting pregnant, and, when she'd married him, Roan had no reason not to believe them. Linc had died of a heart attack a few years ago. Roan had learned to accept his place over the years. He'd even come to relish his job and the fact that no one can equal his skills.

Of late, however, his appreciation has been robbed of him along with his soul. He considers himself dead, more man than machine; if he functions, it's on an instinctive level and the memories are residual past.

Plot Conflict (External):

Roan doesn't know anything about Danny's recruitment. When Perry asks him to help her save their son, and he says he'll do everything in his power to help Danny. Everything in his power might not be enough to save his son from what Roan would easily describe as a fate worse than death

Roan's Evolving Motivations and Goals:

He has to know if Perry ever loved him, or it'd been his brother she loved all along. He goes to her, allows her to know that he is Daniel. He asks her who Danny's father is, and she tells him the truth--Daniel Sands is her son's father, and her son has always known that fact. When he asks Perry why she married Linc, she says she did it because Danny needed a father who would love him almost as much as his real one. She and Linc were never married in the intimate sense of the word. Something breaks loose inside him then. Not feeling--it's how he's existed these past 25 years. Better not to feel anything when he couldn't change his circumstances. Better to control it so it couldn't control him. Now, as he becomes resurrected to the man he once was, he's furious about what the Network took from him, all he could have had if they'd accepted his refusal. In many ways he's coming back to life, yet pieces the Network took from him are missing.

Plot Conflicts (External):

Roan's Network evaluations prove that their best operative is on the edge. He no longer cares if he lives or dies. Time off and relocation won't help. At the time, he's at his peak efficiency and he'll continue to be that way...until something pushes him over the edge completely. And then they won't be able to bring him back. Daniel Sand's son could replace him in time, and that's why they believe his recruitment is vital to the future success of the organization. Even if Roan is able to save their son, he can never save himself.

Perry is fully aware that Roan can never have a regular life, but she's falling in love with this man who is her Daniel and yet is so different. Whatever this organization is, it wants it all. It *takes* it all from those it "employs". Roan can never leave the life they require of him behind to return to the past. He can't have a future. He can't have a family. If her old life hadn't been taken from her, she knows exactly what it would be like now. She and Daniel would have married, they would have had the three children they'd talked about. The only danger to their happiness would have been her job, which carried a degree of risk that she'd accepted and even thrived on. She can't help hating this organization that took all of it away from them. He's given them 25 years--why can't that be enough? But Roan seems unwilling...or unable...to change his life. If they let him go, is he even capable of love anymore?

END STORY SPARK

The current 3rd in Network Command, Head of Operations, Angelo Pluzetti, never wanted to draft Daniel/Roan into service. His predecessor was corrupt had different ideas, just as Angelo now has a conflict about this same thing with the 2nd in Command. He believes an injustice was done with Daniel/Roan and could still be done with the man's son if Danny Sands is also involuntarily inducted into the Network. Behind his superior's backs, Angelo has come up with a plan to give Roan his freedom by convincing Network superiors and operatives, along with their enemies, that the most dangerous man in the world is dead.

Plot Conflicts (External):

R.E.D. is targeting Roan with everything they've got. They've put a bounty on his head with other terrorist groups they work with. They don't care who takes him out, just so someone does.

Inducting Danny involuntarily is a security risk to the Network. Perry's FBI status, along with his grandmother as the FBI director of the Minneapolis field office, make him a containment risk. His family is on the alert. If the Network proceeds now or in a year, they'll suspect, and that could endanger Network anonymity. Besides, Perry and her mother have the skills and resources to find them if they look hard enough. The Network can't risk a breach, especially now that they're so vulnerable because their best operative is on the edge and over a controversial new recruit with a family that will cause them no end of trouble. Perry has already gotten too close to them.

Roan's Conflict (Internal) Resolutions:

As soon as the alpha mission is contained, Roan's superiors plan to relocate him to a retirement facility that, for all intents and purposes, is a prison disguised as paradise. There's no way in or out of the place, no escape. It's the only recourse for operatives since they have more enemies than any other organized justice system in the world. Roan knows he'll never survive in a cage of any kind. His superiors can't simply let him go. Either way, he'll never see Perry or Danny again. Angelo believes that if he and Dr. Celine Hunter, the Network's head of the Medical Department, can convince everyone on the inside and the outside that Roan is dead, it means he's free. Roan isn't so sure.

Angelo's plan for freeing Roan by faking his death and then giving him a whole new, untraceable identity requires outside help. Authenticating Roan's death will be Angelo and Celine's first priority, and only then can they complete his transformation. The only way to give him a new life is not to allow any indication whatsoever that his death isn't genuine--to Network operatives, superiors and enemies. No one on the inside can be involved, but they need someone competent enough to handle his disappearance--someone with training in covert operations. Someone who can aid them in helping Roan disappear while his death is confirmed. Only one person on the outside possessed the skills to help them. Perry. And Roan won't take that risk. If she's seen by anyone, she and Danny will be hunted forever, too.

Perry's Conflict (Internal) Resolutions:

Angelo comes to Perry and tells her briefly about a terrorist organization planning to set off nuclear weapons in ten major cities soon. While preventing this is his organization's first priority, he sees an opportunity to free Roan, whom he'd never had any choice in recruiting. Angelo can't be absent during any phase of the operation. There can be no indication whatsoever that Roan's death isn't genuine--to both their superiors and their enemies. He tells Perry his plan to have Roan taken out of the mission at the last minute. A body will be recovered which will be proved to be his. They need someone on the outside, and Perry has the training to pull it off. #1 will move immediately after the operation to retire Roan. And once he's put out, there'll no way back to the Network or the real world for him. When they confirm when the projected terrorist strike will take place, they'll have to move quickly. She'll have to be ready. This is the last opportunity they'll ever have to get Roan out. Once Roan is in the safe house, she needs to return to her home. If Perry is at home and nothing amiss seems to be happening, then it'll be further conviction to everyone that Roan really is dead. Roan won't be able to come to her right away--possibly not for a year or more--and she won't recognize him immediately either. But, if all goes well, someday they'll be together again and the Network won't suspect a thing.

Perry doesn't know if she can trust the Network or Angelo, but there's no time to do anything but. She wonders if it's worth losing her life and leaving her son without a parent for the chance to have Daniel back, to give Danny the father he so desperately wants.

Perry's Evolving Motivations and Goals:

Maybe it won't be the same, maybe Roan will never love her the way he used to, but it's a risk she believes is worth taking. But what if Roan is too scarred to come back to her when it's safe?

Roan's Evolving Motivations and Goals:

Roan would rather be dead than to put his family at risk. And maybe he should be dead. He hasn't been whole in so long, he isn't sure he can ever be again...not even to be with Perry and to finally get to know his son. He can't have a life, sure can't have *back* what should have been buried twenty-five years ago. Impossible, but he can't fight the knowledge that he's waking from the dead. And, just like the Frankenstein monster, he *wants* to live again. When it's safe and the time is right, he returns as Douglas Lazarus, a man truly risen from the dead, and hands Perry a black rose.

Story Plan Checklist

Title:
I Am Legend, by Richard Matheson

Genre:
Horror

POV Specification:
Robert Neville

Estimated Length of Book/Number of Sparks:
50,000 words/3 story sparks

High-Concept Blurb:

Robert Neville is the last man on Earth. A terrible plague has either killed mankind or transformed them into vampires...and all they want is Robert's blood.

BEGINNING STORY SPARK

For the past eight months, since the plague infected the population--a plague he himself is immune to--Robert has been surviving the only way he can while systematically trying to get rid as many of the vampires (who, along with insects and dust storms, caused the rapid spread of the disease) as he can during daylight. By day, he tries to repair the damage done to his property during the night attacks; he strings together garlic necklaces and places them on all the windows to drive away the creatures; he creates endless wooden stakes to drive into the hearts of the vampires he encounters during his trips for supplies; and he disposes of their bodies in the gigantic fire pit (created by those who initially tried to control the spread of the plague) that always burns in an excavated field. He lives by his watch because as soon as the sun sets, he must be behind the locked doors and boarded windows of his home, where the vampires are drawn, howling, snarling and trying to break through the barriers he's erected to keep them out. They want his blood; they want to make him as they are. He understands little about them beyond that they stay inside by day, avoid garlic, can be killed by a stake through the heart, fear crosses, and dread mirrors. The creatures are white-fanged and powerful, frequently attacking each other because there's no union among them--their need for blood is their only motivation.

Identifying the Main Character: Robert Neville

Character Introductions:

- ***Robert:*** Believing himself to be the last man on earth, he fights to survive when everyone he loves has died or been taken by the plague. With so many things to do, he wonders if he'll get around to figuring out the real problem--how to destroy these things once and for all.

Description (Outside POV):

- ***Robert:*** A tall, blond man born of English-German stock, his features are undistinguished save for a long, determined mouth, and bright blue eyes. His face is gaunt and bearded; he looks older than his thirty-six years.

Description (Self POV):

- ***Robert:*** I'm a man who's had to get used to unnatural things, like the stink of garlic that overwhelms everything from my clothes to the taste of all food to my very flesh. I struggle with trying to convince myself I'm doing the right thing in killing the deadly creatures who, by day, are in an all-but-comatose state and look just like me. I consider myself the "blind-man" type--only accepting the truth a blind man can see when there's no other possibility.

Occupational Skills:

- ***Robert:*** Before the vampires took over, he worked at a plant.

Enhancement/Contrast:

- ***Robert:*** Early in his life, his mother taught him to appreciate music. Now it, and reading, help him fill the terrible void of hours.

Symbolic Element:

- ***Robert:*** None.

Setting Descriptions:

- ***Robert's home:*** His boarded-up house is on Cimarron Street, "proofed" to keep out the vampires. He burned the neighboring houses to prevent the vampires from using them to jump on his roof. He has a giant freezer run by a generator, since there is no electricity anymore, and in what was once his daughter's bedroom is a pantry filled with food. In the backyard, there's a water tank and a hothouse for the garlic he collects.

Character Conflicts (Internal):

His wife, Virginia, and daughter, Kathy, died from the plague. Kathy's body had been thrown in the fire pit. He hadn't allowed them to do that to his wife--he'd tried to bury her, but she came back, and then he had to kill her as he had the others. The face of every child vampire he destroys is Kathy's; the women creatures, Virginia. Virginia is in a crypt, sealed in her casket, in the cemetery, where the creatures can't get at her.

He isn't sure how much longer he can do what he's been doing--little by little trying to reduce their unholy numbers. He wants to die; if only he knew for sure he would be with his wife then.

Evolving Goals and Motivations:

The only sure way to be free of the creatures would be to go out at night, become one of them. The only thing that has prevented him thus far is the possibility that there are others who survived the plague and that they might be looking for their own kind. But how will he ever find them if they're not within a day's drive of his house, which is the only place he's safe at night?

He has no time to slow down and think, because his struggle is never-ending. Nevertheless, the hours of the relentless, nightly attacks are taking their toll on his sense of purpose. He smokes too much and drinks too much. His health is waning and the endless stress is getting to him, preventing him from doing things the way they should be done--the way his father taught him: analytically and scientifically.

Plot Conflicts (External):

Robert discovers that in addition to wooden stakes, sunlight also kills the vampires. He realizes that infrared and ultraviolet rays of the sun do something to the creatures' blood. To test the theory, he drags a second vampire out into the daylight and it dies instantly, just as the first. Realizing he's put off the research he needs to do to find the answer, he rushes toward home only to become aware that he can't be certain the creature really is dead. What if it comes back at sunset? He turns the car around and goes back to get the body to bring home with him. Only then does he look at his watch...and realize that, in his grief remembering his lost family this day, he forgot to wind it...and it's stopped.

Only by tricking the animalistic creatures is he able to return to his home. Repairing the damage over the next few days gives him something to lose his fury in, and then he can begin his investigation. This forces him to remember his last days with his wife and daughter in an effort to find the answers to the plague and the coming of the vampires in the past. He tests several theories but all end in failure. The only thing he's sure of is that having the blood taken from them kills the creatures. With a microscope, he begins testing the blood of a vampire and finally isolates a germ--the cause of vampirism. Sunlight kills the germ. It's too late to cure those who have already been infected, but, if there are others like him, how can he cure them?

MIDDLE STORY SPARK

Robert finds a dog--initially uninfected--roving on his lawn.

Character Conflicts (Internal):

After being completely alone for ten months, after believing that his investigation into how to destroy the vampires is worthless and that he has no reason for staying alive, the possibility of a *life* other than his own, a companion, renews his determination to keep fighting. He's clung to the idea all this time that a human being not infected will come, that he isn't the last person on Earth, and the dog returns to him the ray of hope he's almost lost.

Evolving Goals and Motivations:

The wounded canine is frightened of him after somehow surviving the nightly attacks just as Robert has--by finding a hiding place. Robert wants to heal the dog, get its trust and affection, and he finally succeeds in getting the animal, now infected yet still able to roam in daylight, into his house.

Plot Conflicts (External):

Just a week after he rescues the dog, it dies and leaves him completely alone again.

END STORY SPARK

Three years of survival pass, and Robert meets a young woman--Ruth. Alive. In the daylight.

Character Conflicts (Internal):

Though the possibility of gaining a companion doesn't allow him to leave her and, in desperation, he brings her to his safe house despite her terror, Robert is afraid that she's infected. After all, the dog had been infected and still went about in daylight.

He's never discovered how or why, but he knows now that the germ sets up a symbiosis with the host. The vampire feeds it fresh blood, and the bacteria provides the energy so the creature can get more fresh blood--if indeed there are any more people left to infect. Stakes work to kill the vampire because they allow air into the body. In that environment, the germ becomes virulently parasitic--symbiotic--and eats the host. Treatments don't work because the vampire body can't fight germs and make antibodies at the same time.

The fact that Ruth is awake in daylight and not in a coma like the others confuses him. He shoves garlic under her nose, but she only draws back from the stink and becomes ill. *How can he trust after all the disappointment, all the time alone?* He feels hollow and without feeling, unable to believe anything remarkable can happen in this lost world. If she's infected, he'll have to try to cure her, but he knows eventually she'll die and his life will return to the way it had been before she came. But if she's not infected, if she stays, if they establish a relationship...that possibility is even more terrifying to him. He's afraid to make sacrifices, to accept responsibility for more than himself and, most of all, to give his heart again.

Evolving Goals and Motivations:

Robert asks to check Ruth's blood, and she agrees to allow it in the morning. He tells her he'll try to cure her if she is infected because she's not like the others. He begins to wonder again if others survived and are immune to the plague.

Having Ruth there--alive, destroying his adjustment to the isolation, as well as his sense of security and peace--brings him back from the edge. It's just the two of them together, survivors of a black terror, and they've found each other. And he wants to help her. He'll cure her if she's infected--somehow...or he'll die himself.

Plot Conflict (External) Resolutions:

When Robert tests Ruth's blood in the morning, he discovers she is infected. She slams a wooden mallet down on his head over and over, knocking him unconscious. When he wakes, she's gone, but she's left him a note. She was spying on him, and everything she told him was a lie, save one truth--she had a husband, and Robert killed him. She and others like her are infected, and they want to stay alive now that they're able to live in the sun for short periods. They've found a way to survive--in the form of a pill. With it, the blood feeds the germ and the drug prevents its multiplication. They'll be the new world order, and that means killing the wretched creatures the germ has taken. And there are those, like Robert, who won't allow them to survive, and they must be done away with. But Ruth wants to save him by telling those like her that he's too well armed to attack. Robert must get away and go into the mountains to save himself. Before long, those like Ruth will be too well organized, and she won't be able to stop them from killing him.

Those infected but not overtaken because of the pill come, but Robert has vowed not to fight. He'll surrender because he believes these new humans will allow him to live, and living has become a habit he's become too used to give up easily. But he quickly realizes that's not the case because they fear and hate him for killing their loved ones. He's the abnormal one now, worse than the disease they've come to live with, a black terror that must be destroyed. They shoot him and drag him out into the night, into a world that is theirs, no longer his. He's Robert Neville, the last of the old race, a legend.

Story Plan Checklist

Title:
Harry Potter and the Chamber of Secrets (Year Two)

Genre:
Young Adult Fantasy

POV Specification:
Harry Potter

Estimated Length of Book/Number of Sparks:
85,000 words/5 story sparks

High-Concept Blurb:

All Harry wants is to get back to Hogwarts School for Witchcraft and Wizardry, but he's stuck spending the summer with his only living relatives, the Dursleys. Harry is distressed about not getting any mail from his two best friends, Ron and Hermione. On this twelfth birthday, Harry is visited by the house-elf Dobby, who warns Harry that he'll be in mortal danger if he returns to Hogwarts. Dobby has been intercepting Harry's letters to make it seem like his friends have forgotten him, hoping this will convince Harry not to return to school. A few days later, Ron and his brothers come to rescue Harry from the Dursleys for the remainder of the summer in their father's enchanted, flying Ford Anglia.

In Harry's second year at Hogwarts, he faces an outrageously stuck-up new professor and a spirit who haunts the girls' bathroom. But then the real trouble begins--someone is turning Hogwarts students to stone. Could it be Draco Malfoy, a more poisonous rival than ever? Could it possibly be Hagrid, whose mysterious past is finally told? Or could it be the one everyone at Hogwarts most suspects...Harry Potter himself!

BEGINNING (FIRST) STORY SPARK

Following a pleasant summer together at the Weasley house, Harry, Ron, and Hermione head to Diagon Alley, where Lucius

Malfoy and Arthur Weasley get into a skirmish when Lucius calls Arthur a blood traitor for being a pure-blood (from an entirely magical bloodline) family who associates with non-pure-bloods--"half-bloods" or "Muggle-borns" ("Mudbloods" in the derogatory) with no magical ancestors. With a final remark about the family's poverty--judging by the looks of Ginny's second-hand, battered copy of a schoolbook--Lucius and his son Draco sweep out of the shop.

Later, Harry and the Weasleys arrive at Platform 9 3/4 to take the Hogwarts Express to school. Harry and Ron, the last two to cross over, are unable to enter the barrier between platforms 9 and 10.

Identifying the Main Characters:

Harry Potter, Ron Weasley, and Hermione Granger. *Note that Ron and Hermione--in this book at least; not necessarily in the others in the series--fill the same role, though they're both very well-defined characters with their own distinctive personalities. They are Harry's support and fellow "sleuths". So, for a few of the story spark sequences, Ron and Hermione will be combined, as their conflicts, goals, and motivations are identical. Only the main characters are followed from start to finish in the Story Plan Checklist, with their internal conflicts and goals and motivations. Secondary and minor characters are covered within the story sparks in which they're introduced, along with the villain. For efficiency, I've included outside and self POV descriptions of secondary, minor, and the villain character in the introductions.*

Main Character Introductions:

- ***Harry Potter:*** The twelve-year-old protagonist, Harry is also known as "The Chosen One" and "The Boy Who Lived". The Dark Lord Voldemort killed Harry's parents. A lightning-bolt-shaped scar on his forehead that Harry tries to hide is the result of Voldemort's attempt to murder Harry as a baby with a killing curse. Harry is famous throughout the wizarding world for being the only person to have survived this curse, which brought about Voldemort's first downfall.

Enhancement/Contrast:

Several. One of Harry's best friends, Hermione, is extremely intelligent, but isn't generally a risk-taker (fearing she might be expelled--to her, a fate worse than death), and this enhances Harry's personality. Working together, they usually figure out what's going on and how to fix the problem.

Another enhancement is that Harry has a lot in common with Tom Riddle, who's the villain, which creates an intrigue and conflict within the plot.

In contrast to Harry, who dislikes the fame he's garnered, his other best friend, Ron, longs for recognition.

Another school-mate of Harry's, Draco, serves as a foil, enhancement, and contrast for Harry, also longing for recognition and constantly berating Harry for the fame he doesn't believe Harry deserves.

Symbolic Element:

- ***Harry Potter:*** Harry's lightning-bolt shaped scar serves as both a character- and plot-defining enhancement for reasons mentioned above.
- ***Ron Weasley:*** Sarcastic, passionate, hot-headed, with immense and sometimes surprising wit and optimism, along with a strong tactical ability when it comes to chess. As the sixth of seven siblings, he usually receives little recognition, while Harry's fame almost always puts him at the center of attention, and this brings out Ron's highly ambitious side. Ron wants dearly to be popular and successful.
- ***Hermione Granger:*** Hermione Granger is a Muggle-born (*Muggle* means "non-magic person") witch with dentist parents. She reads vo-

raciously and firmly believes that anything worth knowing about can be learned about in books.

Description (Outside POV):

- ***Harry:*** Harry has a knack for mischief, inquisitiveness, and a certain calculated disregard for the rules. Despite occasional bouts of bad temper and a penchant for risk-taking, he has great courage and a fierce loyalty to all he considers friends.
- ***Ron:*** Ron's suggestions and decisions are often far-fetched, but he also has a rational and calm side--especially in moments of crisis. He's generally loyal, yet lacks much of the magical power Harry possesses.
- ***Hermione:*** Hermione's knowledge and common sense prove valuable in overcoming challenges, and Harry and Ron depend on her. Hermione is brave and loyal to her friends, and she has a fierce political conscience, as evidenced by her disdain for wizards using house-elves as servants.

Description (Self POV):

- ***Harry:*** I'm being raised by the Dursleys, who have no love for me and are deathly afraid of magic. My primary desire is to be with my friends and to keep them safe. My most loyal friends, Ron and Hermione, insist on accompanying me on whatever adventure I undertake. I've also developed close relationships with adults, particularly Rubeus Hagrid and Albus Dumbledore, the headmaster of Hogwarts. The Weasleys have become a family to me, with Mr. and Mrs. Weasley treating me like a son. Similarly, the Weasley siblings treat me as another brother, although the youngest and only girl, Ginny, has a crush on me.
- ***Ron:*** Despite great loyalty to my family, I'm sometimes ashamed of our economic situation, which causes me to feel self-conscious, frustrated, and even resentful,

especially when my rival Draco taunts me for my family's poverty.

- ***Hermione:*** Though I staunchly continue to disapprove of rule-breaking, I knowingly, willingly, and boldly break several school rules in order to discover who's behind the opening of the Chamber of Secrets. Prior to Draco calling me a Mudblood, I've had little if any experience with prejudice against my non-magic parents.

Occupational Skills:

- ***Harry Potter:*** A bright, young but powerful wizard who attends Hogwarts, Harry belongs to Gryffindor house.
- ***Ron:*** A member of Gryffindor, as all the witches and wizards in his family before him, Ron is known for his lack of academic interest and his reliance on fellow second-year Hermione to help him muddle through his studies.
- ***Hermione:*** Also in Gryffindor, Hermione is known as one of the most intelligent students in her year, an achievement that she works hard to maintain.

Secondary and/or Minor Characters:

- ***Ginny Weasley:*** The youngest of seven siblings and the only daughter, Ginny attends Hogwarts for the first time this year and is sorted, to no one's surprise, into the Gryffindor house. Though shy, Ginny rushes to defend Harry when Draco insults him.
- ***Mr. Arthur and Mrs. Molly Weasley:*** The Weasley childrens' parents. An affable, light-hearted man, Arthur allows his wife, Molly, to take the role of authority figure in the family. Arthur works long hours for the Ministry of Magic, in the Misuse of Muggle Artifacts Department. His salary is insufficient to provide for a family of nine. He's obsessed with learning about Muggle customs and inventions, including a Ford Anglia he's enchanted to fly invisibly.

Since they have no magical family, Molly takes Harry and Hermione under her wing and treats them with motherly affection.

- ***Lucius Malfoy:*** Lucius Malfoy is head of a pure-blood wizarding family and suspected to have been a follower of Voldemort during his first reign of terror. Lucius, who's on the Governing Board of Hogwarts, also uses his position in the wizarding world to wield considerable power in the current Ministry of Magic.

Symbolic Element:

Lucius has quite a collection of illegal poisons and Dark Arts objects and artifacts in his house, hidden under the drawing room floor, which he brings to Borgin and Burke's, wanting to sell them in case they're found during a Ministry raid. An item *not* sold at Borgin and Burke's is a small, unassuming book with extraordinary powers: Tom Riddle's diary, entrusted to Lucius by Voldemort shortly before his fall. Lucius intentionally and anonymously passes it off with a battered Transfiguration schoolbook to Ginny Weasley (in an attempt to discredit his bitter enemy Arthur Weasley). This plot leads to the reopening of the Chamber of Secrets.

- ***Draco Malfoy:*** Spoiled by his mother and bullied by the father he worships, Draco is cocky and arrogant. He's Harry's arch enemy at Hogwarts, actively trying to undermine him in any way he can. Draco is in Slytherin, which turns out more Dark witches and wizards than any other house at Hogwarts, and he shares his father's bigotry concerning half-blood or Muggle-born wizards. Draco is constantly frustrated by the attention given to Harry, though his father cautions him not to appear to be Harry's enemy, since everyone in the wizarding world considers him a hero for making the Dark Lord disappear. Following his father's counsel, Draco appears respectable in Hogwarts society but also knows how to advance the cause against Dumbledore, whom Lucius despises. Although Draco often employs bullying tactics (through the use of his thug cronies who follow his every order) to obtain what he wants, he also shows a cunning ability to wield magic to attain his objectives.

- ***Dobby, the house-elf:*** Dobby is a magical creature called a house-elf. Fierce and principled, Dobby adores Harry for his bravery concerning Voldemort and, therefore, will do anything to save his life.

  House-elves are used by wizards as unpaid servants. Most house-elves spend their whole lives serving one family or institution (like Hogwart's); their descendants even carry on their tasks unless they're freed--a state many house-elves view as shameful, as it implies they failed to properly serve. House-elves take pride in their hard work and appear to be happy in their bondage. House-elves must obey their masters, whatever their personal feelings may be. House-elves wear discarded items like pillowcases and tea-towels, rather than conventional clothing. House-elves' masters can free them by giving them an item of clothing. Because of their quiet, subservient natures, some house-elves are abused by their families. Dark wizard families, in particular, make a habit of bullying and mistreating house-elves.

  Unlike most other house-elves, Dobby longs to be free of his servitude to his wizard family--which is revealed to be the Malfoys at the very end. House-elves are unendingly loyal to their human families, so much so that Dobby punishes himself each time he utters a negative remark about his masters.

Symbolic Element:

Dobby's clothing--he wears an old pillowcase, with

rips for arm- and leg-holes--is both character- and plot-defining, as it marks his servitude...and, later, his freedom.

- ***Professor Albus Dumbledore:*** Hogwarts' Headmaster, Dumbledore is considered by many to be the greatest wizard of modern times. He also has the distinction of being the only wizard Lord Voldemort ever feared. Frequently displaying an eccentric sense of humor, Dumbledore retains his whimsical sense even during conflict. A brilliant and wise wizard, he's always patient and calm.

Symbolic Element:

Dumbledore's pet, Fawkes, is both character- and plot-defining. Fawkes is a phoenix--a swan-sized, magical bird with red and gold plumage, and a golden beak and talons. The phoenix has several amazing characteristics: The ability to lift great weight with its tail while in flight; the ability to, in a burst of flames, disappear and reappear at will; the ability to shed tears that have healing properties. The phoenix's most unusual characteristic is that, after its body begins to fail, it dies in a burst of flames, to be reborn momentarily from the ashes. This occurs not only on a phoenix's natural Burning Day, but also if it receives a fatal injury. Given its gentle and loyal nature, it's no surprise that the phoenix will defend someone who shows great loyalty to its master. This powerful creature matches Dumbledore's strengths, and its unique characteristics are important to the latter portion of the plot.

As Headmaster of Hogwarts, Dumbledore holds items that are important to the plot of the book, including:

The Sorting Hat (plot-defining) was originally the pointed wizard's hat of Godric Gryffindor, and was bewitched by all four of the founders of Hogwarts with brains and personality. Its function is to determine which of the four houses--Gryffindor, Hufflepuff, Ravenclaw, or Slytherin--each new student is to be assigned to based on the student's abilities, personality, and aspirations. The hat speaks to the student privately, discussing strengths and weaknesses as it analyzes the mind beneath its brim, before announcing which house the wearer will belong to for the duration of his or her schooling. The Sorting Hat had a difficult time placing Harry, almost putting him in Slytherin before Harry emphatically requested not to be assigned there. The Hat instead placed him in Gryffindor, as it did both his parents before him. The Sorting Hat becomes character-defining when Harry begins to question why the Sorting Hat originally considered putting him in Slytherin.

The Sword of Gryffindor (plot-defining), once owned by Godric Gryffindor, is a goblin-made sword adorned with huge rubies. Only one who is truly a member of the Gryffindor house, one who shows courage in the face of danger, can use the sword. This makes the sword equally character-defining for Harry.

The Sorting Hat and Sword of Gryffindor team up in the latter portion of the book. The Sorting Hat can be used by a true member of the Gryffindor house to conjure the sword from under its brim.

- ***Rubeus Hagrid:*** Hagrid is the Keeper of Keys and Grounds and the gamekeeper at Hogwarts. He was raised by his human (wizard) father; his mother was a giant. As a Hogwarts student, he was a member of the Gryffindor house. When he was orphaned in his second year at the school, Dumbledore looked after him, securing Hagrid's fierce loyalty. Friendly, soft-hearted, and easily driven to tears, Hagrid was the first member of the Hogwarts staff to meet Harry. Harry and his friends frequently discover things by talking to Hagrid, since he has a habit of letting secrets slip.

Symbolic Element:

Hagrid loves animals and magical creatures, particularly those that are unusual or dangerous, and this peculiarity is very character-defining. It's also plot-defining, because Hagrid was expelled during his third year at Hogwarts because of a giant spider he was hiding in the school.

- ***Lord Voldemort/Tom Riddle:*** Tom Marvolo Riddle, a half-blood wizard who later became Lord Voldemort, was raised at a Muggle orphanage. Riddle attended Hogwarts and was sorted into Slytherin house. An extremely handsome and gifted student, he quickly became a staff favorite. He was made a Prefect and eventually the Head Boy, and was even described by Dumbledore as "the most marvelous student ever to pass through Hogwarts." Riddle was a student at Hogwarts at the same time as Hagrid.

- ***Gilderoy Lockhart:*** Lockhart is a celebrity in the wizarding world, having written many books on his fabulous adventures encountering Dark Creatures. A narcissistic, self-obsessed buffoon, his fan base consists mostly of middle-aged women and teenage girls who find him attractive. His honors and awards include Order of Merlin, Third Class; Honorary Member of the Dark Force Defense League; and five-time winner of *Witch Weekly's* Most Charming Smile Award. When Harry arrives at school for his second year, he finds that Lockhart is the new Defense Against the Dark Arts instructor. Lockhart decorates both the classroom and his personal office with smiling portraits of himself. His widely proclaimed secret ambition is to rid the world of evil and market his own line of hair-care products.

Setting Descriptions:

Settings are the charm--and cohesiveness, with characters and plot--in the Harry Potter series. Since there are too many fascinating, magical places to describe, we'll focus on only three (the first two, my personal favorites).

- ***The Burrow:*** The Weasley family lives in a large, ramshackle house, which they call the Burrow, that bursts with the strange and unexpected. Their house, complete with a tumbledown garage, is located to the south of the village of Ottery St. Catchpole. Extra rooms have been added to the house here and there, so it's several stories high and so crooked that it looks like it could only be held up by magic. The red roof has four or five chimneys. A mess of rubber boots and a rusty cauldron are jumbled together around the front door.

  The garden is full of gnomes--knobby, bald-headed creatures that look like potatoes.

  Mr. Weasley has stuffed the shed with various Muggle artifacts that he likes to take apart and enchant just for fun.

  Inside, the kitchen is small and cramped. The clock on the wall has only one hand and no numbers. Instead, it's marked with things like "Time to make tea," and "You're late". A mirror over the kitchen mantelpiece shouts "Tuck your shirt in, scruffy!"

  A narrow passageway leads to an uneven staircase, which zigzags its way up through the house. The paint on the door of Ron's room is peeling. Inside, the ceiling slopes and everything is a violent shade of orange. Nearly every inch of the shabby wallpaper has posters of Ron's favorite Quidditch team. Ron's bedroom is right beneath the ghoul in the attic who's always banging on the pipes and groaning.

- ***Hogwarts School of Witchcraft and Wizardry:*** Silhouetted high on a cliff over a smooth, black, glassy lake stands the many turrets and towers of Hogwarts castle, with its great oak front doors, secret passageways, and ghosts, muttering portraits, and creaking suits of armor.

Across the vegetable patch are the greenhouses, where magical plants are kept. The Gamekeeper's one-room cabin is next to the Forbidden Forest on the grounds.

The Great Hall is a vast chamber with a bewitched ceiling that mirrors the sky outside. The High Table, where the staff sits, is on a raised platform at the front of the Hall and descends to four long tables for the four houses. Innumerable candles hover in midair.

The Caretaker's office is a small room with a single oil lamp hanging from the ceiling. Filing cabinets are stuffed with details of the misdeeds of students.

The Potions professor's office is down a narrow stone staircase and through a cold passageway of the dungeons. The office has shadowy walls lined with shelves of large glass jars, in which all manner of revolting things float.

The secret entrance to the Gryffindor Tower is on the seventh floor hidden behind an oil painting of a very fat woman in a pink silk dress. A password (which frequently changes) is required for entrance into the circular common room. Lopsided tables, squashy armchairs, and a fireplace fill the room. A spiral staircase leads to circular dormitories with high, narrow windows and five four-poster beds hung with red velvet.

A large, extremely ugly stone gargoyle protects the entrance of the Headmaster's office. When the password is uttered, the gargoyle springs to life and hops aside as the wall behind it splits in two. Behind the wall is a spiral staircase that moves smoothly upward like an escalator. At the top of the stone staircase is a gleaming oak door with a brass knocker in the shape of a griffin. The headmaster's office is a large and beautiful circular room with a number of curious silver instruments standing on spindle-legged tables, whirring and emitting puffs of smoke. The walls are covered with portraits of old, snoozing headmasters and headmistresses. The claw-footed desk is enormous, and a high chair stands behind it.

- ***The Chamber of Secrets:*** The Chamber of Secrets within the castle is located in a second-floor girl's bathroom that's out of order. The bathroom is a gloomy, depressing room with worn and poorly-maintained wooden cubicles. The chipped stone sinks form a row under a large cracked and spotted mirror. One of the copper taps (which has never worked) has a tiny snake scratched on the side. When a Parselmouth commands it, the tap glows and spins briefly before the entire sink drops down out of sight to expose a pipe wide enough for a man to slide into. Inside the seemingly endless, slimy, dark hole that twists and turns, more pipes branch off in all directions. Sloping steeply downward, deeper below the school than even the dungeons, the pipe finally levels out, ending on the damp floor of a dark stone tunnel large enough to stand in. From there the tunnel turns and turns. A solid wall appears on which two entwined serpents are carved, their eyes set with great, glinting emeralds. The serpents part when the wall cracks open, the halves sliding smoothly out of sight. At the end of a very long, dimly lit chamber, towering stone pillars entwine with more carved serpents rising to support a ceiling lost in darkness, casting long, black shadows. An odd, greenish gloom fills the place. Level with the last pair of pillars, a statue high as the Chamber itself looms into view, standing against the back wall. A statue of a wizard, ancient and monkey-ish (Salazar Slytherin) with a long thin beard that falls almost to the bottom of sweeping stone robes, stands on two enormous feet on the smooth Chamber floor.

Character Conflict (Internal):

- ***Harry:*** Hogwarts is Harry's home, much more than the Dursleys'. Yet he can't completely ignore Dobby's dire warning not to return to school for his second year. After all, look what happened to him the previous year.
- ***Ron and Hermione:*** Ron and Hermione have been worried sick about Harry all summer, since he hasn't been answering their numerous letters or responding to Ron's repeated invitations for Harry to stay at the Burrow. Their worry is compounded when they learn that Harry received an official warning for using magic in front of Muggles. In desperation, Ron and his older brothers decide to rescue Harry the night of his birthday.

Evolving Goals and Motivations:

- ***Harry:*** Harry assumes the sealed barrier at the train station means he won't be going to school--and the alternative of returning to the Dursleys isn't even an option for him, so he's open to any suggestion at all.
- ***Ron and Hermione:*** Ron can't understand why the magical gateway between Platforms 9 and 10 has sealed itself, barring them from getting on the train. Ron's idea to use his father's flying car to follow the Hogwart's Express train to school very nearly gets them expelled and results in a broken wand for Ron and the enchanted car escaping into the Forbidden Forest. A Howler (a nasty smoking letter that screams at the recipient in the magnified voice of the sender and explodes if not opened immediately) from Ron's mother arrives the next morning, and both Harry and Ron receive detentions. Hermione is disapproving of the means in which the two arrived at school, especially when it's revealed that Arthur is facing an inquiry at work because of the enchanted car.

Plot Conflicts (External):

During his detention with Lockhart (Ron is polishing trophies and Special Awards for Services to the School for Filch), Harry hears a voice inside the walls that the professor doesn't hear. The voice says menacing things about ripping and killing. On Halloween night, Harry again hears the voice, hissing that it's been hungry for so long and that, smelling blood, it's time to rip, tear, and kill.

SECOND STORY SPARK

Following the sound of the menacing voice, Harry, Ron, and Hermione discover writing on the wall of a deserted corridor near a large puddle of water on the floor. The words say, "The Chamber of Secrets has been opened. Enemies of the Heir, beware." Nearby, Mrs. Norris--Hogwarts caretaker Argus Filch's cat--hangs by her tail from the torch bracket. She's been Petrified, a condition that's curable through the use of Mandrake Restorative Draught (which isn't mature yet).

Character Conflicts (Internal):

- ***Harry:*** Harry is accused of Petrifying Filch's cat, the head of Harry's house and the Headmaster defend him. Yet Harry becomes increasingly bothered by the fact that he's been hearing voices when Ron tells him that it's not a good sign to hear such sounds, even in the wizarding world. Something's happening, and he seems to be the chief suspect.
- ***Ron and Hermione:*** Both worry about the voice Harry heard, what the message written on the wall means, Draco's threat "You'll be next, Mudbloods" made at the scene, and the Petrified state of the cat.

Evolving Goals and Motivations:

- ***Harry:*** Harry wonders again why the Sorting Hat seriously considered putting him in Slytherin house. Does he have the potential to be a Dark Wizard? Because Harry was found at the scene of the Petrification, a rumor begins that he's the Heir of Slytherin. He wants to find out the truth about himself.

- ***Ron and Hermione:*** Ron notices that his sister Ginny seems particularly disturbed by the cat's fate, and he attempts to comfort her. Hermione spends a great deal of time reading, trying to find out about the Chamber of Secrets. She asks Professor Binns, the History of Magic teacher, about the Chamber of Secrets, and he tells her that, according to the legend, Salazar Slytherin and Godric Gryffindor argued over whether to allow Muggle-born students into Hogwarts. When Gryffindor apparently won, Slytherin left the school, but not before building the Chamber of Secrets, a secret room constructed to house a monster that would finish his "noble work". Slytherin's true heir would accomplish this by opening the Chamber and releasing the monster to rid the school of non-pure-blood students. Over the centuries, many great witches and wizards searched for the Chamber, but none found it. Eventually, the whole thing was assumed to be purely fiction.
- Harry, Ron, and Hermione revisit the scene of the crime and wonder if the puddle of water came from the bathroom where Moaning Myrtle abides. Moaning Myrtle is a ghost who haunts the second floor girls' lavatory at Hogwarts. True to her nickname, she has a tendency to sob, whine, and wail; therefore, most of the Hogwarts female students avoid her bathroom.

  They also speculate that Draco could be a descendant of the Heir of Slytherin, possibly receiving the key to the Chamber when it was handed down from father to son. Hermione knows a way to find out, too--by brewing up a batch of Polyjuice Potion, a task that will take about a month and will require stealing ingredients from the Potions professor and a bit of "essence" from three Slytherin students they'll temporarily transform into in order to question Malfoy. Hermione doesn't want to break rules, but will if it means protecting Muggle-borns and proving she can perform a complex piece of advanced magic.

Plot Conflicts (External):

At the Quidditch (a wizard sport played on broomsticks) match, a rogue Bludger (a type of ball) chases Harry and breaks his arm, though he does get the Golden Snitch (the most important ball, the capture of which ends the game and usually determines who wins), and Gryffindor is awarded the match. The school nurse heals him, and Harry is forced to spend the night in the hospital wing. Dobby appears and admits that he was the one who sealed the barrier at Platform 9 3/4 and jinxed the bludger--all to keep Harry from returning to Hogwarts and to save him now that the Chamber of Secrets has been reopened. Since Harry isn't Muggle-born (both of his parents were wizards), he's believed himself safe, but now he has to wonder. Dobby tells him that dark deeds are planned at Hogwarts.

THIRD STORY SPARK

A young first-year Gryffindor is Petrified with a camera in front of his face. When Draco conjures a snake during a dueling match, Harry learns that he's a Parselmouth (a speaker of snake language, Parseltongue, not a common wizard gift). Rumors again fly, suggesting that Harry's responsible for the attacks on students, a rumor that's strengthened when Harry stumbles upon the Petrified forms of a fellow second-year student (whom Harry called the snake off when he instinctively spoke Parseltongue to it), and Nearly Headless Nick, the Gryffindor house ghost.

Character Conflicts (Internal):

- ***Harry:*** Reminded of the time he accidentally set a boa constrictor on his cousin at the zoo, Harry is shocked to learn he was speaking a different language. How can he speak a language without knowing he can speak it? Apparently everyone who witnessed the Draco incident thought he was trying to egg the snake on, not call it off. Harry knows so little about his parents, he can't be sure of anything concerning his heritage, but the Sorting Hat tried to put him in Slytherin. Now he wonders if it's because he's related to Salazar Slytherin.

- ***Ron and Hermione:*** Ron and Hermione don't have the answers to Harry's questions, but being able to talk to snakes was what Salazar Slytherin was famous for--it's why the symbol of Slytherin House is a serpent. Now the whole school thinks Harry is his grandson many times removed...and, therefore, Slytherin's heir.

Evolving Goals and Motivations:

- ***Harry:*** Harry is hauled before Dumbledore, where he questions the Sorting Hat about its attempt to place him in Slytherin, but is too afraid to hear the answer. He witnesses Dumbledore's pet, the phoenix, burning, and learns Dumbledore doesn't believe Harry is behind the attacks. When Dumbledore shrewdly asks Harry if there's anything he wants to tell him, Harry thinks about the Polyjuice Potion he and his friends have been cooking up and his dread about being somehow connected with Salazar Slytherin...but he can't get himself to divulge any of it.
- ***Ron and Hermione:*** On Christmas Day, the Polyjuice Potion is ready. Two of Draco's thug friends in Slytherin house are drugged, so that strands of their hair can be stolen and added to the potion. After Ron and Harry drink the potion and are transformed into Draco's thugs, they question Draco. Unfortunately, he says he has nothing to do with the Chamber of Secrets, and his father won't tell him what happened the last time it was opened, since it'll look suspicious if he knows too much. All he knows is that, the last time it was opened, a Muggle-born student died.

Plot Conflicts (External):

Moaning Myrtle's bathroom floods, and, in the pool of water, Harry finds a small, shabby book with the name T.M. Riddle on the first page. From his detention at the start of the year, Ron remembers that T.M. Riddle received an award for special services to the school fifty years ago. Apparently, fifty years ago, someone threw this book belonging to Riddle in the girls' lavatory. Harry also shows the otherwise empty book to Hermione, and they begin an avid search to verify the true owner.

FOURTH STORY SPARK

On Valentine's Day evening, Harry learns the secret of the diary, goes back in time, and discovers--or so he believes--that it was Hagrid who last opened the Chamber of Secrets after being caught in possession of a dangerous acromantula--a vicious, gigantic black spider with a poisonous bite and the ability to talk--named Aragog. Only after a young girl attending Hogwarts was killed did staff and Ministry officials come to the conclusion that Aragog was Slytherin's monster, kept inside the Chamber until it was released and commanded to kill. A few months later, after a period of no attacks at the school, Harry returns to his dormitory after Quidditch practice to find his belongings ransacked and the diary gone. Soon after, Harry hears the voice in the walls again, and Hermione and another girl are attacked and Petrified. A small, circular mirror is found on the floor near them. It's likely the school will close unless the culprit behind the attacks is found.

Character Conflicts (Internal):

- ***Harry:*** Horrified about what's happened to Hermione, Harry is also afraid that the school will close and he'll end up in an orphanage.
- ***Ron:*** Ron is also distressed about Hermione. Without her to guide them, he isn't sure they'll be able to figure out who's behind all the attacks, let alone stop them.

Evolving Goals and Motivations:

- ***Harry:*** Though he finds the idea that Hagrid could be responsible for all these attacks unimaginable, Harry determines that he and Ron will confront Hagrid.

While in Hagrid's hut, they overhear a conversation between Hagrid, Dumbledore, Cornelius Fudge (the Minister of Magic), and Lucius. The school governors are worried, and, feeling the pressure, Fudge has Hagrid taken away to Azkaban, the wizarding prison. Before he goes, Hagrid drops a hint to Harry and Ron about following the spiders. Dumbledore is suspended as Headmaster of Hogwarts, since he's been unable to stop all these attacks. Dumbledore, too, drops the hints to Harry and Ron that he'll only truly leave the school when none there are loyal to him, and help will always be given to those who ask for it.

- ***Ron:*** Acting on Hagrid's hint isn't easy for Ron, who harbors a great fear of spiders. Against his own better judgment, he goes along with Harry into the Forbidden Forest to find Aragog. Aragog reveals that it was believed Hagrid opened the Chamber of Secrets to free the spider and command it to kill a young girl in a school bathroom, but what really lives in the castle is an ancient creature spiders fear above all others.

Plot Conflicts (External):

Ginny is terrified about something, and she tries to tell Harry and Ron, but she's interrupted when her eldest brother appears. While visiting Hermione, Harry finds a scrap of paper in her petrified hand. It's torn from a library book and contains information about basilisks. Spiders, including acromantulas like Aragog, fear the basilisk above all other living things, and they flee before it. Scrawled on the scrap in Hermione's handwriting is the word "pipes". This is one of the words Harry has been hearing whispered from within the walls of the castle--but why can only *he* can hear it? Slytherin's monster is a basilisk--and its master speaks Parseltongue to command it to move through the pipes. The basilisk kills people by looking them in the eye. No one has died because no one looked the creature straight in the eye. The cat saw it reflected in the pool of water on the floor. The first year student saw it through his camera lens. Harry's classmate saw it through Nearly Headless Nick. Hermione warned the Ravenclaw Petrified to use a mirror to look around corners before proceeding, but her advice clearly wasn't heeded. Harry realizes that it was Moaning Myrtle who died the last time the Chamber of Secrets was opened, and that the entrance to the Chamber must be in Moaning Myrtle's bathroom.

END (FIFTH) STORY SPARK

The Heir of Slytherin has left another message right underneath the first one: "Her skeleton will lie in the Chamber forever." A student has been taken by the monster into the Chamber--Ginny Weasley. Since he's been boasting that he's known all along where the entrance to the Chamber of Secrets is located, Lockhart is called upon to find her.

Character Conflicts (Internal):

- ***Harry:*** Ginny's capture is the worst horror Harry has ever felt.
- ***Ron:*** Ron essentially collapses when he hears about his sister. He realizes that Ginny must have known something about the Chamber of Secrets--she was thwarted in telling them. Is she even alive?

Evolving Goals and Motivations:

- ***Harry:*** Wanting to do something, anything, he suggests they help Lockhart get into the Chamber. Lockhart is packing, preparing to flee the scene rather than rescue Ginny. He admits he didn't really do all the things his books claim he did. He took other wizard's stories, then put a Memory Charm on them so they wouldn't remember what he'd done. Harry and Ron force him to accompany them to Moaning Myrtle's bathroom. They ask Moaning Myrtle how she died, and she tells them she saw the glowing eyes of the basilisk. When she tells them where she saw them, they find and unlock the secret of the entrance. The reason no one could find the Chamber is because only a Parselmouth can open it.

Slytherin spoke Parseltongue and, a thousand years later, his heir, Tom Riddle, also had the skill. Now Harry is able to open it through his own, similar ability.

- ***Ron:*** Once in the Chamber, Lockhart attempts escape once more by using Ron's broken wand, but it backfires and blocks the tunnel, separating Harry from the two of them. Harry has no choice but to go on alone to save Ginny.

External Plot Conflict Resolutions:

Harry finds the unconscious Ginny and meets Tom Riddle, a memory preserved in a diary for fifty years. Back when he was in school, Riddle spent several years discovering how to open the Chamber and, when he did, he unleashed the monster on the school. Riddle could control the basilisk, since it's a great serpent, and can be commanded with Parseltongue. There were a number of attacks on Muggle-born students, ending in the death of Myrtle. However, Riddle's plan backfired on him. When the girl died, the headmaster decided to close the school. Riddle came from a Muggle orphanage, and therefore would have to return to it. In order to prevent the school from closing, Riddle framed Hagrid for the crime of opening the Chamber. Hagrid was expelled and Hogwart's remained open. Dumbledore alone saw through Riddle, though he could never prove anything. Riddle's had Ginny in his power through the diary, which Lucius dropped secretly into her cauldron at the bookstore before school started. She opened her heart and spilled all her secrets to an invisible stranger. Riddle grew stronger on a diet of her deepest fears and darkest secrets, which emptied her, while he poured a little of his soul back into her--too much. The exchange was enough to let Riddle leave the pages of the diary. Unknowingly, Ginny opened the Chamber of Secrets and set the Serpent of Slytherin on the Muggle-born students. When she realized the diary was controlling her, she grew afraid and tried to dispose of it. Harry was the one who picked it up--the very one Riddle wanted to meet. Riddle is Lord Voldemort, brought back by Ginny's helpless and ignorant use of the diary.

When Riddle proclaims himself to be the greatest sorcerer in the world, Harry disputes the boast by saying Dumbledore is the greatest wizard alive. At that moment, Fawkes the phoenix arrives with the Sorting Hat. Inside is the Sword of Gryffindor. Riddle calls the basilisk to kill Harry, but Fawkes intervenes by blinding the serpent. Harry uses the Sword of Gryffindor to kill the basilisk. In the process, one of the creature's fangs drives into Harry's arm. Fawkes tends the injury with healing tears, then drops Riddle's diary into Harry's lap. Harry plunges the basilisk fang into the diary, destroying the memory and substance of Riddle.

Ginny revives, and Fawkes carries her, Harry, Ron, and Lockhart to safety. Dobby is revealed to be the Malfoy house-elf, and Harry tricks Lucius into freeing him from servitude when Harry puts a sock into the destroyed diary and hands it to Lucius. Lucius callously and carelessly shoves the diary off on his abused servant Dobby, thereby releasing him from bondage.

Dumbledore is reinstated as the Headmaster of Hogwarts and assures Harry that the reason he was put in Gryffindor house is because he *chose* to be put there. Only a true Gryffindor could pull the sword out of the Sorting Hat. Voldemort must have transferred some of his powers to Harry when he tried to kill him...which is why Harry can speak Parseltongue.

The Mandrake potion is finally ready, and those Petrified are brought back, including Hermione. Hagrid is released from Azkaban. Ginny is perfectly happy now, and Draco is sullen and resentful.

After a full school term, Harry returns to the Muggle world for another summer with the Dursleys.

Story Plan Checklist

Title:
The Friday Night Knitting Club, by Kate Jacobs

Genre:
Mainstream Literary Fiction

POV Specifications:
Georgia Walker, Peri Gayle, Anita Lowenstein, Darwin Chiu, K.C. Silverman, Lucie Brennan, and Cat Phillips

Estimated Length of Book/Number of Sparks:
At least 100,000 words/3 story sparks

High-Concept Blurb:

Once a week, seven women with an interest in knitting meet in a New York City yarn shop to share their lives...

The owner of the Walker and Daughter shop, Georgia juggles the store and her young daughter, Dakota. She eagerly looks forward to her Friday Night Knitting Club. The man who broke Georgia's heart re-enters her life in hopes of connecting with his daughter. That's when the unthinkable happens, and the knitting club becomes a sisterhood.

BEGINNING STORY SPARK

Walker and Daughter has become something of a mecca for knitters of all skill levels and dispositions. What begins as a disorganized Friday night gathering of Georgia's most loyal customers turns into a regular meeting of minds and hearts, as each woman discovers there's much more to be found here than tips on knitting technique. These women gather once a week to work on their latest projects and to chat--and occasionally to clash--about love, life, and everything else.

When the knitting club first forms, Georgia makes it clear that everyone has to knit...but not everyone has to use yarn (i.e., everyone has stories to share to knit their friendships). Entrepreneurs, single moms, and a seventy-something undergoing a sexual reawakening--the women of the knitting club are hardly traditional, although a highly traditional woman's craft brings them together each Friday.

Just when business is really looking up, the Georgia's long-forgotten nemesis--the father of Georgia's daughter--suddenly resurfaces. James is a successful architect in a major Manhattan firm. He dumped Georgia just before she found out she was pregnant because he "just wasn't into exclusivity". His reappearance causes Georgia's orderly world to fall to pieces. Soon enough, she learns that she isn't the only Friday Night Knitting Club member who sees it as the only constant in her life--and her saving grace.

Identifying the Main Characters: Georgia, Peri, Anita, Darwin, K.C., Lucie, and Cat

Combined Character Introductions, Descriptions *(just Outside for efficiency)***, and Occupational Skills:**

Many of the main characters in this book have very sparsely fleshed out character introductions, descriptions, and even occupational skills. Naturally, I can only use what I found in the book, and, in some cases, there wasn't much to find. For that reason, it made more sense to combine all of these areas into one section for all the main characters.

- ***Georgia:*** A single mom in her late thirties, an entrepreneur, and a knitwear designer, Georgia has her hands full juggling the demands of running her yarn store with the challenges of raising her twelve-year-old daughter, Dakota, who also loves to knit and bake for the knitting club. Georgia is a listener, not a sharer, and oversensitive to boot. Her entire adult life has been centered around work and her daughter for so long that she feels awkward with women her own age until the knitting club forms and eases her loneliness. She longs to take Dakota to Scotland, where the grandmother who taught her to knit still lives.
- ***Peri:*** Georgia's employee, who works at the shop by

day and goes to school by night. She's a pre-law student turned knitted handbag designer, and she's always up on the latest fashion trends.

- ***Anita:*** The wealthy, unpaid employee who encouraged Georgia to use her gift of knitting to make a life for herself, this silver-haired uptown widower is a talented knitter who takes on the informal role of teacher to the knitting group. With her sons grown, married, and moved away, her family has become Georgia and Dakota and the knitting club gals.
- ***Darwin:*** A struggling, all-business grad student in a long-distance marriage who doesn't actually know how to knit, yet is a keen observer. When she is in search of a dissertation topic for her doctorate in women's studies, the knitting club becomes her primary resource for thesis research. She finds the thought of living up to traditional expectations makes her want to scream herself hoarse. She sees knitting as a throwback that holds modern women back...at first.
- ***K.C.:*** In her late forties, Georgia's longtime friend and an out-of-work editor looking for inspiration, K.C. is a born-and-bred New Yorker always full of energy; brash outside with a surprisingly soft center. She's a master at starting new knitting projects, but not so expert at finishing them. Nevertheless, she always seems to land on her feet and isn't one to get stuck in a rut.
- ***Lucie:*** A single, freelance producer. Lucie is a superfast knitter who loves to make cardigans and pullovers for friends, family, and herself. Lucie is a trooper who keeps trudging along in life but might never get to the front line. She decides to make a series of knitting videos that capture the essence of the shop and the fun of knitting together.
- ***Cat:*** Georgia's former high school friend, Cat occasionally attends meetings--though she refuses to use her own hands to knit. Cat is the typical bored trophy housewife with money to burn. Cat hires Georgia to

make her knitwear designs.

Enhancement/Contrast:

The book is sectioned with knitting steps and advice, which mirror and enhance the state of the knitting club member friendships:

- ***Gathering:*** Choosing and gathering wool is likened to choosing and gathering friends who, though so very different, help create and hold pieces of the soul.
- ***Casting on:*** The knitting process begins with a leap of faith and is likened to friendships being knitted by simply starting something.
- ***Doing the gauge:*** Making a practice piece in knitting is likened to measuring yourself against expectations and making adjustments in creating friendships.
- ***Knit and purl:*** The fundamental stitches in knitting are likened to what friends show the world in contrast to what's kept inside.
- ***Mastering a complicated stitch:*** In knitting, a pattern begins to take shape, a reward for perseverance, likened to developing friendships and seeing how far they can go.
- ***Ripping it out:*** Taking out stitching in knitting is likened to forgiving in relationships.
- ***Starting again:*** A project left unfinished in knitting, one that has a secret hope that keeps the knitter holding on to it, is compared to friendships that are held on to.
- ***Binding off:*** In knitting, eventually a garment has to exist on its own, supporting itself, but the stitches must be done so they can be pulled off the needle without the garment coming apart. Friendships are knitted in the same way.
- ***Sewing it all together:*** In knitting, garments are done in sections, then blocked to get out wrinkles that prevent it from having a smooth, finished look. In relationships, friends are made in sections before coming together to iron out problems.

- ***Wearing what you've made:*** Putting on something you've knitted to celebrate the hard work and love involved in its creation is likened to celebrating the friends you've made and infused with your love.

Symbolic Element: None

Setting Descriptions:

- ***Walker and Daughter:*** The coziest knitting shop in New York City. Located above busy Broadway, the shop offers all knitting essentials including the widest arrange of premium yarns in the city. A sandwich board displays the hours of the shop at the top of the stair landing. The shop, and the apartment Georgia and Dakota live in, are above Marty's deli.

Character Conflicts (Internal):

Throughout the middle and end story sparks of this Story Plan Checklist, I'd like very much to provide more than what's given in the various sections, since some items may seem more like events, or even goals, than conflicts, but, again, the book didn't provide the answers--I can't even speculate. The Friday Night Knitting Club *doesn't follow the standard rules about these things, but don't get confused by this. Keep in mind what you've learned about internal conflicts and goals and motivations throughout this reference. Oddly enough, most of the characters mentioned in the book (even minor ones I haven't included) were given point-of-view scenes at one time or another, yet some of these POV characters didn't have fully fleshed out internal monologues throughout each story spark.*

- ***Georgia:*** Georgia has a history of being burned by the people closest to her. Cat's decision to attend Dartmouth meant breaking a pact of friendship, and James abandoned her for another woman. He didn't just break her heart, though--she holds him responsible for stealing her ability to trust as well. She doesn't understand why he's suddenly back. Though he's wired money into a custodial account he set up for Dakota, he hasn't pursued a role in his daughter's life all these years. Unfortunately, his presence also forces Georgia to realize how much she'd liked James, how she built her life around him. Now he's back and he's everywhere--in her shop, with her daughter, and in her thoughts.

- ***Peri:*** Knowing her parents want her to take a law career path, Peri has thus far kept her design ambitions to herself. She considers her job at the knitting shop her toe in the fashion world. She hopes to land a big account at Barneys and have her bags featured on *Oprah*.
- ***Anita:*** Anita hasn't let go of her husband, yet she's lonely and wants to fall in love again.
- ***Darwin:*** She's married to the perfect man, but then the universe tipped its hand and Dan got into med school at NYU and Darwin got into a top women's-history program at Rutgers. When he finished school, his residency ended up being in Los Angeles while Darwin is still fighting her way through her dissertation. Their mature, long-distance relationship isn't going the way either of them planned.
- ***K.C.:*** Nearly broke, K.C. doesn't have a clue what to do now that she's been laid off. She's too expensive for her old position, yet too mature for potential employers to risk hiring her for a lower position, because they believe she'll bail for something better at the first opportunity.
- ***Lucie:*** After learning that love could smother a person, that men wanted too much of her time and more of her soul, she's decided she doesn't mind being independent. Lucie's decision to become pregnant without telling the man she conceives with flies in the face of social convention and her mother's expectations, to say nothing of her Catholic upbringing. But having a baby is at the top of her list of things she wants to do, and she's ready to make it happen on her own before her

body is too old.

- ***Cat:*** Uneasily wishes to renew her former bond with Georgia. Cat considers that her life became sidetracked with lust and love with her now-husband Adam and the life he offered her. Now she sees that he doesn't care about her--long ago, he stopped thinking of her as something separate from him. Cat is jealous because Georgia is independent and lives by her own rules, yet she regrets her treacherous treatment of her best friend in the past.

Evolving Goals and Motivations:

- ***Georgia:*** She knows James wants something, but she doesn't know what. She makes it clear how the getting to-know-Dakota situation will work because she's calling all the shots. Deep down, she's terrified he's going to make a power play for Dakota's affection...maybe even for custody.
- ***Peri:*** Despite working hard toward her goals, Peri isn't enjoying herself. She's lonely and hasn't learned how to get to know herself or understand her conflicting emotions and insecurities. She makes a deal with K.C.--she'll tutor her in exchange for a meeting with a cousin of K.C.'s who's a buyer for Bloomingdale's.
- ***Anita:*** When Georgia's landlord--Marty, the owner of the deli--asks Anita out, she's thrown but believes she's ready to begin a new relationship.
- ***Darwin:*** Darwin has a problem with the outdated idea of knitting; however, after spending time with these women, she decides to write her thesis about the positive impact of knitting in the lives of modern women rather than criticize it as a "throwback" that prevents women from focusing their energy on professional success. Besides, the knitting club is the only place she has to go. A one-night stand throws her into conflict, making her think she'll lose her husband. Darwin's husband grows distant in contacting her--does he sus-

pect her infidelity?

- ***K.C.:*** K.C. decides to give up bad knitting for a more noble pursuit--she's going to take the Law School Admission Test.
- ***Lucie:*** Though her baby will be well loved by herself, Lucie hasn't spoken to her family in a year and she longs to go home to her mother. But she's not ready to risk her family's reaction.
- ***Cat:*** In an effort to mend fences with Georgia, Cat commissions her to make a one-of-a-kind, designer knit dress. The dress she asks Georgia to make for her is her excuse to spend time with her, and she's willing to pay any amount to have her old friend's attention. She plans to wear the dress to the Guggenheim, then dump her husband in front of his friends, family, and colleagues--and her plan goes off without a hitch when she serves him divorce papers. But then she crashes, believing herself to be all alone with no one to turn to and nowhere to go unless she's willing to make a stand and find her own way in the world. After she tells her husband she wants a divorce, she talks to Georgia about their past. Cat wants her and Georgia to be friends like they used to be--real friends. Georgia agrees.

Plot Conflicts (External):

Georgia kisses James and begins to fall into the ease of his presence. But then he announces his plan to take Dakota away for a weekend to meet his parents in Baltimore, and she wonders where things will go from there. Plus, James doesn't think to ask her first, nor to invite her along, leaving her to play the bad guy with her daughter.

MIDDLE STORY SPARK

Georgia can't find her daughter--all she finds is a note in her room in Dakota's handwriting: "GONE TO BALTIMORE." James hasn't seen Dakota--when Georgia nixed the idea of taking her to

Baltimore, he gave it up. But he joins Georgia's quest to find her--and they do find her at Penn Station. Dakota insists that she ran away to see her family; to know where she comes from. If she needs to know her roots, Georgia will show her herself. She'll take Dakota on a trip to meet her grandmother in Scotland.

Character Conflicts (Internal):

- ***Georgia:*** Georgia aches to reconnect with her daughter, spend some time with her, before James comes between them. But when she reads the letters that he sent to her right after he initially left her--letters she hadn't let herself read before--she's tormented to realize that he'd always regretted his actions and wanted to be with Georgia and their child. She's spent years nursing resentment of him, yet he'd cared even then. She knows in her heart that sometimes people just don't get things right, and then you're left to decide how you're going to react to what they offer because you can't make them change. Somehow she has to forgive the unforgivable.
- ***Peri:*** K.C.'s cousin at Bloomingdale's buys fifty of Peri's bags, and life is good.
- ***Anita:*** She's in love with Marty--at her age! She worries what everyone will think.
- ***Darwin:*** She admits to Lucie that she had a miscarriage a year ago and couldn't talk to her husband about it. Being around Lucie and her impending baby has made her feel better.
- ***K.C.:*** A little terrified about what's she's decided to do by becoming a lawyer, she worries who would ever want to hire someone her age.
- ***Lucie:*** Lucie asks Darwin to be her labor coach. The bigger she gets, the more she realizes she hasn't thought her plan out well. She's afraid of all the things she hadn't allowed herself to think about when she made her decision.
- ***Cat:*** Cat tells herself she shouldn't miss Adam. She hat-

ed him for years. So why does she long for him now? At the very least, she expected him to make a play to win her back, and the fact that he isn't doing so stings. Adam's settlement is simple: A considerable sum of money and an apartment up to five million dollars on her agreement to waive alimony rights.

Evolving Goals and Motivations:

- ***Georgia:*** Georgia makes amends with the past and takes James back because she loves him simply and completely.
- ***Peri:*** Peri enlists all her friends to help her fill the handbag order from Bloomingdale's to make her dream happen.
- ***Anita:*** Anita is ready to take the next step in her relationship with Marty, and a trip to gynecologist is in order. Georgia agrees to go with her support, but is also talked into having her own exam, considering her age.
- ***Darwin:*** Darwin decides she, who barely knows how to knit, is going to make a sweater.
- ***K.C.:*** With a little encouragement from her friends, K.C. continues to study hard for the LSAT.
- ***Lucie:*** Lucie finds she needs the support of friends more and more as her pregnancy progresses.
- ***Cat:*** Cat is learning, but it's not easy to get beyond the past. Life is nothing like she imagined it would be now that she's left Adam, and she finds herself terrified in some ways. Yet she believes her old friend Georgia can teach her how to have it all, like she does. Georgia tells her she needs to be her own safety and security, and that life is what you make it. Cat knows she needs to follow that advice--easier said than done. And she needs to find out what she's meant to do in life. The trip to Scotland is the same one she and Georgia always said they'd take together after college, so she decides to go with Georgia and Dakota.

Plot Conflicts (External):

Georgia and James talk about moving in together...and marrying. With Dakota, they're a family. Life is good.

END STORY SPARK

Georgia is diagnosed with cancer--a malignant tumor in her ovary.

Character Conflicts (Internal):

- ***Georgia:*** When James brings up moving in together again, she puts him off because she's not ready to face the reality of her illness. In essence she's pushing away the two who matter the most to her because she can't bear for them to see her weak. It's one thing to lean on Anita and the other women in the knitting circle, but she doesn't want James and Dakota to see her as anything but strong and in charge. She even wonders if that's part of why people like her--that she's always so capable, confident, and certain. She worries whether she'll live.
- ***Peri:*** Peri isn't sure how to juggle her job and the yarn store and filling orders for her handbags.
- ***Anita:*** Anita puts aside her own devastation to help Georgia--finding doctors, taking care of her, providing a quick hug or a pep talk. If they do enough research, find answers, they can change the course of this thing.
- ***Darwin:*** Unable to stand her shame another minute, Darwin talks to Dan, admits she never wanted the baby she miscarried--she fears she lost it because she wished it so. But when she confesses she cheated on him, he hangs up.
- ***K.C.:*** K.C. is oblivious to all that's going on around her as she crams with Peri for her upcoming test, but she is getting cold feet about it.
- ***Lucie:*** Lucie finds herself in need of advice--from Georgia--on having a baby solo. Her pregnancy has also made her consider her spiritual needs. Though she's

always believed in God, now, with her pregnancy, she's thinking about maybe returning to the church and getting her baby baptized.
- ***Cat:*** Cat has been worried how she'll take care of herself after the divorce is final. Finding out Georgia has cancer dissolves everything but the needs of her best friend. Forgoing her own concerns for a better life on her own, she tells Adam she'll sign the divorce papers without a fight if he gets Georgia in to see the top doctor immediately. She's willing to pay any price to save Georgia. She wants to repay Georgia, not out of guilt, but for the faith Georgia had had in her all along.

Evolving Goals and Motivations:

- ***Georgia:*** Georgia encourages James to take Dakota for a weekend to Baltimore to visit his family to help them bond in case something happens to her. He knows something is wrong, but he agrees. While they're gone, Georgia confides in the Friday Night Knitting Club about her illness, and they rally around her. It feels good and right that she shares with them how her body's betraying her. She needed to reach out, open her heart, and share her pain. They're there for her--they truly and genuinely care for her. And, after her surgery, when she's home and recovering, her knitting club presents her with an afghan they knitted together--beautiful because it's made with love.
- ***Peri:*** Peri spends most of her free time and working hours on her bag line, which has become a front-window item at Bloomingdale's.
- ***Anita:*** Anita decides to move in with Marty and asks Cat, who's been sleeping at Georgia's, to be a house-sitter.
- ***Darwin:*** Darwin is almost finished with her sweater for Dan. To finish it, she has to put all the pieces together--what knitters call "making up". She sends the finished sweater to Dan.

- ***K.C.:*** K.C. gets her results on the LSAT back and she passed with flying colors. Now she's going all the way--Columbia Law or bust.
- ***Lucie:*** Lucie e-mails her mother about her pregnancy...but her mother only checks if someone calls to tell her to do so. And she's completed the how-to knitting videos. The group plans to invite the public to an official "premiere" of the finished product.
- ***Cat:*** Cat has finally decided what she wants to do with her life. She spent her junior year in Italy for her art history degree. Her fantasy was becoming a curator dealing with antiquities. Georgia encourages her to hang up her shingle in Manhattan.

Plot Conflict (External) Resolutions:

Georgia dies, and James transitions into becoming a full-time parent to Dakota as he mourns.

Peri keeps the yarn store open, making room for her purses.

Anita gives Dakota the first sweater she commissioned Georgia to make and the journal in which her mother put all her knitting secrets.

Darwin starts her thesis, and Dan appears in the ill-fitting sweater, forgives her and takes her back.

K.C. begins law school in the fall.

Lucie goes into labor just as Georgia collapses from an obstructed bowel. She has a baby girl with her mother at her side. Lucie's documentary is aired at the Friday Night Knitting club. She plans a new cut of the documentary to submit to the Tribeca Film Festival.

Taking everything she learned from her dear friend to become the woman she's always wanted to be--that Georgia always believed she *could* be--Cat opens her antiques shop in a little town within commuting distance of Manhattan.

APPENDIX E
Story Plan Checklist Exercises

INTRODUCTION

In this section of the book, I'm going to present three story sparks (beginning, middle, and end) to you. For each spark, you'll perform exercises to come up with Story Plan Checklist essays for each area on the worksheet. By doing this, you'll flex your story-building muscles. Work from the beginning spark. If an entire story becomes very clear to you with that spark, or if you already have story sparks that are more cohesive than the suggestions, feel free to use yours. (And bravo!) Otherwise, use the sparks I suggest and build from there.

But don't forget: Your goal in using the Story Plan Checklist is to come up with *cohesive* ideas for character, setting, and plot, so you won't just be brainstorming random ideas and putting them together. You *must* make each of the items on your Story Plan Checklist cohesive. Your character(s) must be in an occupation that fits the beginning story spark. The external and internal conflicts must fit together in the strongest ways possible. You must find organic ways to link them. In other words, in each area, build on what you've done before in such a way that everything fuses.

Also, remember what I said in chapter two--you're free to mix up the elements on the Story Plan Checklist. (For the purpose of completing these exercises, though, follow the most logical order--the one provided in the blank Story Plan Checklist found in Appendix B.)

Each exercise will include instructions, plus cohesiveness tips for the beginning items on the checklist, which will apply to middle and end sections as well. Additionally, I'll include a bonus at the end of this appendix to show you possible cohesive elements for the story spark examples you'll use in the pages to follow.

Good luck!

EXERCISE 1: BEGINNING STORY SPARK

Writer, this story spark is rife with possibilities. Regardless of your genre, you should be able to brainstorm unique and intriguing scenarios to fit this spark. You're ready to begin on the next page. Feel free to revise this beginning spark in any way you choose.

Beginning Story Spark

As an eight-year-old child, the main character was kidnapped and held captive in the woods for a period of ten days until he or she was rescued. When your story opens, this main character is an adult (twenty-eight years old), and he or she has just heard the devastating news that another eight-year-old child has been kidnapped.

EXERCISE 2: BASIC STORY INFORMATION

Write down something basic to get you started.

Title:

Genre(s):

POV Specification:

High-Concept Blurb:

Estimated Length of Book/Number of Sparks:

EXERCISE 3: MAIN CHARACTER IDENTIFICATION AND CHARACTER INTRODUCTIONS

Now we come to the external monologues section. If you need some help coming up with ideas for this section, you might try using a character sheet you like to help you.

Once you've got some ideas rolling, put the basic information below. To identify the POV characters, simply state their full names. Under character introductions, your goal is to identify in general terms who the characters are when the story opens. If you need help, turn back to Layer II and review the examples from Death on the Nile, *or read through the other Story Plan Checklist examples included in Appendix C. Also, remember that you can identify secondary characters and villains in both sections if they're important enough to play a significant role in the story.*

Identifying the Main Character(s):

Character Introductions:
First Character:
Second Character:
Third Character:

EXERCISE 4: CHARACTER DESCRIPTION (OUTSIDE AND SELF POVS)

Building on the beginning story spark, blend in character descriptions. Remember, these are not physical descriptions, like you'd include in a basic character sketch. Instead, these are essays on how other people see the main character(s) and how each one sees himself. Flip back to Layer II and review the examples from Death on the Nile, *or read through the other Story Plan Checklist examples included in Appendix C. Feel free to include secondary characters and villains in both sections.*

Cohesiveness Tip: Any character type--vulnerable, jaded, or otherwise--would work well in the scenario suggested in the beginning story spark, so the trick is to make whatever character type you decide on blend with the rest of the items in the Story Plan Checklist, or to find an intriguing contrast. Remember, to be cohesive is not to be predictable!

Description (Outside POV):
First Character:

Second Character:

Third Character:

Description (Self POV):

First Character:

Second Character:

Third Character:

EXERCISE 5: OCCUPATIONAL SKILLS

Building on the beginning story spark, blend in the occupational skills of your main character(s). Remember, your character's job must match the situation he is facing in the beginning story spark. For examples, flip back to Layer II or look at Appendix C. Generally, you wouldn't need to include secondary characters and villains in these sections, but do so if you feel it's necessary.

Cohesiveness Tip: Any main character who doesn't have an occupation that suits his internal conflicts and plot conflicts can't be truly cohesive, nor will readers sympathize with (and love) him. But that doesn't mean that a character's occupation has to be predictable. For instance, for the beginning story spark presented here, the most obvious occupation for the main character would be that of a cop. But you can turn that plot on its ear if the main character is a priest or pastor, or even a reformed criminal. Both of these suggestions are completely cohesive with the internal conflicts and plot conflicts. In real life, you can find lawyers who are predictably ruthless and greedy. You can just as easily find doctors and nurses who don't really care about patients. Even these stereotypes usually have families who love them. Just remember, fiction isn't always like reality.

Occupational Skills:
First Character:

Second Character:

Third Character:

EXERCISE 6: ENHANCEMENT/CONTRAST AND SYMBOLIC ELEMENT

Building on the beginning story spark, blend in the enhancement/contrast for your main character(s), then add a symbolic element for each that is character- or plot-defining, or both. But note that you don't need either an enhancement/contrast or a symbolic element--include these only if they fit the plot and characters. Remember, enhancement is a subtle, balanced, or extreme element that complements a character's established traits. A contrast, which can also be subtle, balanced, or extreme, is an element in opposition to a character's established traits.

If you decide to include a symbolic element, remember that it must be something that defines a character, defines the situation he's in, or both. Whether it's tangible or intangible, the symbolic element should enhance and/or contrast, thereby developing the character and plot in deeper ways. Cohesion with what you've done previously is a must! If you need more help with this section, return to Layer II, or look at Appendix C. Generally, you wouldn't need to include secondary characters and villains in these sections, but do so if you feel it's necessary.

Cohesiveness Tip: Consider your characters in the scenario suggested in the beginning story spark. Whatever type you've decided on will help you choose whether they need an enhancement or contrast. A balanced character will probably only need something (or someone) to better define his character or the plot. If a character has any quality to an extreme, he'll need a corresponding opposite quality. A hard character will need softness. Someone uptight will need something or someone that mellows. Remember, too, that these enhancements and contrasts should blend well with the character's occupational skills (though they don't necessary have to *match*).

Enhancement/Contrast:
First Character:

Second Character:

Third Character:

Symbolic Element:
First Character:

Second Character:

Third Character:

EXERCISE 7: SETTING DESCRIPTIONS

Building on the beginning story spark, blend in your settings in such a way that they're cohesive with your characters and plots. Make them larger than life--settings readers will want to return to in the future in other books (even if you don't write a series). Generally, you don't need to include secondary characters and villains in these sections, but do so if you feel it's necessary. For examples, see Layer II, or study Appendix C.

Cohesiveness Tip: Think carefully about your setting--there are lots of details to consider. For instance, if the main character lived in a small town and was held in the woods at the edge of town, would it make more sense for him as an adult to get away from a small town and move to a big city, where there aren't so many trees? If you intend the main character to save the child who's been kidnapped in the current story, does it make more sense for him to know the town well in order to find the child? If so, perhaps he shouldn't move. The latest missing child could be kidnapped not in the main character's childhood home town, but in his current town, should he have relocated--you choose which works best for your story.

Setting Descriptions:
First Character:

Second Character:

Third Character:

EXERCISE 8: CHARACTER INTERNAL CONFLICTS

We've reached the internal monologues section of the checklist. Building on the beginning story spark, blend in your characters' internal conflicts in such a way that they're cohesive with your settings and plots, and that they intrinsically increase the tension and suspense. Internal monologues are free-form essays that deep-delve into a character's internal conflicts. You're building a story from the inside out with these. They must be cohesive with external conflicts, as they work together to form a complete story. Again, keep in mind that you don't need to include secondary characters and villains in these sections, but do so if you feel it's necessary. For examples, see Layer II or Appendix C.

Cohesiveness Tip: The scenario that may be most effective in this situation is the obvious one (and maybe that's the best reason you should find something different here but equally cohesive): The main character has never truly gotten over what happened to him as a child. (You'll have to decide whether what happened to him included mental, verbal, physical, or sexual abuse and torture.) While he might hide it and not really face that fact himself, it's clearly his internal conflict. The possibilities are endless, but those possibilities should be cohesive with his internal conflicts and the plot conflicts.

Character Conflicts (Internal):
First Character:

Second Character:

Third Character:

EXERCISE 9: EVOLVING MOTIVATIONS AND GOALS

Building on the beginning story spark, blend in your characters' evolving goals and motivations. Give them reasons and incentives to keep fighting. For examples, see Layer II or Appendix C.

Cohesiveness Tip: Characters succeed because they rise above their fears, and this requires goals and motivations that are cohesive with the characters you've equipped for this task. For a character to succeed, you must set the stage *from the beginning* for the particular skills your main character uses in rescue, escape, defeat, and villain-battling (in whatever way makes sense in light of the character you've created--intellect to intellect, strength to strength, etc.). Don't try to pull a fast one by expecting the reader to believe, for instance, that a man who can barely get out of bed in the morning and who is afraid of his own shadow can suddenly knock down walls and take on an armed man with nothing more than a rubber band and a rock. Remember, when David fought Goliath, he'd already killed a lion with his bare hands.

Evolving Goals and Motivations:
First Character:

Second Character:

Third Character:

EXERCISE 10: EXTERNAL PLOT CONFLICTS

Now blend in your external plot conflicts in such a way that they're cohesive with your characters and settings, and intrinsically increase the tension and suspense. For examples, see Layer II or Appendix C.

Cohesiveness Tip: Putting twists into each story spark is a sure-fire way to turn a suspenseful story into a nail-biting one. Ask yourself, *In light of the rest of my story and the cohesiveness I must provide, what's the most shocking thing I could have happen at this point? What is the reader absolutely not expecting?* This twist must be set up properly from the very beginning of the book to make it believable. And resolutions must fit perfectly with every angle this twist presents.

Plot Conflicts (External):

EXERCISE 11: MIDDLE STORY SPARK

Writer, this second story spark is rife with new possibilities. However, if you prefer to make up your own because it's more cohesive or simply fits your previous structure better, feel free. Otherwise, get started on the next step.

Middle Story Spark

The eight-year-old child who was kidnapped still hasn't been found. Your main character is kidnapped and held captive. His or her kidnapper seems familiar.

EXERCISE 12: CHARACTER INTERNAL CONFLICTS

Building on the middle story spark, blend in your characters' internal conflicts in such a way that they're cohesive with your settings and plots, and intrinsically increase the tension and suspense the beginning story spark set off. For examples, see Layer II, or Appendix C.

Character Conflicts (Internal):
First Character:

Second Character:

Third Character:

EXERCISE 13: EVOLVING MOTIVATIONS AND GOALS

Building on your middle story spark, blend in your characters' evolving goals and motivations. For examples, Layer II or Appendix C.

Evolving Goals and Motivations:
First Character:

Second Character:

Third Character:

EXERCISE 14: EXTERNAL PLOT CONFLICTS

Blend in your external plot conflicts in such a way that they're cohesive with your characters and settings, and that they intrinsically increase the tension and suspense the beginning story spark set off. For examples, see Layer II or Appendix C.

Plot Conflicts (External):

EXERCISE 15: END STORY SPARK

Writer, this final story spark is rife with new possibilities that should cohesively merge with all that you've built into this story previously. However, keep in mind that all story threads must be tied up in this final section of the book, and resolutions must be logical, based on what you've set up in the beginning and middle of the story. For that reason, the final spark should enlighten (though it should also enliven in the process!). Include how each conflict is tied up and resolved. If you prefer to come up with your own spark, feel free. Otherwise, jump in!

End Story Spark

Your main character recognizes his or her captor...and suddenly nothing--and everything--makes sense.

EXERCISE 16: CHARACTER INTERNAL CONFLICTS

Building on the end story spark, blend in your characters' internal conflicts in such a way that they're cohesive with your settings and plots, and that they increase the tension and suspense the middle story spark set off. Include in these areas how you'll resolve any lingering internal-conflict loose ends. For examples, see Layer II or Appendix C.

Character Conflicts (Internal):
First Character:

Second Character:

Third Character:

EXERCISE 17: EVOLVING MOTIVATIONS AND GOALS

Blend in your characters' evolving goals and motivations. Include in these areas how you'll resolve any loose ends related to character goals and motivations. For examples, see Layer II or Appendix C.

Evolving Goals and Motivations:
First Character:

Second Character:

Third Character:

EXERCISE 18: EXTERNAL PLOT CONFLICT RESOLUTIONS

Blend in your external plot conflicts in such a way that they're cohesive with your characters and settings, and that they resolve the tension and suspense the beginning and middle story sparks set off. Be specific about how external-plot loose ends are tied up with satisfying resolutions. For examples, see Layer II or Appendix C.

Plot Conflict (External) Resolutions:

SUGGESTIONS FOR MAKING YOUR STORY PLAN CHECKLIST ITEMS COHESIVE

These are the most obvious scenarios that could be developed in response to the story sparks introduced in the exercises, but remember to always generate the unexpected in your readers. Discombobulate them within the confines of logic, satisfactory resolutions, and cohesion. Also note: To cut down on the number of "he or she" references here, all references below are to "he", though of course I mean "he or she" in every case.

Beginning Story Spark:

As an eight-year-old child, your main character was kidnapped and held captive in the woods for a period of ten days until he was rescued. When your story opens, the main character is an adult (twenty-eight years old) and he has just heard the devastating news that another eight-year-old child has been kidnapped.

Cohesive Main Character Introductions:

Though you can include a minor romance in any genre, if you're writing a story with a romance element, a cohesive heroine for your main character might be his partner on the job, someone who knows what he's been through (like his therapist), or someone from the past (a childhood neighbor who's come back to town, one he either confided in or who simply knew what happened to him).

Cohesive Occupational Skills:

In any genre you can think of (contemporary, historical, science fiction, fantasy, futuristic, time-travel), a law enforcement occupation would blend wonderfully with this scenario. Any type of military, spy, or secret agent profession would also work. A position within the justice system would match well. Any type of therapist works. If your imagination takes you beyond these suggestions, bravo!

Cohesive Enhancement/Contrast:

In the scenario above, you could easily have a character who, jaded from his experience as a child, is now a cop ruthless in his pursuit of capturing criminals. His soft contrast could be that he counsels children who have been kidnapped.

Alternately, you may have a vulnerable character who's never really gotten over his own experience. His "enhancement" might be a self-destructive vice he falls into whenever he feels the world is too dark and claustrophobic, such as sex (with the work partner, therapist, or childhood acquaintance he may otherwise turn away) or alcohol. Or maybe he feels insanely safe in a dark and claustrophobic world now, and this is what sets off destructive vices.

Cohesive Symbolic Element:

Your main character's symbol in the scenario above could be any number of tangible or intangible items, such as a rock or object he used to try to escape or held for comfort when he was held captive as a child.

It could work very well to make his symbol tangible, too--perhaps he carries a gun (or takes along something else that makes him feel safe--a dog?) at all times now.

He might have a scar or other disability or disfigurement caused in the course of his captivity.

Or, intangibly, his symbolic element might be singing a certain song or type of song when he's afraid or overwhelmed--the same one he sang when he tried to block out his fear as a kidnapped child.

Or he might physically walk away whenever anything heavy happens. He simply can't face conflict because of his experiences.

Cohesive Setting Descriptions:

In terms of your main character's setting, would it be more likely that he stayed in the town where his own kidnapping took place, or that he moved long ago? *What* about the town he lives in now should either contrast or enhance his internal conflicts and the plot you're about to unveil?

Now let's narrow the setting and consider his home--think about the elements you've already created. If you have a character who's running from the past, in which he was held captive in a claustrophobically tiny, dark room, he'd probably live in a big house with lots of windows, possibly no curtains. A house that he can't stand to have dark--and he may even leave the lights on when he goes out so he doesn't have to come home to darkness. He may have taken all the doors off the closets, etc. if he was held in a closet, or even blocked all the doors to the basement. In a romance, his love interest's abode might be too dark and closed-in for him to remain there comfortably.

On the other hand, if it's more cohesive with what you've built previously, maybe he's gotten to the point that his experience has so twisted him that he prefers darkness and closed-in quarters. In a romance, his love interest's abode might be too open and bright for his tastes.

Cohesive Character Internal Conflicts:

Since it's obvious that his childhood trauma is his internal conflict, let's explore the possibilities in this. If he's romantically involved with his work partner, his therapist, or childhood neighbor, he may be forced to face his own demons and may rebel for part of the story if he's jaded and unwilling to accept his vulnerability.

Does he avoid the woods at every turn (even for a simple walk)?

Maybe he even hides the fact that he was kidnapped as a child because of the fame he inadvertently received after his rescue, possibly going to the extent of changing his name.

And what of the child who's just been kidnapped? The main character remembers poignantly what happened to him when he was kidnapped. If this child isn't rescued soon, the same things might happen to this innocent child.

Cohesive Evolving Goals and Motivations:

In the scenario presented, the main character may start the story refusing to get involved, refusing to put himself in the position of remembering what he went through. He may even search and present valid arguments about why he can't become involved in this, and your beginning may focus on these--and his unending torment in voluntarily (and both justifiably and selfishly) removing himself from this situation.

Cohesive External Plot Conflicts:

The external plot conflict in the scenario presented is the parallel between the kidnapping of a young child in the present and the kidnapping of the main character in the past. You may expand this to make the kidnappings a serial scenario in which each instance includes many elements that are similar to what the main character faced in his kidnapping.

Your character can be a cop investigating, or a civilian called in because of his past, but either angle will organically produce both internal character and plot conflicts.

Middle Story Spark:

The eight-year-old child who was kidnapped still hasn't been found. Your main character is kidnapped and held captive. His or her kidnapper seems familiar.

Cohesive Character Internal Conflicts:

The main character could experience flashbacks or nightmares about his kidnapping, and, during these, he feels as though he should know who kidnapped him. The face and name eludes him through the beginning and middle of the book. He may see glimpses in his mind--vague and unformed. Or maybe he remembers a voice or a gesture. Something along these lines desperately needs to be set up from the get-go of the story (in flashbacks, nightmares, or hazy memories that the main character allows only in snatches), and should be cohesive with the other elements.

While originally the main character may not be able to go beyond his own past trauma, the internal conflict involves a child in trouble *now*. He may wish to, but he can't sit back idly--this fact will drive him nearly to the edge of his sanity. He doesn't want to return (mentally or physically, or both) to the place that caused him so much horror. It's the horror that haunts him even now that causes his internal conflicts, years after he was rescued. But your character may experience physical or mental "pieces" of that horror (which could be an injury caused during the kidnapping, or mental images that traumatize him), in a sense implying that he's never really escaped in all this time. Ultimately, he has to accept there is no choice for him. He has to get involved.

Cohesive Evolving Goals and Motivations:

Based on the main character's internal and external conflicts, he'll have no choice but to "evolve" his original goals and motivations into more proactive ones. Whatever his occupation, he'll no doubt put himself on the case, and ruthlessly and actively pursue the kidnapper in any possible scenario you can think up.

Going back to where his own kidnapping took place could set off several things: a traumatic reliving of the past, which gives him both sympathy and drive for the recently kidnapped child; and the return of his captor, who again kidnaps him (per our middle story spark). Presumably but not necessarily, this person is also the one who kidnapped the child and is currently holding him in the same place as the main character.

Cohesive External Plot Conflicts:

Internal character conflict and plot conflict will build throughout the final two sections of the book to include other conflicts that stem from the story sparks. The middle spark set off a new conflict--the main character is kidnapped as an adult (as we said, this could be by the same kidnapper as when he was a child, the same kidnapper who took the child in the current situation, both, or neither).

The plot conflict suggested is that the main character believes he knows who the kidnapper is, but he may rebel against the idea either because he doesn't have enough facts or because he knows this person and trusts him. Figuring out the identity of the kidnapper will give him the (hopefully shocking!) answers he needs. And possibly the means to escape and/or rescue the eight-year-old.

End Story Spark:

Your main character recognizes his captor...and suddenly nothing--and everything--makes sense.

Cohesive Character Internal Conflicts:

While reassuring the child held captive with him, bonding with him, the character may be experiencing a newfound sense of control in the situation--a control he didn't have as a child. He's now in the position of being the therapist he needed all those years after he was rescued--he alone can help this child! Whether or not the control lasts or comes in spurts depending on what the kidnapper does, the main character is working through his past trauma by being proactive in whatever scenarios you come up with for him to deal with.

Cohesive Evolving Goals and Motivations:

The only way for the main character to succeed is to rise above his fears. This drive produces organic goals and motivations. Rescuing the eight-year-old child is the main character's most important goal. He's going to save this child--or die trying.

In later portions of the book, if he believes this kidnapper is the same one who held him captive, his evolving goals and motivations will include discovering who this person is and going after him--whether that means escaping or setting some sort of trap.

We talked about downtime and the black moment in Layer II. Keep in mind that this is the place you'll be including both. The main character may put his all into an escape attempt, only to have it fail. Perhaps his failure almost brings about the death of himself or the child he's trying to rescue. This is his downtime--he's lost all hope. But then the black moment--the worst thing that could possibly happen--arrives, and the showdown begins. He'll find a way to win, whatever the cost, and this time nothing can stop him...although the villain will definitely give him a challenge.

Cohesive External Plot Conflict Resolutions:

With the middle and end story sparks, finding the means to save the child will be pivotal, along with determining how the identity of the kidnapper can help or hinder the rescue.

Remember, this is the very best place to put in a wonderful twist. You could give the main character a trusted ally who's come into the story multiple times. You've set this ally up as someone the main character trusts implicitly--leading the reader to do the same. Now is the time to unveil the truth: How foolish to have trusted this madman who'd seemed so normal before. If the twist is set up properly, the reader will remember the times he had doubts, or when the evidence of just this was right before his eyes, yet he never saw it any more than the main character did.

Resolutions come in logical sequence as the main character battles the ally, saves the child, and, of course, resolves his own internal conflicts.

***

Cohesion of elements reigns throughout this Story Plan Checklist and should produce a story that will blow your reader away.

APPENDIX F
Editing and Polishing Exercises

In the following six editing and polishing exercises, I've taken passages from my novel *Dead Drop* and rewritten them with all the classic blunders of lazy, passive, and (perhaps amusingly) poor writing. Below each exercise, you'll find the published version. Review Layer III to refresh yourself on tips, then edit and polish the paragraphs to follow.

Good luck!

EXERCISE 1

She nodded, joining her fists in front of her mouth and wishing Daniel's brother Linc was here with her. She had married him shortly after Daniel had disappeared, as, at the time, the reasons to do so had all made sense. Linc was always sensible. Linc always knew just what to do in a crisis. She had relied heavily on his strength, although they had not lived together in a way that was typical of other married couples. She wondered what she would do if she eventually found out that this organization was not a white hat one. She wondered why else they would presume to take away everything a recruit knew and cared about.

- - - - - - - - -

She nodded, joining her fists in front of her mouth, wishing Daniel's brother Linc was here. She'd married him shortly after Daniel's disappearance, for reasons that had all made sense at the time. Linc was always sensible, always knew what to do in a crisis. She'd relied on his strength, though she hadn't lived together with him in a way typical of other married couples.

What if this organization isn't a white hat one? Why else would they presume to take away everything a recruit knows and cares about?

EXERCISE 2

Surprising Perry, her petite, lovely mother smiled, raising one dark, elegant eyebrow. "I could not tell you that if I did know, Parris. But I can say emphatically that it is risky to interfere with such an organization."

Perry demanded out loud whether her mother was blatantly implying that she should just stand by and let this organization that may or may not be evil steal her son from her, the way they had the man she loved twenty five years and to this very day.

Her mother's shrewd instincts picked up on what Perry hadn't intended to admit out loud. Somehow her mother realized that she still loved Daniel as much as she ever had all those years ago. She lifted Perry's hand and held it comfortingly in her lap. She pointed out that Perry didn't know for certain that Daniel had been stolen by the organization attempting to recruit Danny now. That, from all appearances, Daniel Sands had died in a freak car accident. His blood was found at the scene. Despite this coincidence, there was no clear evidence to disclaim that theory. She then squeezed Perry's hand and told her the very thing she did not want to hear: That she could not go on living in denial. Such a state could never be considered healthy.

- - - - - - - - -

Surprising Perry, her mother smiled, raising one dark, elegant eyebrow. "I couldn't tell you if I did know, Parris. But I can say emphatically that it's risky to interfere with such an organization."

"Are you saying I should just stand by and let them steal my son from me, the way they did the man I love?"

Her mother's shrewd instincts picked up on what Perry hadn't intended to admit out loud--that she still loved Daniel as much as she ever had. She lifted Perry's hand and held it in her lap. "Sweetheart, you don't know that Daniel was 'stolen' by them. From all appearances, he died in a freak car accident. His blood was found at the scene. Despite this coincidence, there's no evidence to disclaim that theory. You can't go on living in denial, Parris. It's simply not healthy."

EXERCISE 3

During the agonizingly slow passage of hours in which Roan knew that Perry was nearby, close enough for him to touch, he was watching her. Watching her had been utter torment for him. The past was most certainly gone, gone like a tumbleweed in the wind. So why could he not get the bittersweet memories out of his too-full head now? He recalled almost too sharply the softness of her peach-colored, fragrant skin; how his rough cheek felt cradled against her smooth forehead, her silken hair, through the mocking hours of the dark night--a blessed dream world with her sweet body completely enveloped in his strong, loving arms. How they had slept so tangled up with each other, separating them would have divided them body and soul. They were yin and yang. They were male and perfect female. They were devil and angel, his mind mocked as cruelly as a sword thrust ruthlessly through his heart.

- - - - - - - - -

The slow passage of hours, knowing Perry was nearby--watching her--had been utter torment for him. The past was gone. So why couldn't he get the memories out of his head now? He recalled almost too sharply the softness of her skin. How his rough cheek felt cradled against her peach-soft forehead, her silken hair, through the hours of the night. A blessed dream world with her completely enveloped in his arms. How they'd slept so tangled up with each other. Yin and yang. Male and perfect female. *Devil and angel.*

EXERCISE 4

Roan shrugged uncaringly. "When I'm, like, *dead* and buried six feet under, dude, I ain't gonna *be* concerned with no half-assed *escape*."

"Dude, ya've served too long and too loyal for our head honchos to *cancel* ya with a red-hot bullet, like ya *dissed* us, man. That rumor...yeah, dude, ya know the one...the one that keeps newborn baby recruits believin' there *is* no retirement in here without a red-hot bullet. But you, man, *ya* know better. McKee and I've never agreed on what to do 'bout you, dude, any more than I ever agreed with what Jameson did when he brought ya in against yer will."

"Does McKee, like, *know* ya didn't agree with my recruitment, dude?" Roan asked wryly.

"Yeah, man, but it was *outta* her hands then, just like it was yours truly's. It's too late to turn back now, dude. Ya know we can't simply *let ya go*. And, like, sendin' ya off to retirement...well, that kinda thing, dude, it causes problems for both you and yours truly."

- - - - - - - - -

Roan shrugged. "When I'm dead, I won't be concerned with escape."

"You've served too long and too loyally for us to cancel you with a bullet, Roan. That rumor keeps young recruits believing there *is* no retirement in here without a bullet, but you know better. McKee and I have never agreed on what to do about you, any more than I ever agreed with what Jameson did when he brought you in against your will."

"Does McKee know you didn't agree with my recruitment?" Roan asked wryly.

"Yes, but it was out of her hands then, just like it was out of mine. It's too late to turn back now. You know we can't simply let you go, Roan, and sending you off to retirement...causes problems for both you and me."

EXERCISE 5

It went against her every instinct to agree, but, as soon as she did, he slid out of the car and disappeared into the woods surrounding the park while she questioned what she'd done and whether all this was worth the chance of having a not-whole Daniel back; of giving her son the father he still wanted and needed desperately. She knew their lives wouldn't be the same, wouldn't be the "happily ever after" life she'd imagined as a young girl, and Roan might never even love her, might not stay with her or become a father to Danny, and so her grief might never end--yet she had to risk it; if there was any chance at all for Roan to be free, she had to save him.

- - - - - - - - -

It went against her every instinct to agree. As soon as she did, he slid out of the car and disappeared into the woods surrounding the park.

What had she done? Was all this worth the chance of having a not-whole Daniel back? Of giving her son the father he still wanted and needed desperately? She knew their lives wouldn't be the same, wouldn't be the "happily ever after" life she'd imagined as a young girl. Roan might never even love her, might not stay with her or become a father to Danny. Her grief might never end. Yet she had to risk it. If there was any chance at all for Roan to be free, she had to save him.

EXERCISE 6

Perry went to hide behind the structure she had emerged from a moment earlier. She fully expected it when Roan came bursting after her. She reached for the ski mask she was wearing.

Roan began swearing when she pulled it off, but she turned his attention to the body on the ground by pointing to it. The first time she had seen it, she had gagged. The man was the same height and weight as Roan was, with the same hair color and skin tone he had. If not for how badly damaged this body was, she might have thought he was a twin of Roan's.

Unfortunately, Samuel Crawford had told her more than she had wanted to know about the carefully preserved body of an operative who had recently been killed in the line of duty. An explosion had left him nearly in pieces. Fingerprints could not be matched to the body. Crawford had said a colleague of his would be performing the autopsy and would, at that time, plant samples from Roan's own body on the decoy, along with the transponder he had had implanted in him when he was first inducted. This transponder apparently had a unique signature that his superiors would use to identify it as belonging to Roan. How Samuel had managed to "fix" the transponder so his superiors would recognize its signal as Roan's own signature, she could not even begin to guess.

- - - - - - - - -

Perry darted behind the structure she'd emerged from a moment earlier. She fully expected it when Roan burst after her. She reached for the ski mask she wore.

Roan swore when she pulled it off, but she pointed to the body on the ground. The first time she'd seen it, she'd gagged. The man was the same height and weight as Roan, with the same hair color and skin tone. If not for how badly damaged this body was, he might have been Roan's twin.

Unfortunately, Samuel Crawford had told her more than she'd wanted to know about the carefully preserved body of an operative who'd recently been killed in the line of duty. An explosion had left him nearly in pieces. No fingerprints could be matched to the body. Crawford had said a colleague of his would be performing the autopsy and would plant samples from Roan's own body on the decoy, along with his unique-signature, implanted transponder. How they'd fix the transponder, she didn't know.

APPENDIX G
Sample Submission Elements

Sample 1: The Query Letter
Sample 2: The Synopsis
Sample 3: The Partial

The Query Letter

Karen Wiesner
PO Box 0
City, State, and Zip
000-000-0000
E-mail Address
https://karenwiesner.weebly.com/

Jane Doe, Senior Editor
Best Fiction Publishing
100 E. Best St.
New York, NY 00000

January 1, 2014

Dear Ms. Doe:

After being approached by a recruiter, a man is unwillingly inducted into a covert government organization. Daniel Sands was inducted at the age of 20 against his will. Parris "Perry" L'Engle, the only woman Roan ever loved, was never convinced that the car accident that took his life was legitimate, regardless of the evidence to the fact. She's never stopped searching for him. Alone, Perry gave birth to a child Daniel never knew she was carrying. Twenty-five years later, when their son is approached by the same covert agency that tried to recruit Daniel before his disappearance, Perry knows the man she loves isn't dead. As an FBI agent, Perry is determined to find Daniel--the only man who can save their son from the same fate that destroyed both of their lives.

Dead Drop, Book 4 of the Incognito Series, an action/adventure romantic suspense novel, is complete and is approximately 60,000 words in length. Please find enclosed a brief synopsis of *Dead Drop,* as well as a partial of the manuscript.

Karen Wiesner is an accomplished author with 105 books published in the past 16 years, which have been nominated for and/or won 128 awards, and has 40 more titles under contract. My books cover such genres as women's fiction, romance, mystery/police procedural/cozy, suspense, paranormal, futuristic, gothic, inspirational, thriller, horror, chick-lit, and action/adventure. I also write children's books, poetry, and writing reference titles such as my bestseller, *First Draft Outline* and *Cohesive Story Building*. My third writing reference was *Writing the Standalone Series*. My previous writing reference titles focused on non-subsidy, royalty-paying electronic publishing, author promotion, and setting up a promotional group like my own, the award-winning Jewels of the Quill, which I founded in 2003.

I look forward to discussing *Dead Drop* with you. Thank you for your time and consideration.

Sincerely,

Karen Wiesner

Enclosures:
Dead Drop Partial
Dead Drop Synopsis

The Synopsis

Dead Drop, Book 4 of the Incognito Series
Synopsis
by Karen Wiesner

Roan Emory, double agent for the Network, was recruited at the age of 20 against his will. Parris "Perry" L'Engle, the only woman Roan ever loved, was told he was dead. Now, 25 years later, he's a man on the edge with the face of a fallen angel and the heart of a machine. Alone, Perry gave birth to the child he never knew she was carrying. When their son is approached by a covert agency--the same one Perry knows approached Roan just before he disappeared, Perry knows the man she loves isn't dead. As an FBI agent, Perry is determined to find Roan--the only man who can save their son from the same fate that destroyed both of their lives.

Daniel Sands, 20 years old when inducted, taught microbiology at the university, but his real love was his research into strengthening the human immune system to resist multiple diseases. He'd accumulated a massive body of work and was much touted in the academic field. He was blessed with genius level IQ that had justifiably caught the attention of some of the largest intelligence networks in the world, including NASA and the American government.

Roan Emory (the former Daniel Sands) is a Network operative. The Network is the most covert organization in the world with branches all over the globe. It's funded by a major technology corporation that designs innovative equipment both for public use--computers, cell and satellite phones, software and the like--and devices to which only the Network has access. The corporation, Expanding Technology Industries--ETI--functions exactly as a real business does and is the perfect cover for the Network. Below the ETI skyscraper in Chicago, in an underground bunker deep in the earth, is the Network headquarters, inaccessible to anyone without clearance. The American government sanctions the organization, but only the highest officials know about it, including the President and a select committee in the White House, called Oversight. Having the unchallenged authority and skill to disable and destroy criminals the way few other law enforcement agencies can, the Network takes over where regular law enforcement leaves off. The organization represents an absolute justice in a world overrun with evil. The price for that justice is high, requiring the life of every man and woman who serves it. For them, there is no life and no love, only duty.

Trained to disappear into thin air, Roan kills with the stealth and precision of an otherworldly being. If he doesn't want to be found, he won't be. He's the most dangerous man in the world. He's been trained to be an emotionless, calculating machine, silky-smooth and sensual in his manner. Restless, reckless, he nevertheless never fails to do what he needs to.

For the past few years, the Network's Alpha Mission had been to bring down the most dangerous terrorist group in the world--R.E.D. R.E.D. is an invisible, highly militant terrorist group out of Mexico. They're both elusive and vast, spread out all over the world in small groups called remote command centers. R.E.D. is led by a man called 'the Black Pope', a ruthless killer who seems to have God--or the devil--on his side. Roan was to infiltrate and then destroy R.E.D. from the inside out. That's what he's been doing for the past year, but his contact, whom he passes information to, never leads him to the next level within the group. He hasn't gotten anywhere near the Black Pope because the R.C.C.'s are self-contained. Only the highest figures within the organization have access to him. All the information Roan has passed to his contact has panned out. Roan has also been able to get valuable information from them without his contact knowing. Nevertheless, his contact had gotten suspicious of him not long ago for no accountable reason and pulled out of their deal. Befitting his role as a traitor, Roan has retaliated and the Network has descended on R.E.D., destroying R.C.C.'s one after another with a vengeance. Roan has vowed to take them apart a piece at a time. Roan and his team have just retrieved a briefcase nuclear weapon R.E.D. has developed.

But Roan is an operative on the edge. Death is the only way to end the pressure, the oppression, the lack of freedom the Network offers him. He'll never be completely free of the Network, especially not to return to the life he had with Perry. They'll never let him go. Having his freedom out in the world would be dangerous for them. Even if they willingly let him go and cut all ties with him, wiped away his memories of them and his years in service, enemies of the Network will see him as collateral. His presence outside could cripple them in a short time. Only legitimate death will free him. The only way to keep himself sane in this insane place was to shut down his emotions and put everything into his work. Nothing has challenged those safeguards in the twenty-five years since he was inducted. But, after so many years on the edge, he wants out or wants it to end.

Parris "Perry" L'Engle is a highly respected woman, mother, daughter and FBI agent. She has a love of growing roses, particularly lush, blackish-red blossoms in a hybrid tea rose called Ink Spots. Perry has an inextinguishable fire, an ambitious drive to keep plugging on until the answers eluding everyone else come to her through sheer force of will or seduction. As both of her parents are also FBI agents, they believe that if they haven't found an explanation for Daniel's disappearance 25 years ago, then it truly must have been an unfortunate accident. Perhaps, they believe, Perry is projecting unrealistic wishes into the situation. To Perry, admitting to the car accident is admitting that Daniel really is dead. She's nowhere near ready to do that.

A week before Daniel disappeared, Perry overheard a voice just outside his office door. Later, Daniel told her that the man refused to give his name or the government organization he worked for, had told Daniel to tell no one anything about the meeting where Daniel had been propositioned to join a covert government organization. Daniel had been promised the moon. The price? His life. He would have to give up everything he knew, even his family. Those he loved. Stopping short of laughing in the man's face, Daniel had turned him down flat. Though Perry had only just completed her FBI training at that time and had accepted a job at the Minneapolis field office, she'd spent a lifetime with two FBI agents. At the time she'd assumed the fact that she came up with absolutely nothing on this supposed government agent was because she didn't have the skills or the clearance to find him. Now, 25 years later, she's discovered that the man is an enigma. She has no idea who he was, and she's never been able to locate him.

On the heels of the strange, hush-hush attempt to recruit Daniel, Perry had come up with endless scenarios about what could have taken place that day. Almost all of those she'd come up with pointed to the fact that Daniel Sands wasn't dead. Yet she's been unable to locate him and solid evidence--however slight--that the only man she's ever loved is still alive. Nevertheless, there are too many strange things about Daniel's death for Perry to let it go. He was on a rural road in the middle of nowhere--there wasn't a house for over a mile. He was over 25 miles from home, in an area where he didn't know anyone. His teaching assistant had confirmed that a call had come in at about 5:30 that day, and Daniel had left immediately after it, looking extremely upset. Perry herself had had a last-minute doctor's appointment. That appointment had confirmed her suspicions for the past few weeks--she was pregnant. The cause of Daniel's accident had never been discovered, but the front end of his car had been badly damaged before it'd blown up. His body hadn't been recovered, but his blood had been found in the smoking hull of his car.

Like his father, Danny Sands, Perry and Daniel's son, applies himself to his research, which makes him a fanatical workaholic. He's strong, independent, capable, not afraid to face anything in life. He won't hide behind his mother if the recruiter steps beyond request. Danny teaches microbiology at the university, but his real love was his research. Danny had become interested in the massive body of work his father left behind early on, and he's taken over his father's much touted work in the academic field. Danny is also blessed with genius level IQs that has justifiably caught the attention of some of the largest intelligence networks in the world, including NASA and the American government.

Outside Danny's office, she hears voices. One of them is her son's, the other makes her go stock still and cold. She recognizes it as belonging to the recruiter who'd propositioned Daniel 25 years ago. She listens to him give the same recruiting pitch to

Danny. Horrified, she vows to protect her son at all cost. But how?

Perry realizes she might be able to find Daniel after all these years, by following this recruiter. Upon following the recruiter, Perry meets the man called Roan Emory...quite possibly Daniel Sands. She's horrified by the ramifications. This unemotional man who'd held her throat in his powerful hand and promised he'd kill her if she didn't do what he told her to could be the man she'd loved, a man who'd once held her heart completely in his sway. The grief Perry has never fully allowed herself to feel--because she couldn't accept Daniel was truly dead--comes over her, and she's immobilized and overwhelmed by it. Even if that man is Daniel, she now knows he's truly dead to her.

There's a good possibility Perry had never really known Daniel Sands at all and an even better possibility Daniel willingly gave up his life to join this secret government organization. He'd gone along with the faked car accident, surrendered his very blood to make it look authentic. He'd willingly given her up, their love and life together. He'd conceded loss on all of it for the chance to discover more than he could 'ever have believed possible'. As hard as she rebelled against it, there are plenty of reasons Daniel would give up everything. His research had been so important to him. His thirst for knowledge was unbearable even for him. He'd spent his life meeting problems head-on--problems that had been insurmountable for nearly everyone who came before him--and solving them. If the recruiter had given Daniel an utterly compelling, impossible problem to solve and the resources to solve it, Perry can imagine that Daniel would have given up his life as he knew it to discover what had been hidden from him in that life. His confident, almost cocky mind no doubt convinced him he'd return to his original life when he finished. For the first time, he may have met his match and discovered there was no going back.

Perry has to find out the truth and possibly face that Daniel had given up the life he knew voluntarily. He might be aware the organization he works for is trying to recruit his son. He could very well be willing to do anything to see to it personally that his son follows in his footsteps. She has to protect her son, possibly from his own father. She realizes she has to make plans, but she's at a complete loss as to how. Her mother has done her a favor by putting Danny and Aimee in protective custody, but it's a temporary solution. Her son won't live his life, running, living in fear, anyway. Perry now knows that there is no fairness with this organization. If they want Danny, they'll have him, one way or another.

Roan's Network evaluations prove that their best operative is on the edge. He no longer cares if he lives or dies. R.E.D. is targeting Roan with everything they've got. They've put a bounty on his head with other terrorist groups they work with. They don't care who takes him out, just so someone does. The Network knows that time off and re-location won't help Roan. At the time, he's at his peak efficiency and he'll continue to be that way...until something pushes him over the edge completely. And then they won't be able to bring him back. Daniel Sand's son could replace him in time, and that's why they believe his recruitment is vital to the future success of the organization.

Roan doesn't know anything about Danny's recruitment. When Perry asks him to help her save their son, and he says he'll do everything in his power to help Danny. Everything in his power might not be enough to save his son from what Roan would easily describe as a fate worse than death. Even if Roan is able to save their son, he can never save himself.

Knowing that Perry married Lincoln Sands, the late Daniel Sands' older brother, less than six months after his death, Roan believes Danny is Linc's son. He'd never had any real choice about joining the Network. Once they'd decided they wanted him, everything had been arranged without his approval, including Parris being out of contact that day so he couldn't verify the car accident he'd been told she'd been in wasn't real. By the time he'd figured that out, it was too late to do anything about it, outside of fighting them and making his training hard on them, making them regret bringing him in against his will. They'd told him Perry betrayed him by being secretly in love with his brother and getting pregnant, and, when she'd married him, Roan had no reason not to believe them. Linc had died of a heart attack a few years ago. Roan had learned to accept his place over the years. He'd even come to relish his job and the fact that no one can equal his skills. Of late, however, his appreciation has been robbed of him along with his soul. He considers himself dead, more man than machine; if he functions, it's on an instinctive level and the memories are residual past.

Roan has to know if Perry ever loved him, or it'd been his brother she loved all along. He goes to her, allows her to know that he is Daniel. He asks her who Danny's father is, and she tells him the truth--Daniel Sands is her son's father, and her son has always known that fact. When he asks Perry why she married Linc, she says she did it because Danny needed a father who would love him almost as much as his real one. She and Linc were never married in the intimate sense of the word. Something breaks loose inside him then. Not feeling--it's how he's existed these past 25 years. Better not to feel anything when he couldn't change his circumstances. Better to control it so it couldn't control him. Now, as he becomes resurrected to the man he once was, he's furious about what the Network took from him, all he could have had if they'd accepted his refusal. In many ways he's coming back to life, yet pieces the Network took from him are missing.

Perry is fully aware that Roan can never have a regular life, but she's falling in love with this man who is her Daniel and yet is so different. Whatever this organization is, it wants it all. It *takes* it all from those it "employs". Roan can never leave the life they require of him behind to return to the past. He can't have a future. He can't have a family. If her old life hadn't been taken from her, she knows exactly what it would be like now. She and Daniel would have married, they would have had the three children they'd talked about. The only danger to their happiness would have been her job, which carried a degree of risk that she'd accepted and even thrived on. She can't help hating this organization that took all of it away from them. He's given them 25 years--why can't that be enough? But Roan seems unwilling...or unable...to change his life. If they let him go, is he even capable of love anymore?

The current 3rd in Network Command, Head of Operations,

Angelo Pluzetti, never wanted to draft Daniel/Roan into service. His predecessor was corrupt had different ideas, just as Angelo now has a conflict about this same thing with the 2nd in Command. He believes an injustice was done with Daniel/Roan and could still be done with the man's son if Danny Sands is also involuntarily inducted into the Network. Behind his superior's backs, Angelo has come up with a plan to give Roan his freedom by convincing Network superiors and operatives, along with their enemies, that the most dangerous man in the world is dead.

Inducting Danny involuntarily is a security risk to the Network. Perry's FBI status, along with his grandmother as the FBI director of the Minneapolis field office, make him a containment risk. His family is on the alert. If the Network proceeds now or in a year, they'll suspect, and that could endanger Network anonymity. Besides, Perry and her mother have the skills and resources to find them if they look hard enough. The Network can't risk a breach, especially now that they're so vulnerable because their best operative is on the edge and over a controversial new recruit with a family that will cause them no end of trouble. Perry has already gotten too close to them.

As soon as the alpha mission is contained, Roan's superiors plan to relocate him to a retirement facility that, for all intents and purposes, is a prison disguised as paradise. There's no way in or out of the place, no escape. It's the only recourse for operatives since they have more enemies than any other organized justice system in the world. Roan knows he'll never survive in a cage of any kind. His superiors can't simply let him go. Either way, he'll never see Perry or Danny again. Angelo believes that if he and Dr. Celine Hunter, the Network's head of the Medical Department, can convince everyone on the inside and the outside that Roan is dead, it means he's free. Roan isn't so sure.

Angelo's plan for freeing Roan by faking his death and then giving him a whole new, untraceable identity requires outside help. Authenticating Roan's death will be Angelo and Celine's first priority, and only then can they complete his transformation. The only way to give him a new life is not to allow any indication whatsoever that his death isn't genuine--to Network operatives, superiors and enemies. No one on the inside can be involved, but they need someone competent enough to handle his disappearance--someone with training in covert operations. Someone who can aid them in helping Roan disappear while his death is confirmed. Only one person on the outside possessed the skills to help them. Perry. And Roan won't take that risk. If she's seen by anyone, she and Danny will be hunted forever, too.

Angelo comes to Perry and tells her briefly about a terrorist organization planning to set off nuclear weapons in ten major cities soon. While preventing this is his organization's first priority, he sees an opportunity to free Roan, whom he'd never had any choice in recruiting. Angelo can't be absent during any phase of the operation. There can't allow any indication whatsoever that Roan's death isn't genuine--to both their superiors and their enemies. He tells Perry his plan to have Roan taken out of the mission at the last minute. A body will be recovered which will be proved to be his. They need someone on the outside, and Perry has the training to pull it off. #1 will move immediately after the operation to retire Roan. And once he's put out, there'll no way back to the Network or the real world for him. When they confirm when the projected terrorist strike will take place, they'll have to move quickly. She'll have to be ready. This is the last opportunity they'll ever have to get Roan out. Once Roan is in the safe house, she needs to return to her home. If Perry is at home and nothing amiss seems to be happening, then it'll be further conviction to everyone that Roan really is dead. Roan won't be able to come to her right away--possibly not for a year or more--and she won't recognize him immediately either. But, if all goes well, someday they'll be together again and the Network won't suspect a thing.

Perry doesn't know if she can trust the Network or Angelo, but there's no time to do anything but. She wonders if it's worth losing her life and leaving her son without a parent for the chance to have Daniel back, to give Danny the father he so desperately wants. Maybe it won't be the same, maybe Roan will never love her the way he used to, but it's a risk she believes is worth taking. But what if Roan is too scarred to come back to her when it's safe?

Roan would rather be dead than to put his family at risk. And maybe he should be dead. He hasn't been whole in so long, he isn't sure he can ever be again...not even to be with Perry and to finally get to know his son. He can't have a life, sure can't have *back* what should have been buried twenty-five years ago. Impossible, but he can't fight the knowledge that he's waking from the dead. And, just like the Frankenstein monster, he *wants* to live again. When it's safe and the time is right, he returns as Douglas Lazarus, a man truly raised from the dead, and hands Perry a black rose.

The Partial

Dead Drop, Book 4 of the Incognito Series

60,000 words

by Karen Wiesner
PO Box 0
City, State, and Zip
000-000-0000
E-mail Address
https://karenwiesner.weebly.com/

Chapter 1

Parris L'Engle jumped as the phone on her desk rang, then laughed slightly at her own deep focus in searching for a man who'd been lost to her for twenty-five years. She realized when she looked away from the computer screen that her office had become dark in the hours since her partner had left for the night. She should have been long gone herself. Her eyes felt dry, and her stomach reminded her how late it was with a hollow rumble.

Taking a deep breath, she lifted her phone, murmuring, "Agent L'Engle."

"Hi, Mom," came the sound of her son's long-time girlfriend Aimee. "I knew I'd find you there."

Perry laughed a little sheepishly at how predictable she was to those who knew her best. She tucked back a strand of sleek mahogany hair that'd fallen out of the twist at the back of her neck. "You caught me." Reluctantly, she pushed away from her desk, turning her back on her computer. "What's up, sweetie?"

"Actually, I was hoping you could do me a favor."

"Name it."

Perry could hear the affectionate frustration in Aimee's voice when she said, "I haven't been able to get that son of yours out of his office. He's five minutes late for our date tonight. I know nothing short of the old Mom-Oust will get him away from there anytime soon. I'm going through withdrawal, I miss him so much."

Chuckling at the reminder of young love, Perry was glad to have an excuse to push herself away from her desk. She reached beneath it to get her discarded pumps. "I'd be happy to help. I'll drop by the college on my way home and make sure he heads out to you pronto."

"You're the best, Mom! We'll see you tomorrow for lunch, right?"

"I'm counting on it. You have a good night."

"Love you."

Perry smiled, straightening after slipping her shoes on. "Love you, too, Aimee. 'Night."

Replacing the receiver, Perry glanced back at her computer screen. In twenty-five years of searching, she'd found nothing to prove conclusively that Daniel might still be alive. Tonight surely wouldn't see a change in that. She closed out the browser on her screen, then shut down the machine.

Once she slung her purse over her shoulder, she walked through the empty halls and out of the Minneapolis FBI field office to her car. The drive to the university, where her son was up for tenure, was short and refreshing. Perry looked forward to seeing him. Though either Danny or Aimee called her every day and she saw them several times a week, she suffered from empty-nest syndrome. Living alone hadn't been easy for her. She missed having a houseful of people. More than once, she'd considered asking Danny and Aimee to move into the house with her. She could present it as a way for them to save on rent, but knowing they both liked their independence too much kept her quiet. She was the one who could use a little less of it.

In the habit of an experienced FBI agent, she walked lightly on her feet. Barely an echo sounded as she strolled down to the basement office Danny occupied. Her son taught microbiology at the university, but his real love was his research into strengthening the human immune system to resist multiple diseases. Danny had become interested in the massive body of work his father left behind early on, and it'd never been any surprise to Perry when he'd taken over Daniel's much touted work in the academic field.

At this time of night, the halls were dark and shadowed. An overwhelming sense of *deja vu* washed over Perry. The halls she'd walked to meet Daniel twenty-five years ago were similar to these. It seemed like yesterday. Relating to Aimee's agony in wanting to be with the man she loved made it only too easy for Perry to remember. More than two decades ago, she'd been in the role of the girlfriend, desperately trying to get her workaholic, genius fiancé to come out and play for the night. Daniel had usually put up something of a fight before he could be coaxed into it, too.

Perry recalled walking a hall similar to this one, knowing no one else but Daniel remained in the building. She remembered carrying a cassette player into the office adjoined to his laboratory, slipping out of her shoes so she wore only a thin, gauzy slip of a dress. She remembered pouring wine for them before turning on the sensual Latin music they both loved. She hadn't actually gotten Daniel out of his office that night, of course...

Her body alive with the memories, Perry felt tears behind her eyes even as her face burned. She shook her head as if to cool them, angry with herself for dwelling on the past, on bittersweet memories that only made her lonelier. Daniel was gone. She should move on. *Had* to. How to get herself to do that was the question she'd never been able to answer.

As she neared Danny's office, a strange male voice floated out to her. It didn't belong to Danny. There was something familiar about it anyway. Some instinct--no doubt borne out of her years in the FBI and from growing up with parents who were both agents--made her stop short. She put her back against the wall outside her son's office, listening intently.

Danny said something in a soft, suspicious tone that had Perry reaching instinctively for her gun. Only uncertainty made her hesitate.

The other man spoke authoritatively: "You have the skills we're looking for, Daniel."

The very breath in Perry's lungs halted. That deep voice. Now she knew where she'd heard it before. Outside of Daniel's office at the college, a day before he disappeared. The day before he died. She'd overheard it then just as she was overhearing it now.

Her heart thumping wildly, Perry silently eased herself closer to the door. The pebbled glass with gold writing showed her the blurred yet recognizable form of her son with his dark hair and tanned skin. He stood six foot two inches tall with a lean, muscular frame. The man with him was an inch or two taller. Blondish-brown hair, she guessed. Wide shoulders. Wearing a suit.

No, he wasn't someone she knew. Yet Perry didn't second-guess herself. She needed to know about him--to use him to find out what happened to the man she loved. It was possible he was the only person alive who knew something about Daniel's death...

Find out more:
http://www.writers-exchange.com/dead-drop/

If you enjoyed this author's book, then please place a review up at the site of purchase and any social media sites you frequent!

You can find ALL our books up at Amazon at:
https://www.amazon.com/shop/writers_exchange

All our Non-Fiction:
http://www.writers-exchange.com/category/genres/nonfiction/

COHESIVE STORY BUILDING
Bonus Companion Booklet

Frequently I'm asked whether the worksheets, checklists, charts, examples, exercises, and/or other aids from my writing reference titles are available in a usable download format. While the original publisher of the main book did offer free copies of some of these in PDF format on their website, naturally these were only "usable" if they were printed out and written on by hand.

My publisher and I wanted to offer a download of all of these in an editable format (RTF) that allows you to type right into the document and use it over and over as needed.

Cohesive Story Building Bonus Companion Booklet contains all the blank worksheets from the main book along with detailed exercises and examples. Download the free ebook now at http://www.writers-exchange.com/cohesive-story-building/. For those who prefer print, a paperback equivalent is available for purchase.

www.ingramcontent.com/pod-product-compliance
Ingram Content Group UK Ltd.
Pitfield, Milton Keynes, MK11 3LW, UK
UKHW022028190726
13853UKWH00005B/2165